Confessions of a Swadeshi Reformer

Celebrating Holi—the author and Atal Behari Vajpayee

Confessions of a Swadeshi Reformer

My Years as Finance Minister

YASHWANT SINHA

PENGUIN
VIKING

VIKING
Published by the Penguin Group
Penguin Books India Pvt. Ltd, 11 Community Centre, Panchsheel Park,
New Delhi 110 017, India
Penguin Group (USA) Inc., 375 Hudson Street, New York, New York 10014, USA
Penguin Group (Canada), 90 Eglinton Avenue East, Suite 700, Toronto,
Ontario, M4P 2Y3, Canada (a division of Pearson Penguin Canada Inc.)
Penguin Books Ltd, 80 Strand, London WC2R 0RL, England
Penguin Ireland, 25 St Stephen's Green, Dublin 2, Ireland
(a division of Penguin Books Ltd)
Penguin Group (Australia), 250 Camberwell Road, Camberwell,
Victoria 3124, Australia (a division of Pearson Australia Group Pty Ltd)
Penguin Group (NZ), 67 Apollo Drive, Rosedale, North Shore 0632,
New Zealand (a division of Pearson New Zealand Ltd)
Penguin Group (South Africa) (Pty) Ltd, 24 Sturdee Avenue, Rosebank,
Johannesburg 2196, South Africa

Penguin Books Ltd, Registered Offices: 80 Strand, London WC2R 0RL, England

First published in Viking by Penguin Books India 2007

Copyright © Yashwant Sinha 2007

Photographs courtesy of the author

All rights reserved

10 9 8 7 6 5 4 3 2 1

The views and opinions expressed in this book are the author's own and the facts are as
reported by him which have been verified to the extent possible and the publishers are not in
any way liable for the same.

ISBN-13: 978-0-67099-952-1   ISBN-10: 0-67099-952-0

Typeset in *Sabon Roman* by SÜRYA, New Delhi
Printed at Gopsons Papers Ltd, Noida

To my dearest ones who inspired me to write this book—
Nilima, my wife,
Sharmila and Ashok, my daughter and son-in-law,
Jayant and Sumant, my sons, and
Punita and Vaishali, my daughters-in-law.

Contents

Acknowledgements

Grateful acknowledgements are due to my wife and children—they not only persuaded me to undertake this exercise but made their own contributions to both the content and the language of the book. I have fond memories of the intellectually stimulating discussions I had with my children during the writing of this book. My wife was the resident editor who read the manuscript repeatedly, many more times than I did, correcting mistakes and removing imperfections.

Thanks are due in no small measure to Vimala Veluchamy, a business research analyst. I 'spoke' the book to her, which she then transcribed. She also helped me recall many more incidents, comments and responses. Her contribution is invaluable.

I owe an enormous debt of gratitude to my secretary Gajender Sharma who worked incessantly on the draft and spent long hours at the computer. I am also grateful to Krishan Chopra, but for whom I may not have undertaken this exercise at all.

And, finally, thanks to Sumitra Srinivasan, for her patience.

Prologue

It was another hot and sultry day in Patna. I had just returned home after hectic election campaigning, tired to the core. Darkness had descended, but without bringing any relief from the heat and humidity. The short-lived Chandra Shekhar government had fallen in just four months and the country was in the throes of fresh Lok Sabha elections in less than eighteen months, well short of the normal period of five years. I was a candidate of the newly formed Samajwadi Janata Party, from the Patna Lok Sabha constituency. The constituency was a mixed one, with a large urban population and a larger rural population.

Outside, a crowd waited as usual, to give me all the news of the day and receive instructions for the next day's campaigning. The presence, in the waiting crowd, of a senior officer from the Ministry of Finance was unusual. I immediately judged that he must have come with something very important, needing urgent attention, because such were my instructions. Only the most important and unavoidable work was to be brought to me at Patna, where I was locked in a tough election battle with strong contenders like I.K. Gujral, foreign minister of the V.P. Singh government that had preceded ours, from the Janata Dal, Dr C.P. Thakur, a leading physician of Bihar and a former member of Parliament (MP) from Patna, from the Congress party, and Dr Shailendra Nath Srivastava, a well-known professor of Patna University and the sitting MP from Patna, from the Bharatiya Janata Party.

The file brought for my consideration and approval was not only important, it contained a proposal on which I was called upon to take one of the most difficult and controversial decisions of my life. India was facing its worst economic crisis ever. It had been building up over the years, neglected by the previous governments and had now reached an unavoidable flashpoint. Our foreign exchange reserves were down to the barest minimum. As finance minister, I had already taken all the steps I could to tackle the crisis, within the limitations that the Chandra Shekhar government suffered from, dependent as it was on the support of the Congress party for its survival. Knowing fully well that all other options were now closed, Prime Minister Chandra Shekhar and I had decided that, if push came to shove and the country had to be saved from defaulting on its external commitments, we would not hesitate even to mortgage our gold reserves.

The dreaded moment had arrived. The file brought to me in Patna contained a proposal to mortgage twenty tonnes of gold held by the State Bank of India on behalf of the Government of India to the Bank of England for a sum of around $400 million. We had decided that this gold, which was not a part of our foreign exchange reserves, would be offered for mortgage first, though we would not hesitate to mortgage our gold with the Reserve Bank of India (RBI), which formed part of our foreign exchange reserves, should that become unavoidable.

I approved the proposal, signed the file, and marked it to the prime minister for his final approval. The deed was done. We were mortgaging our most precious asset, gold, which Indians are sentimental about, to save something even more precious—our honour and prestige.

Flashes of the past came to my mind. I was born in a middle-class family. My father was an advocate of the Patna High Court and had a fairly flourishing legal practice. Unfortunately, in the early 1940s, he fell seriously ill and could not work for over a year. This largely destroyed his practice as his clients shifted their loyalty to other lawyers. This was also the time when the country experienced unprecedented and galloping inflation as a result of the Second World War. We were a large family of seven brothers and four sisters. My father had to work very hard to make both ends meet. I remembered how, in those difficult days, when we were left with no money and did not know when or from where the next meal would come, he had to sell or mortgage the family assets. I remembered the pain I felt then as a child. Now, many decades later, as finance minister of India, I was facing a similar situation. It was not of my making. But I was at the helm at the time, and the decision was for me to take; the responsibility was mine.

That day I made a commitment to myself and to the nation, and resolved India must become economically strong. It should be a lender, rather than a borrower. We should never again have to look to others for help; instead we should try to be secure and self-reliant. I thought to myself: If ever I get the chance again, the most important task before me will be to try and achieve this goal.

Seven years later, fate came knocking at my door.

PART 1

THE FINANCE MINISTER PRESENTS

1

The Original Reformer?

The year 1989 was a tumultuous year in Indian politics. Well before the general elections which were due that year, the centrist parties, mainly the Janata Party, the Lok Dal and the rebels of the Congress party who had formed a new outfit called the Jan Morcha, came together to form the Janata Dal. V.P. Singh, the former finance and defence minister in Rajiv Gandhi's government, was chosen as the president of the party in the unity convention held at Bangalore. In the general elections, the Congress party led by Rajiv Gandhi, the then prime minister, was decisively defeated. A new government was formed, with V.P. Singh as prime minister, supported from the outside both by the Bharatiya Janata Party (BJP) and by the Left parties. As general secretary of the Janata Dal, its main spokesperson, in-charge of its central office and its chief campaign manager, I played a very important role in the victory of the party in the elections of 1989. Unfortunately, while most of my colleagues who worked alongside me were appointed as cabinet ministers by V.P. Singh, he decided to offer me the post of a state (junior) minister. This was a deliberate snub to Chandra Shekhar and his followers in the party. The offer was not acceptable to me and I walked away from the swearing-in ceremony at Rashtrapati Bhavan. Chandra Shekhar also strongly felt that V.P. Singh had acted unfairly, and fully endorsed my decision not to join the V.P. Singh government. Nor did I join the government later despite personal persuasion by V.P. Singh. Subsequently, he offered me the governorship of Punjab, which was in the grip of militancy and under President's rule. Since I did not want to leave the Rajya Sabha and move out of Delhi, I did not accept this offer either. I never regretted my decision because the government collapsed after ten months.

Chandra Shekhar became the prime minister of India in November 1990 under unusual circumstances, to say the least. The reasons for the split in the Janata Dal, the collapse of the V.P. Singh government and the political arrangement worked out by Chandra Shekhar with the Congress are all chapters of another story on which I shall not dwell here. Chandra Shekhar took oath as prime minister in the forecourt of Rashtrapati Bhavan on 10 November 1990. His cabinet, however, was sworn in many days later, the reason for the delay being the hectic negotiations that had to be held to accommodate the various factions, even within this small party. The expectations of individual MPs had to be managed in a manner which did not ruffle too many feathers. Ultimately, as the price of Congress support, the list had to be shown to the Congress party president, Rajiv Gandhi.

Subramanian Swamy was determined to become finance minister. Others were against the very idea. So, he had to be placated by the offer of two portfolios, those of commerce, and law and justice. My own preference was for the Ministry of External Affairs. But Chandra Shekhar was keen that I take the finance portfolio, in view of the gathering economic crisis. As a result, external affairs went to V.C. Shukla and I became the finance minister.

I was familiar with economic issues. I had studied economics at the intermediate level (the first two years of college in those days in a four-year degree course). I must confess, however, that I did not care much for the subject at that stage and had given it up after two years, in favour of history. I graduated in history and chose political science for my master's. Later, in my career as an IAS officer, I worked in three important economic ministries—commerce, industry and what was then the Ministry of Shipping and Transport. I was also posted as First Secretary in Bonn and later Consul General in Frankfurt to look after commercial and economic work, in the early 1970s. I realized that economic work was far more interesting than any other work in government. But the finance ministry was an entirely different proposition. I had not bargained for the challenges that I faced in this ministry, either in 1990 or later in 1998.

The Indian economy was in dire straits in 1990. As I.G. Patel, a world-renowned economist, former finance secretary and former governor of the Reserve Bank of India, explained in a lecture he delivered at the Indian Institute of Management, Bangalore on 28 October 1991: 'If the present crisis is the greatest we have faced since independence, it is for no underlying economic factor which is more adverse now than what we have had to contend with in the past several decades. It is because successive governments in the 1980s chose to abdicate their responsibilities to the nation for the sake of short-term partisan political gains and indeed out of sheer political cynicism.'

In the same lecture, he said about previous regimes:

With the new wave of ushering in the twenty-first century, we had a series of financial excesses—large increases in defence expenditures, unbridled growth of subsidies, a quantum jump in public salaries and indeed a philosophy stated in so many words that money did not matter. It was already clear by 1986 that we were in an internal debt trap which would soon engulf us in an external debt trap. Rather than take any remedial action, we went merrily along, borrowing more and more at home and on shorter and shorter terms abroad. The climate for official and concessional capital had turned irretrievably adverse for many years. But our response to that was not to strive harder for self-reliance but to increase the amount as well as the proportion of short-term debt in our total external indebtedness. Borrowing short-term is like inviting sudden death—with the slightest adverse turn in confidence, these loans will not be renewed and we will be faced immediately with a liquidity crisis. Yet nothing was done to take corrective action or to buy time for such action and create confidence, for example, by going to the IMF [International Monetary Fund]. This was obviously politically inconvenient in 1988 and 1989 when winning elections was the only concern. The government of Mr. V.P. Singh could not but be aware of the writing on the wall. But it preferred to add its own fuel to the fire à la loan waivers and the red herring of reservations.

This is the most apt description of the economic mismanagement by the two governments which preceded the Chandra Shekhar government, especially by the Rajiv Gandhi regime. The crisis after Iraq invaded Kuwait, and the resulting Gulf War when the United States got militarily involved in this conflict, caused a sharp increase in petroleum prices. It was the immediate trigger for a first-rate balance of payments crisis in India. In the history of independent India it was perhaps the worst time to shoulder the responsibility of the finance ministry.

When the Chandra Shekhar government assumed office in November 1990 the foreign exchange reserves of the country had dropped to Rs 3142 crore, sufficient only to finance imports for one month. On account of rising oil prices these meagre reserves were also depleting fast. The fiscal situation was alarming. It had to be attended to on an urgent basis. I introduced immediately, in December 1990, a package of measures to mobilize additional revenues. It included both direct and indirect taxes. The tax proposals were prepared in great secrecy. I remember a senior excise official in Mumbai telling me that it was, perhaps, the first time that a leading industrial house of India was taken completely by surprise by the announcement. Normally, its executives were the ones who used to inform the revenue officials about changes that could be expected. This was the first time that they came to his office to inquire about them.

At the Ministry of Finance, we were engaged in a fire-fighting exercise. We had two immediate priorities. First, to secure whatever assistance we could from the IMF on an emergency basis and, second, to prepare a path-breaking budget that would address the accumulated problems of the Indian economy. My senior officers made trips to Washington to negotiate assistance from the IMF. They were successful. Though the amount received was small, it was enough to see us through until the regular budget was presented. The IMF was looking at the policy measures that we proposed to initiate. We could therefore begin serious negotiations with the IMF for assistance only after the presentation of the budget. To quote I.G. Patel once again:

> It was left to the feckless Chandra Shekhar government to start serious negotiations with the Fund when it was almost too late . . . the Chandra Shekhar government began to behave more responsibly than most people had expected. But the rug was pulled from under its feet when it was not allowed to present a Budget which, I am sure, was discussed with the Fund and contained at least some features of sensible adjustment. It is no secret that IMF assistance was widely assumed to be forthcoming as soon as the Budget was passed by the Chandra Shekhar government. But our political masters willed otherwise.

Years later, when I presented my first regular budget in 1998 as the finance minister of the Vajpayee government, Dr Arjun Sengupta, another eminent economist and now an independent member of the Rajya Sabha, was critical of my budget. He said:

> Very few people know that Yashwant Sinha as finance minister of the Chandra Shekhar government had prepared a most revolutionary budget in 1991. In many ways, that budget was more radical than the budget that was presented later that year by Dr Manmohan Singh when he introduced the Narasimha Rao package of economic reforms. For reasons quite well known, Yashwant Sinha's budget could not be presented to Parliament. If it were, it probably would have been a major Indian response to the 1991 crisis. I thought that this time again, when we are facing another major crisis, Yashwant Sinha would rise to the occasion and present an

equally radical budget. He did not and that is why I was disappointed.

On 10 March 2006, participating in the budget debate in the Rajya Sabha, Arjun Sengupta said, 'I must admit that Shri Yashwant Sinha is one of the country's very famous reformers. There is no doubt about it. As finance minister, I think, we should admit, he was the original reformer . . . His first budget—which he prepared, before Manmohan Singh's budget, I happened to have seen that—was a unique budget. That was the first original reform budget.'

If I had ever made such a claim, Manmohan Singh and his admirers would have been most critical. But we now have the testimony of two leading economists, I.G. Patel and Arjun Sengupta. I will leave it at that.

*

While the Ministry of Finance was engaged in this life-and-death struggle, politics was taking its own inexorable course. Chandra Shekhar had set out to solve the three most difficult problems the country faced—the Ram temple issue at Ayodhya, the militancy in Punjab and the rising disaffection in Jammu and Kashmir. Chandra Shekhar is not only a leader but a statesman in the true sense of the word. He has deep insight into the problems confronting the nation. He also has a clear vision of how to resolve them. He is determined and confident. He pursues his goal doggedly. Even as prime minister he continued with his informal style of working and, though he had never served as a minister in the government, his disposal of files was quick and competent. He handled Parliament with great aplomb.

Soon after assuming office, Chandra Shekhar set up a committee of chief ministers cutting across political party lines, to tackle the Ayodhya issue. He came very close to finding a solution. He was also making progress on the other two issues. This started to cause Rajiv Gandhi much concern. Should he allow Chandra Shekhar to become the man of destiny for India? The answer was a resounding no.

The Congress therefore began to create problems for the government. I was told that the party felt concerned about the management of the economy. They wanted to be informed about the budget that I was preparing, but they did not tell Chandra Shekhar or me whom I should talk with. When I met Rajiv Gandhi in a meeting, I asked him whom I should talk to about the state of the economy and the budget. He named senior Congress leader Pranab Mukherjee, who had held the finance portfolio earlier.

I contacted Mukherjee and invited him home for lunch. My wife made rohu fish curry, in typical Bihari style, especially for him. We had a long and pleasant chat. I apprised him of the challenges we faced, and my approach to budget-making. I was careful not to share the actual budget with him. Mukherjee appeared to be satisfied with my approach. But his satisfaction apparently was very short-lived.

It is pertinent at this point to quote from the book *My Presidential Years* by President R. Venkataraman, himself a former finance minister:

> I was desperate to save the ministry for at least another six months. I wanted the financial business authorizing expenditure beyond April 1 to be adopted before a crisis enveloped the country. It appeared to me that no one understood the gravity of a situation where the administration could come to a standstill without adequate financial provisions being made. Hence, I reminded Rajiv Gandhi of the unconditional support he had promised to the ministry and the loss of credibility he would suffer by acting contrary to his words. He hastened to say that he was not contemplating the fall of the ministry and that he would continue to support it.
>
> The next day newspapers reported that there was a thaw in the relationship between Chandra Shekhar and Rajiv Gandhi. But this was short-lived for Rajiv Gandhi again called on me on February 11 and expressed apprehension that the Budget the Finance Minister Yashwant Sinha was

preparing might contain a massive dose of taxation which, if supported by the Congress (I), would lead to the party losing popularity at the time of next elections.

On February 13, Rajiv Gandhi again called on me with Pranab Mukherjee, my successor as Finance Minister in 1982. Pranab Mukherjee told me that he had a discussion with Yashwant Sinha and that he felt a harsh budget would be inappropriate at that time. He was also worried that inflation would be sparked off and bring unpopularity to the Congress if it supported those measures. Since Yashwant Sinha had earlier discussed the economic situation with me, I told Pranab Mukherjee of some of the compulsions of the Finance Minister. As an old colleague of mine I explained to him that the current inflation was not due to cost-push or demand-pull but largely due to excessive liquidity and that budgetary action was unavoidable to control inflation. The whole discussion was in the nature of an academic exercise rather than consultation on programmes to be adopted.

Obviously, Rajiv Gandhi was not convinced by the arguments advanced by President Venkataraman or me, because he decided to prevent me from presenting the budget. I was aghast when I was informed of this decision. Given the crisis the country was facing, it was criminal to prevent the government from presenting a regular budget. Only after presenting the budget could we have approached the IMF for the further assistance which the country sorely needed. Non-presentation of the budget was bound to push the country into bankruptcy. Only the most cussed could have taken such a decision. This issue came up for informal discussion in one of the cabinet meetings. I detailed the economic situation and the crisis we faced. I also said that in such a situation the only alternative for us was to quit rather than cling to office at any cost. If we gave in to blackmail on the budget, I said, the Congress party would find some other issue with which to pull us down. Chandra Shekhar was not happy with my blunt views. After returning from that meeting, I sent a handwritten letter of resignation to Chandra Shekhar and stopped going to office. Chandra Shekhar sent his private secretary, C.B. Gautam, a couple of days later to personally escort me to meet him at 7 Race Course Road, where he tore my letter of resignation and asked me to continue in government. I did not have the heart to say no to him.

I was not wrong, however, about the designs of the Congress party. The government was brought down a few weeks later on the ridiculous and unfounded allegation that two constables of the Haryana police had been posted outside Rajiv Gandhi's house to spy on him.

Chandra Shekhar's success as prime minister turned out to be his biggest failure.

Left without an alternative, I presented the interim budget for 1991–92 on 4 March 1991. The opposition parties protested vehemently, both at the non-presentation of the regular budget and on the presentation of an interim budget. The BJP was the main opposition party, so L.K. Advani led the attack, followed by Somnath Chatterjee, Inderjit Gupta and others. Each of them condemned the government roundly for the injustice it was doing to the economy by not presenting a regular budget. They made their point and walked out of the House.

I felt really humiliated. Some blamed the Congress for the situation. But members of that party added insult to injury by asserting that it was the decision of the government to present an interim budget and not a regular budget and they had nothing to do with it. After the walkouts, I proceeded to read my budget speech. I shall quote only the first few paragraphs of my speech here to emphasize how I saw the prevailing economic situation.

1. The new Government, which assumed office in mid-November 1990, inherited an economic situation of crisis proportions. The budget deficit of the Central Government [had] reached a level of Rs. 13,000 crore, on 30th November, 1990, as a consequence of revenue shortfalls and expenditure overruns. The Wholesale Price Index registered an increase of 8.5 per cent, while the Consumer Price Index rose by 11.9 per cent, during the first eight

months of the current financial year. The sharp deterioration in the balance of payments situation led to a rapid depletion of foreign exchange reserves, which [had] dropped to Rs 3142 crore at the end of November 1990 and this sum was not even sufficient to finance imports for one month.

2. These developments were not an unfortunate coincidence, but were the outcome of shortcomings in the macro-management of the economy in the past. I say this neither in a spirit of acrimony nor with a desire to apportion blame. But the time has come for the Government to share its concerns with Parliament and the people, in an endeavour to evolve a national consensus, so that the restoration of the health of the economy is perceived as a collective responsibility.

3. Macro-economic imbalances which have been large and persistent are at the root of the problem. The fiscal deficits of the Government had to be met by borrowing at home. The current account deficits of the economy were inevitably financed by borrowing from abroad. The burden of servicing the accumulated internal and external debt has now become onerous. I need hardly stress that neither the Government nor the economy can live beyond its means for long. The room for manoeuvre, to live on borrowed money or time, has been used up completely. The soft options have been exhausted.

4. It is not surprising that the persistent fiscal imbalances have accentuated inflationary pressures in the economy and strained the balance of payments. Thus, even at the beginning of the current financial year, the economy was in a serious fiscal crisis and faced a very difficult balance of payments situation. These problems have been sharply exacerbated by the oil shock and the dislocations caused by the crisis and the war in the Gulf. We have experienced a deterioration in the fiscal situation. Consumers are faced with double-digit inflation. The economy is faced with a balance of payments crisis. The impact of the Gulf

(war) on the economy, in the year to come, is difficult to assess fully at this point of time. The level at which international oil prices would stabilize thereafter cannot be predicted.

5. On assumption of office, we could not have waited and allowed a further deterioration in the budgetary situation. Therefore, without losing any time, I introduced a package of measures to mobilise additional revenue. Steps were taken to improve tax compliance and revenue collections. The strictest possible control was exercised on expenditure. At the same time, I had also assured Parliament that the Government attached a very high priority to fiscal consolidation, even if it meant hard decisions and difficult choices which had been postponed for long. I would like to stress, once again, that my commitment to fiscal adjustment in 1991–92 remains firm and irrevocable.

But what I said in the seventh paragraph was the best reason that I could offer for the political compromise that we had made and the decision not to present a regular budget.

In the difficult set of circumstances, where the uncertainties remain, we shall need some more time to evolve a comprehensive strategy for restoring the health of the economy. In formulating the Budget, we want to ensure that such a macro-economic adjustment does not disrupt the rhythm of the growth process and does not place a burden on the poor. What is more, the process of fiscal correction needs to be situated in a medium-term perspective. We are engaged in the formulation of a comprehensive approach which would provide a satisfactory and sustainable solution to these problems. This needs time. I would, therefore, plead with the House to wait until the regular Budget for 1991–92 is presented in May 1991.

Although it was an interim budget, some elements of the new approach were:

1. The concept of fiscal deficit, which represents the gap
   between the total expenditure and the total receipts of
   the government minus borrowings, was mentioned for
   the first time. Earlier finance ministers only mentioned
   the budget deficit in their budget speeches after taking
   into account the amount of money they proposed to
   borrow from the market or from the RBI. The fiscal
   deficit is a truer reflection of the state of government
   finances than the artificial concept of budget deficit. I
   talked of both in my speech.

2. I mentioned my intention of setting up a Bharat Bachat
   Bank to deal with national savings schemes so that these
   transactions between the centre and the states did not
   burden the budget of the Government of India. Later, as
   finance minister of the Vajpayee government, though I
   did not set up the Bharat Bachat Bank, I transferred the
   entire account of national savings schemes from the
   consolidated fund, which is part of the budget, to the
   public account, which is outside the budget and represents
   more the role of a banker that the Government of India
   performs.

3. I talked about public sector disinvestment: 'It has been
   decided that the Government would disinvest up to 20
   per cent of its equity in selected public sector undertakings,
   in favour of mutual funds and financial or investment
   institutions in the public sector. The disinvestment, which
   would broad base the equity, improve management and
   enhance the availability of resources for these enterprises,
   is also expected to yield Rs 2500 crore to the exchequer
   in 1991–92. The modalities and details of implementing
   this decision, which are being worked out, would be
   announced separately.'

4. I talked of rationalizing expenditure on subsidies and
   reducing allocations on major subsidies. I also talked of
   better targeting of subsidies for the poor and the needy,
   combined with an improvement in management to achieve
   better results.

5. I stated my commitment to fiscal discipline in unambiguous terms, a principle by which I tried to live in my next tenure as finance minister.

This was as far as I could go in an interim budget. All other ideas remained buried and never saw the light of day during my tenure as finance minister of the Chandra Shekhar government.

I have already mentioned how the ridiculous issue of two Haryana policemen spying on Rajiv Gandhi was invented to put the Chandra Shekhar government on the mat. Parliament was in session. The President's address was under discussion in the Lok Sabha. On the morning of 5 March, I got a call from Rangarajan Kumaramangalam, one of the whips of the Congress party in Parliament. He informed me that in the meeting of the Congress Parliamentary Party's strategy group that morning it had been decided that the issue of spying by the Haryana constables would be raised in a big way in both Houses of Parliament. I informed Chandra Shekhar of this development. He had no inkling of it. We were both in the Lok Sabha that morning. So, when the Congress members raised the issue in the House, Chandra Shekhar condemned the alleged surveillance and offered to institute a parliamentary inquiry into the matter and take stern action against the guilty. But the Congress members were not satisfied and staged a walkout, threatening not to return to the House until action was taken against the guilty.

After question hour in the Lok Sabha, we went to the Rajya Sabha. On our way through Central Hall, we were told that Congress members led by its shouting brigade—a description given to a group of loud-mouthed Congress party members who believed more in the strength of their vocal chords than the strength of their arguments—had already forced an adjournment of the Rajya Sabha.

We walked into the Rajya Sabha chairman's room, where our members gave a first-hand account of what had happened. Chandra Shekhar wanted to talk to the leaders of the Congress party in the Rajya Sabha. Since S.S. Ahluwalia was the only Congress member present in Central Hall, he was invited to join the discussions. We told him about the statement Chandra Shekhar had made in the Lok Sabha. Chandra Shekhar offered to make a similar statement in the Rajya Sabha. However, as he had to leave for Ahmedabad for a function immediately, it was suggested that the House could be allowed to function normally and he would make the statement the next day. We thought that the Congress party would consider his suggestion seriously and allow the Rajya Sabha to function. Chandra Shekhar then left for Ahmedabad.

However, when the House reassembled after lunch the Congress members continued to disrupt the proceedings. I was the leader of the House, but my pleas fell on deaf ears. Order could not be restored and the House had to be adjourned for the day. What followed was even worse. The Congress party made it clear that they took the issue of spying so seriously that they could not allow the government to continue in office.

The next day Chandra Shekhar had to reply to the discussion in the Lok Sabha on the motion of thanks to the President for his address to Parliament. The motion had to be carried by a majority of the House. Failure to do so would amount to no confidence in the government and Chandra Shekhar would be left with no option but to resign. It was indeed a long night. Several emissaries shuttled between 7 Race Course Road, where Chandra Shekhar lived, and 10 Janpath, where Rajiv stayed. Among them were Subramanian Swamy, a minister in our government, and T.N. Seshan, who had already been appointed the chief election commissioner. They brought messages from Rajiv and took back replies. Chandra Shekhar's core team, which included me, was at 7 Race Course Road. I was very clear in my mind that there was no point in a compromise and that we should quit. Rajiv insisted that the Haryana chief minister, Om Prakash Chautala, who belonged to our party and was the son of Choudhary Devi Lal, the deputy prime minister in Chandra Shekhar's government, must resign for unleashing his policemen to spy on him. It was nothing but pressure tactics and meant to humiliate Chandra Shekhar and the rest of us. To me, it was totally unacceptable.

I left 7 Race Course Road in the wee hours of the morning. The rest of the core team and Chandra Shekhar were still awake and active, Swamy and Seshan engaged in their shuttle diplomacy. Chandra Shekhar had not yet made up his mind. I hoped and prayed that he would stand firm and not give in to the political blackmail of the Congress party once again.

Chandra Shekhar kept his counsel to himself until almost the last moment. The Lok Sabha convened as usual at 11 o' clock. The Congress members stayed away from the House and waited in the lobby for their leader's instructions. We ourselves barely constituted the quorum of the House. We were subjected to great ridicule by the opposition benches, who mocked us and made insulting remarks. Finally, after question hour, Chandra Shekhar stood up to reply to the debate on the motion of thanks to the President. It was one of his best speeches ever. As he proceeded with his speech, the Congress members in the lobby perhaps had some inkling that he might announce his resignation at its conclusion. Messages were conveyed to some of us inside the House to dissuade Chandra Shekhar from doing so. Talks could still be held to save the government. I had no interest in any such proposal. I therefore waited for Chandra Shekhar to finish his speech and announce his resignation. Others in our party, however, felt that further talks with the Congress could be held. They tried to convey this to Chandra Shekhar as he spoke. Chandra Shekhar, like me, must have realized that it was already too late for such a move. If Congress members did not come inside the House and vote with us to carry the motion of thanks, Chandra Shekhar had no choice but to resign. There was no time for further negotiations.

Chandra Shekhar finished his speech. To my great relief he finally announced that he was proceeding immediately to Rashtrapati Bhavan to submit his resignation to the President and asked the Speaker to adjourn the House.

When Chandra Shekhar submitted his resignation, the

President asked him to continue as caretaker prime minister. The financial business before the House was passed without discussion, thus averting a constitutional crisis. The President dissolved the Lok Sabha. Elections were announced for May. Everyone started preparing for them.

Another government had fallen, this time within six months. I was about to face the most difficult challenge of my life. I had to ensure that during this period, that is, until the next government was sworn in after the elections, India did not default on its external commitments, that the economy was kept going and that we duly paid for our imports, especially oil imports. All this had to be done without any tools of policy at my disposal, without any room for manoeuvre. I was not wrong therefore when I told my friends that it was like being thrown into the deep end with one's hands and feet tied and be expected to float.

It was not merely the economic situation that was worrisome. The introduction of reservation in government jobs for other backward classes (recommended by the Mandal Commission set up by the Janata Party government in the late 1970s and taken out of cold storage by V.P. Singh to shore up his political fortunes) had split society vertically. Rajiv Gandhi, by his irresponsible action, worsened the turmoil by forcing a general election.

A more miserable set of circumstances could not be imagined. I was the finance minister of a caretaker government. Hence, I could not take any policy decisions. The country was getting ready for general elections. While nobody expected us to win the elections, we at least had to survive politically. Hard decisions like rationing of petroleum products or raising administered prices were thus out. The short-term debt of over $5 billion acquired during earlier regimes had to be serviced. Any default in the instalment payments of either interest or the principal amount would have made India a basket case. It would have destroyed our credibility for years to come.

We had to work out effective solutions to save the country in this situation. My top team in the finance ministry consisted of three IAS officers—S.P. Shukla of the Bihar cadre as finance secretary, K.P. Geethakrishnan of the Tamil Nadu cadre as expenditure secretary and Pradip Lahiri of the Madhya Pradesh cadre as revenue secretary. Deepak Nayyar, an eminent economist, was the chief economic adviser. S. Venkitaramanan was the RBI governor. It was a first-rate team. Together we had to tackle independent India's worst economic crisis.

After detailed consultations amongst ourselves, we evolved a strategy which included the following steps:

1. There had to be the strictest control on government expenditure.
2. Collection of revenue had to be stepped up.
3. Foreign exchange outgo had to be closely monitored. Foreign exchange restrictions had to be further strengthened and strictly enforced.
4. Our short-term debt had to be rescheduled wherever possible, and paid, if not rescheduled. But in no case should the country be allowed to default.
5. All efforts had to be made to prepone aid receipts from outside, including from multilateral agencies such as the World Bank and the Asian Development Bank, because no fresh loans could be taken by a caretaker government.
6. The NRIs had lost confidence in India. There was a run on their deposits. That had to be prevented to the extent possible. Renewed efforts had to be made to get sizeable deposits in foreign exchange, even if temporarily.
7. Importers had to be encouraged to negotiate long-term letters of credit for their imports. Exporters had to be asked to bring their earnings home without losing time.
8. States had to be persuaded to submit the utilization certificates and expenditure statements of foreign-aided schemes as quickly as possible, so that foreign exchange flows could come in unimpeded.
9. The RBI had to keep a tab on all foreign exchange transactions, almost on a 24/7 basis, to ensure avoidance of any mishap.

10. The ministry and the RBI had to work as closely as possible to prevent any disaster.

The World Bank and the IMF spring meetings are held in April. I led the Indian delegation. It gave me a good opportunity to have detailed discussions with the managing director of the IMF and the president of the World Bank. At the meeting with the IMF we talked about how a new government in India could negotiate a longer term facility with the IMF. With the World Bank, the emphasis was on the expeditious release of already committed funds.

I also held bilateral discussions with representatives of several countries that were providing aid. The request was the same. We faced a balance of payments crisis. Could they help by releasing their assistance quickly and speedily? I recall particularly my meeting with the US treasury secretary, Jim Baker, because he offered to meet me in the office of India's director on the board of the IMF, instead of my calling on him.

I was carrying a letter from Chandra Shekhar for President Bush, Sr. We had already requested our ambassador, Abid Hussain, to seek an appointment with President Bush so that I could deliver the letter to him personally. When I reached Washington I was informed that while no time could be fixed for such a meeting with the President, I could call on the national security adviser (NSA), deliver the letter to him and maybe even meet the President and have a photo-opportunity with him if he decided to drop into the office of the NSA. I was not particularly keen to visit the White House if I could not meet the President and hand over the letter personally to him. I rather preferred to leave the letter with the ambassador to be sent to the President. I mention this incident because it aroused some comment in the Indian media—that I did not know the ways of Washington and therefore did not call on the NSA.

My exertions in Washington were helpful. If I remember right, we ended up securing commitments for the early release of about $500 million over the next few months.

Japan was a major aid donor to India. It was suggested that I should visit Japan to seek their help. I must confess that I was a little touchy about protocol. I still am. I sent word to our ambassador, Arjun Asrani, that a trip to Japan would be worthwhile only if I could meet the flamboyant finance minister of Japan, Ryutaro Hashimoto. When a confirmation to this effect was received, I decided to visit Japan. I met quite a few friends of India in Japan. My meeting with Hashimoto did take place, but was very brief. Hashimoto told me that he had to leave for some urgent business in the Diet. The discussions, however, went on with his senior officials. Hashimoto went on to become the prime minister of Japan. Many years later, when I became finance minister again in 1998, he came on a visit to India, though not as prime minister but as an influential member of the Liberal Democratic Party. He asked for an appointment with me, which I readily gave. He walked into my North Block office with arms outstretched, saying, 'Oh, my dear old friend!' Sometimes, even brief encounters can be memorable.

My efforts in Japan resulted in India receiving commitments for the early release of another $500 million or so of Japanese aid.

I also used the opportunity to meet those bankers in Tokyo who managed the short-term debt portfolios of our lenders. I requested them to agree to rescheduling our commitments and to keep their faith in India. This personal request had an impact and many of them agreed to the rescheduling.

I remember the Tokyo trip for the back-breaking schedule that the embassy had prepared for me, the feeling that I had gone there literally with a begging bowl and my very brief meeting with Hashimoto. The cherry trees were in full bloom, especially in front of the Indian embassy. Alas, one did not have the leisure or the mood to enjoy the splendid sight.

There was nothing more that I could do abroad as far as the foreign exchange crisis was concerned. The rest of the struggle was in India. With the announcement of the dates of the Lok Sabha elections, political priorities changed completely. The Samajwadi Janata Party, to which I belonged, had only limited prospects in the elections. Our strategy was to win enough seats in a hung Parliament to become the balancing factor in the formation of the new government. So, all those in the party who had any chance of winning were drafted for the contest. After careful thought, I decided to contest from the Patna parliamentary constituency. Though Patna was my hometown and I was born and raised there, I was not familiar with the entire constituency as it was a large one that included a vast rural area. It was also a tough constituency, made tougher still by the candidates who were arrayed against me.

The elections, and my participation in them, added to my cares and worries. I had to spend most of my time in Patna and yet keep track of what was happening in New Delhi.

Summer was already upon us with the day temperature soaring to 40 degrees Celsius and more. Campaigning was tiring. I used to return home exhausted, with the prospect of an early morning start and a strenuous schedule again the next day. And yet, if some officer was visiting me from New Delhi with official files and papers, I had to find time to attend to the work. Life could not have been busier or more demanding.

On one of my visits to New Delhi during this period, I was told by my officers that despite all our efforts matters were going from bad to worse. It was the incumbent government's responsibility to ensure that the coffers were not completely empty when the next government took office. Something had to be done, and urgently, to keep the wheels turning, at least for a few weeks after the installation of the next government. The only way to do it was to mortgage our gold reserves against payment in foreign exchange. It was a difficult decision to take. Indians are more attached to gold than anything else. It is also a symbol of honour. A family will sell its gold ornaments only as a last resort. But the choice was clear. Mortgage gold or face the danger of defaulting on our external commitments. We chose the first option. Perhaps a less responsible government may have avoided taking such a drastic decision and left a succeeding government to fend for itself. The irony is that the people who benefited most from this step turned out to be its most virulent critics.

We decided not to touch the gold reserves with the RBI in the first instance. There was some gold lying with the State Bank of India. Smuggling of gold was rampant because of the restrictions placed even on legitimate gold imports. The customs authorities often succeeded in detecting and confiscating such consignments. The confiscated gold was kept with the State Bank of India. It was also disposed of from time to time in the domestic market. There was nothing sacrosanct about this gold.

Negotiations were held with the Bank of England to mortgage the confiscated gold. For twenty tonnes of gold we expected to get around $400 million. The Bank of England, however, insisted on the gold being shipped to London. It was a momentous decision, unprecedented in the annals of India's economic history. While I was in Patna, Chandra Shekhar, I understand, discussed this with President Venkataraman. Perhaps, he also sounded Rajiv about it. They agreed that in the given situation this was the only option left. After details of the deal were finalized, the file was brought to me in Patna in a sealed cover by an officer of the Ministry of Finance.

After Chandra Shekhar's approval, the deal was put through. The RBI looked after the details. The gold was put on a chartered aircraft and shipped to London. An intrepid newspaper reporter who got wind of the shipment rushed to Mumbai airport, took some photographs and broke the story. All hell broke loose after that. The ongoing elections added fuel to the fire.

The Lok Sabha election results were disastrous from our point of view. We won only five seats out of 543. The winners were Chandra Shekhar, H.D. Deve Gowda from Karnataka, who went on to become prime minister in another government, and three more candidates from Uttar Pradesh. My own election in Patna was countermanded by the Election Commission because of the large-scale rigging resorted to by the ruling Janata Dal in the state. Most tragically of all, Rajiv was assassinated by LTTE terrorists from Sri Lanka while he was campaigning in Tamil Nadu.

The news was broken to me by my driver when I landed in Delhi from Patna that evening. A special air force plane was taking Sonia Gandhi and family members just then to Madras. I remembered my last meeting with Rajiv. I had sought an appointment with him, though our alliance was over. He invited me to come to 10 Janpath at 10 p.m. When I reached there, I found two people I recognized waiting in the room outside—P.V. Narasimha Rao and P.C. Alexander. I was lucky because I was ushered in at the appointed time. Rajiv and I had a long conversation that day. I told him about the economic crisis that we faced and its long-term implications, as also how the political crisis created by his decision had made management of the economic situation that much more difficult. I mentioned how easy it would have been to remove the misunderstanding between him and Chandra Shekhar. Rajiv listened to me carefully. He inquired about how we were managing the economic situation. He expressed regret over the political misunderstanding between Chandra Shekhar and him. He also regretted that he had not talked to me earlier. He wished he had.

The Congress party was returned to power after the 1991 elections. Narasimha Rao took over as prime minister and appointed Chandra Shekhar's economic adviser, Dr Manmohan Singh, as his finance minister. This was the end of our tryst with governing India.

2

A Chance Encounter

The course of events in my life has often depended on chance encounters and accidental meetings. Many of my decisions have therefore been impulsive, taken on the spur of the moment and without a care for the consequences. Surprisingly, most of these decisions have proved to be correct in the long run. In this chapter I shall deal with one such chance encounter which helped me make up my mind on an important issue and put an end to uncertainty.

After the May 1991 elections, I continued as a member of the Rajya Sabha and leader of the Samajwadi Janata Party in the House. I was still an important and active MP though the party to which I belonged had largely become irrelevant.

The party had to look for a future for itself. The responsibility fell largely on Chandra Shekhar to ensure that we, his followers, still had a place under the political sun. The Janata Dal, like the Janata Party earlier, had come unstuck and broken up into its various constituents. The Chandra Shekhar faction was the first to break away. This was followed by the Ajit Singh faction. In 1993, as important assembly elections were round the corner, fresh attempts were made to reunite the three factions of the Janata Dal. Chandra Shekhar nominated me, along with Om Prakash Chautala, to negotiate the terms of the merger. The other negotiators were Sunil Shastri and Rasheed Masood on behalf of Ajit Singh, and S. Jaipal Reddy,

Sharad Yadav and I.K. Gujral on behalf of the original Janata Dal. We had a few meetings at the residence of I.K. Gujral. I was unhappy with the attitude of some of my erstwhile colleagues. I also had serious reservations about merging with a party which was increasingly being dominated by Laloo Yadav who, as chief minister of Bihar, had used his rustic style to create a larger than life image for himself. He completely dominated the proceedings when the unity conference was held and treated everyone as his subordinate. He had no qualms about ill-treating people, even insulting them. I knew that I could not get along with such an individual even for a day. In fact, I remember telling Chandra Shekhar in a party meeting earlier in Haridwar that if the party had to make compromises in order to survive in politics, each one of us should be allowed to make our individual compromises instead of being forced into a collective compromise.

Narasimha Rao, whom fate had catapulted into the position of prime minister after the 1991 elections, was very keen, for some reason, that I join the Congress party. He sent his emissaries to me several times inviting me to meet him. The plea given by these intermediaries was that their stock would go up if I accompanied them for a meeting with Rao. I had my reservations about joining the Congress. I could have exercised that option way back in 1984 itself and reaped the benefit of joining the ruling party, but my rebellion was against the style of functioning and the style of governance of the Congress party. I could not compromise on that. I knew, in my heart of hearts, that I could go anywhere, join any political grouping, but never the Congress party, not even under Rao. Why did I agree to meet him then? I went along just to satisfy my curiosity and help these friends of mine in the Congress party improve their stock with Rao. Naturally, these meetings did not yield any result.

A common friend, who was keen that I join the BJP, had in the meanwhile arranged a meeting with L.K. Advani. Over lunch, Advani and I discussed a number of issues but the question of my joining the BJP was brought up neither by him nor by me.

Things continued to drift until a chance encounter with Laloo Yadav. I was flying to Delhi from Ranchi, via Patna, with my wife. At Patna airport there was a flurry of activity. We were informed that preparations were being made for Laloo Yadav to board the flight. Laloo Yadav entered the aircraft like a monarch of all he surveyed. He glanced at me but refused to show any sign of recognition. Even while alighting at Delhi airport, when we stood side by side, he deliberately ignored me. His behaviour confirmed my worst fears about him. Whatever little possibility had remained of my returning to the Janata Dal evaporated that day. I made up my mind. Even my personal loyalty to Chandra Shekhar could now not persuade me to join the Janata Dal or stop me from going ahead with my plans.

As soon as I reached home, I rang up Advani and requested him for an urgent meeting. He said he was on his way to some election meetings and would contact me either late that evening or early the next morning. He phoned me at around 5.30 a.m. the next day to inquire if I could see him then. He was about to catch a flight out of Delhi and would be back only a few days later. I thanked him and told him that I could wait for a few days and we could meet when he returned. When he did, I told him that I had decided to join his party. The rest was up to him. The issue was handled expeditiously by Advani and I joined the BJP on 13 November 1993. We had just celebrated Diwali, and Advani described me as a Diwali gift to the BJP. A chance encounter had once again determined an important part of my life—my political future. But for it, I may have continued to drift for some more time.

Advani gave me his fullest support. He made me an invitee to the national executive of the party, a body of about 150 senior leaders from all over the country, and also appointed me the spokesperson of the party on economic issues. The drafting of the party's economic resolutions was generally left to me. A newcomer to the party could not have asked for more.

Towards the beginning of 1995, I was informed by

Kailashpati Mishra, the seniormost BJP leader of Bihar, that the party wanted me to contest the Bihar assembly elections. Laloo Yadav had ruled Bihar for five years from 1990 and made a mess of it. But politically he was in a strong position. He had been able to carve out for himself a sizeable vote bank of Muslims and Yadavs during this period. He had also emerged as a champion of the poor, though he had done precious little for them. He was not an easy adversary to tackle.

I was greatly surprised at this move and sought a meeting with Advani to understand the party's strategy better. Advani told me that Bihar was going to witness a four-cornered contest between the Janata Dal, the BJP, the Samata Party (of George Fernandes and Nitish Kumar) and the Congress party, and the division of votes might lead to a hung assembly, and possibly a coalition government. As such, they wanted the BJP legislature party to be led by a person who would have wide acceptability. They were keen therefore that I should contest the assembly election. I agreed and proceeded to Ranchi, the summer capital of Bihar and now the capital of Jharkhand, from where I was to contest the election. I was accompanied by Gulshan Lal Ajmani, the sitting BJP MLA from Ranchi, who had been sent by Advani to invite me to contest the election from there instead of him. A grand welcome awaited me at Ranchi airport. My win was a foregone conclusion, and I was elected by a handsome margin.

Contrary to Advani's expectation, however, the elections did not produce a hung assembly. Laloo Yadav secured an absolute majority, the Samata Party led by Nitish Kumar performed poorly, securing only seven seats, and the BJP emerged as the second largest party with around forty seats. I was elected leader of the legislature party and became the leader of opposition in the Bihar assembly.

I did rather well as leader of opposition and got the better of Laloo Yadav on more than one occasion. My 1995 speech on the Bihar budget is still considered a landmark. The comment from the treasury benches, though, as I proceeded with the speech, was that it was too technical. Laloo Yadav could not reply to even a single serious point that I had raised. Instead, he spent his time telling irrelevant stories, and at the end of his two-hour-long speech put a bunch of papers on the table of the House which he claimed dealt with all the points I had made. I protested, as it was not a permissible parliamentary practice. My objection, however, was not given much weight by the Speaker. I found that in many ways the practice followed in the Bihar assembly was totally at variance with the practice followed in Parliament. In fact, on one occasion, when I raised an issue of procedure, Laloo Yadav got up and told the Speaker that my problem was that I did not know enough about parliamentary norms and practices! I told him that I could teach him the practices and procedures of parliamentary democracy for the next twenty years. This made front page news the next day in all the newspapers in Patna.

Soon I became some kind of a celebrity in Bihar, so much so that when I stopped for tea at a roadside dhaba, the owner would recognize me and refuse to accept payment. I was thoroughly enjoying myself in this new capacity. But it was not to last.

In January 1996, while on an election tour for the party in the Barak valley of Assam, I learnt that I had been chargesheeted, along with Advani and many others, in the notorious hawala case. The entire case was based on some private diary entries made by a business house which mentioned some initials and a certain sum of money against those initials. A large number of Congress party leaders were also chargesheeted in the case. It was a virtual who's who of Indian politics. Advani promptly resigned as leader of opposition in the Lok Sabha. K.N. Govindacharya, BJP general secretary, rang me up in Silchar to tell me that the party had decided that I should not resign. I was greatly upset. Far away from home, with no one to talk to or confide in, I could not sleep the whole night. For my local party colleagues, however, it was business as usual the next day. I noticed that my agitation was hardly shared by anyone else. I went through the programmes indifferently and took the first flight out of Silchar to Delhi. Immediately on arrival in Delhi, I rushed to meet Advani and insisted on resigning from the Bihar assembly. He told me that while he had no objection, Atal Bihari Vajpayee, who was the seniormost leader of the party, would also have to be convinced about this move. I met Vajpayee and repeated my request to be allowed to resign. He agreed reluctantly. Thus ended my all-too-brief stay in the Bihar assembly.

The hawala case, Narasimha Rao's last political gambit to win the 1996 Lok Sabha elections by bringing discredit to a large number of political leaders and, in turn, projecting himself as a knight in shining armour, ended ingloriously for him. Not only did he lose the elections, the court refused to even frame charges in the case. All of us were discharged without the case reaching the trial stage. CBI's appeal to the high court and the Supreme Court also failed. The case, however, caused great mental agony to me and many others. It also interfered with our political careers. For example, not only did I resign from the membership of the Bihar assembly with over four years of my term still left, I also refrained, like Advani, from contesting the 1996 Lok Sabha elections, as the case was still pending. This is not the usual norm followed in politics, certainly not today, but I still believe that Advani and I behaved with dignity in the face of adversity and followed our conscience, if not the political ethics of the day.

In the 1996 elections, the BJP emerged as the single largest party in the House for the first time. The President invited Atal Bihari Vajpayee to form the government, which he did. But Vajpayee was not able to prove his majority in the Lok Sabha and had to resign after a few days. The Third Front led by H.D. Deve Gowda was then able to form a government with the outside support of the Congress party. I remember writing an article in the *Indian Express* in which I recounted the experience of the Chandra Shekhar government and concluded that the Deve Gowda government would also be ditched by the Congress, sooner rather than later, once its purpose had been served, namely, to prove that no political party or formation could rule India except for the Congress. My prediction proved correct and Deve Gowda had to resign as prime minister within a year. The Third Front accepted the humiliating condition of the Congress party to change the prime minister in order to continue in government. I.K. Gujral became the next prime minister. But the Congress party did not allow even this government to continue for long and withdrew its support, forcing the government to resign, again within a year.

While all this political drama was going on in Delhi, the BJP was quietly working hard to consolidate its electoral base across the country. As part of this exercise, the party decided to appoint me as president of the Bihar state unit in October 1997. The hawala case was over by then and I was in a position to resume full political activity, including holding a formal party position. By early next year the Gujral government had resigned and general elections were held in March 1998.

We started preparing feverishly for the elections. During one of my trips to Delhi, Advani, who was party president, told me that he would like me to contest the Lok Sabha elections. I told him that since I was heading the party in Bihar, which had fifty-four Lok Sabha seats, I considered it my duty to work for victory in the whole state rather than concentrate on winning only my seat. But Advani insisted that I contest. Finally it was decided I would contest from Hazaribagh, a constituency adjacent to Ranchi. I was keen on Hazaribagh not only because I had contested the 1984 election from there as a candidate of the Janata Party but also because I had been continuously in touch with that constituency since then. Early in my career, I had been posted as a sub-divisional officer in Giridih, the famous mica town which was then a sub-division of Hazaribagh district. Hazaribagh is a picturesque district and during my first posting itself in the area I had made up my mind to settle there after retirement.

I worked hard for my election, moving from place to place, addressing scores of meetings and leaving nothing to chance. The hard work paid off and I won by a record margin of about 164,000 votes. I led from all the six assembly segments of the constituency. The party also did well in the rest of Bihar.

3

'Who Will Prepare the Budget?'

Once all the results had been announced it became clear that a BJP-led government would be formed at the centre. A frequent question that people started asking in the media, especially on television channels, was who would be the country's next finance minister. Various names were mentioned. While still in Patna, I was invited to join a panel discussion on a TV channel which was being broadcast from Delhi. The anchor asked me the same question. My reply was that it was up to the prime minister to decide, but it would not be a difficult decision. 'I am sure he will be able to find a suitable person for the job,' I added. Then, as if straining his memory, the anchor asked, 'Did you also not hold the post once?' I mention this just to emphasize how short public memory is. People, by and large, had forgotten that I was ever a finance minister.

I left for Delhi after a couple of days. There was great excitement there. TV channels were vying with each other to come up with interesting political analyses. The composition of the new government, its policies and programmes, and the allocation of portfolios—all were hot topics of discussion. Once the channels learnt that I was in Delhi, I was inundated with requests to participate in their programmes. The favourite question was who would be the next finance minister and whether I was a candidate. After a while, I got so fed up with the speculation that I decided to go back to Patna and wait there for news of government formation and word, if any, of my place in it.

I learnt from the media that the prime minister and his cabinet were likely to take the oath of office on 19 March. I waited for word from the party regarding my inclusion in the cabinet. But there was no call from anyone in Delhi. Govindacharya did speak to me over the phone on the morning of 18 March and asked me to come to Delhi. But his call could not be taken as an authoritative invitation. Although unsure, I decided to go to Delhi that day nonetheless. After reaching Delhi around 10 p.m., I asked my wife if either Vajpayee or Advani had called. There had been no call, she told me. It was a scene straight out of *Yes Minister*, the popular BBC serial. Clearly, I was not going to be a part of the new cabinet.

Within half an hour of coming to this conclusion, I got the all-important call from Advani. He invited me for the swearing in at Rashtrapati Bhavan the next morning. Late in the night, a generally well-informed friend told me that I would get the commerce portfolio. I was quite happy. Commerce was a subject I was familiar with, since I had worked in that ministry for seven long years in India and abroad. Early on 19 March, the same friend called up again and informed me that it had been decided that I would get the finance portfolio. I was quite surprised at the development because it was almost certain that Jaswant Singh would get the portfolio. Vajpayee too was keen to include him in the cabinet and make him the finance minister. The rumour was that the Rashtriya Swayamsewak Sangh (RSS) had suggested to Vajpayee that those who had lost in the elections should not be included in the cabinet. This ruled out both Jaswant Singh and Pramod Mahajan, at least for the time being.

On the day of the swearing in, I went to Rashtrapati Bhavan, the third time I was going there for such a function. The first was when V.P. Singh was prime minister and I had walked away from the ceremony; the second when Chandra Shekhar was the prime minister and I had taken oath as a

cabinet minister. The ceremony was held in the forecourt of
Rashtrapati Bhavan and not in the Ashoka Hall. Seats for the
would-be ministers were arranged in alphabetical order and,
with my surname starting with the letter 'S', I found myself
almost at the end of a long queue. Atal Bihari Vajpayee was
the first to be administered the oath by President K.R.
Narayanan. He was followed by L.K. Advani and then the rest
of the cabinet. During the function, I ran into Najma Heptullah,
deputy chairperson of the Rajya Sabha. She was happy to see
me included in the cabinet and told me jokingly that I would
have to get myself elected to her House within six months to
retain my cabinet berth. She did not know that I had already
been elected to the Lok Sabha. I smiled and told her that the
contingency would arise only if I resigned my Lok Sabha seat!
She felt happier on hearing this. As presiding officer, she was
very considerate to me in the Rajya Sabha and often invited
me to her room for sandwiches and coffee during long hours
of duty in the House.

*Taking the oath of office as cabinet minister. The author was
later given the finance portfolio.*

A formal cabinet meeting was held that afternoon. The cabinet room in South Block was not an unfamiliar place for me. The meeting itself was very brief. The only decision taken that day was that the next meeting of the cabinet would be held after four or five days. When the meeting ended, I approached Vajpayee and inquired whether, in the meanwhile, I could go to my constituency to thank my voters. Vajpayee looked at me intently, then smiled, and said, 'If you go away who will prepare the budget?' His words left me speechless. Vajpayee had told the media earlier in the day that he would keep the finance portfolio himself. Imagine my surprise therefore when he told me to prepare the budget. It was the first indication that he was planning to give me finance.

The portfolios were announced late that evening and the news was flashed prominently on all the television channels that I was to be the new Finance Minister of India.

Some in the party circles felt that it was the RSS that had suggested my name since I was a supporter of 'swadeshi'. I shall deal with the concept of swadeshi later, but suffice to say here that in earlier years I had participated in various programmes organized by the RSS to promote the concept of swadeshi. I had even undertaken a cycle yatra of over 250 kilometres all the way from Hazaribagh to Patna, along with hundreds of party workers, to protest against the Dunkel draft. Dunkel was the director-general of GATT and his draft of a trade treaty had met with strong opposition in India as it was considered to be against our interests.

The next morning I called on Vajpayee to thank him for the trust he had reposed in me. During the meeting, I also told him that, as per my earlier experience, a finance minister could function effectively only when he had the complete confidence of the prime minister. 'Poora vishwas hai,' he said, assuring me of his complete confidence. I was reassured beyond any doubt. After my meeting with the prime minister, I went confidently to North Block, which houses the Ministry of Finance. There was a large number of mediapersons waiting outside the office. They asked questions about the Indian economy and my plans

for the future. The most important question was about my
ideas about kick-starting the Indian economy. I did not want
to answer this all-important question in a hurry and promised
to respond later after I had given it serious thought. Suddenly,
I was bang in the centre of things.

The next day I was again asked to meet Vajpayee at his
residence. Jaswant Singh was also present. There was a problem.
Jayalalitha, the head of the AIADMK, which was supporting
the government, was insisting that the minister of state from
her party attached to the Ministry of Finance be given
independent charge of the revenue department of the ministry.
I was expected to agree to this arrangement. I told Vajpayee
and Jaswant Singh that I did not think it was a good idea. It
would be unwise to divest the finance minister of the charge of
revenue. If revenue was under the charge of another minister,
the finance minister would find it very difficult to prepare the
annual budget. Jaswant Singh went out to have a word with
Jayalalitha on the phone. I do not know what he said to her,
but when he came back he told me that I could perhaps draft
the order of work allocation to the minister of state in such a
way that it would make Jayalalitha's minister happy and at the
same time ensure that he would continue to work under me.
So, we settled the issue through a well-drafted order allocating
responsibilities to the two ministers of state who had been
appointed in my ministry. R.K. Kumar, who is unfortunately
no more, was the minister from the AIADMK. A chartered
accountant by profession, he was a very reasonable and decent
person, and I had no problem working with him.

4

A Dream Budget Gone Sour

The first task I had to attend to was the preparation of an interim budget. I had to go to Parliament for a vote on account for the next four months, which would give me enough time to prepare a regular budget and get it passed in Parliament. Though an interim budget is a routine affair dealing mainly with the expenditure estimates, some serious thought does need to go into its preparation; also since it would be the first important economic policy statement of the new government I had to devote enough attention to it. I was assisted by the core budget team in the finance ministry, which consists of the finance secretary, the revenue secretary, the expenditure secretary and the chief economic adviser. They are present in every discussion. Besides them, the additional secretary, budget, the chairmen of the Central Board of Direct Taxes (CBDT), the Central Board of Excise and Customs (CBEC) and others are involved on a need-to-consult basis.

For my first budget, I made no changes in the existing team. Montek Singh Ahluwalia was the finance secretary and was also in charge of the economic affairs department, N.K. Singh was the revenue secretary, C. Ramachandran the expenditure secretary, Shankar N. Acharya the chief economic adviser and J.S. Mathur the additional secretary in charge of budget. This was the core team which prepared both the interim and the regular budgets of 1998.

While preparing the interim budget of 1998, I was fully briefed by my officers on the prevailing economic situation. There were two issues of serious concern which seemed to confront us. First, there were indications that the growth rate in 1997–98 was likely to drop sharply compared to the previous year. Agriculture was likely to register a negative growth and industry was doing poorly for want of demand and huge capacity creation in the previous years. Second, the East Asian crisis was raging, bringing massive economic and financial disruption to several fast-growing economies. The huge inflow of foreign capital, much of it short term, in the previous years had now started reversing as investors had started exiting from these countries at the first signs of trouble in their economies. Since even the short-term capital was employed in long-term projects, repaying these investors caused serious problems, leading to a massive devaluation of the currencies of these countries.

Inevitably, the East Asian crisis exerted pressure on our foreign exchange position also. Foreign funds began to be withdrawn from India. Though we had a reasonably comfortable foreign exchange position with reserves of around $29 billion, they started depleting fast, mainly because there was no inflow of fresh funds. The general global situation was one of gloom and doom. To prevent the outflow of foreign currency, the RBI had raised interest rates and had imposed certain other curbs during P. Chidambaram's tenure as finance minister. When this kind of a situation develops—where the rupee depreciates against the dollar—people tend to delay bringing their money into the country beyond the normal waiting period. The RBI had taken various steps to control the situation, but these steps were affecting investor confidence, which was eroding fast. The interim budget had to be prepared under these difficult circumstances.

I presented the interim budget on 25 March 1998 and promised to get back to Parliament with a regular budget very soon. I particularly remember the comment of one MP who said that, just by placing expenditure proposals for four months in a four-page statement, I had succeeded in drawing the attention of the news media of the whole country. The interim budget was passed by Parliament without much discussion.

The interim budget of 1998 revealed the true state in which the previous government had left the country's finances. The *Statesman* of 26 March 1998 said 'Sinha tears apart Chidambaram's claims'. *The Hindu* titled the budget and the analysis of the economy in my speech as 'Nightmare of 1997–98', while some others said 'New Credo in North Block: Pragmatic Swadeshi'. I may mention here that Chidambaram's budget of 1997–98 had been hailed as a dream budget by the media and the chambers of commerce.

I decided to attend the spring meetings of the World Bank and the IMF in April. There was a lot of curiosity about us abroad: We were the first 'pure' non-Congress government; there was the swadeshi tag attached to us; and most of the cabinet ministers were unknown. Naturally, people were anxious to know more about us. I stopped over in London briefly on my way to Washington, DC. My younger son, Sumant, who worked for Citibank, was posted in London at the time. I used the opportunity to borrow some decent ties from him for my trip. In Washington and New York, I met a large number of investors. The atmosphere was quite optimistic and I was happy to see the 'unprecedented' interest shown in India by American investors and NRIs. My elder son, Jayant, who lived in Boston and worked for McKinsey, came down to New York to meet me. He also bought me some good shirts, which I definitely needed.

Our concept of swadeshi was clearly creating a great deal of apprehension in the minds of people abroad. They were unsure of our policies, especially with regard to foreign investment. I was aware of these apprehensions and tried to calm their fears. Montek Ahluwalia's presence by my side was, no doubt, reassuring to them because he had been in the Ministry of Finance for many years and was fairly well known in the financial and business circles abroad. At one of the meetings I remember saying, in response to a question, that Montek represented continuity while I represented change. I explained that that was how our system worked. We had permanent civil servants and politicians who could change from election to election. I explained swadeshi as a very modern and dynamic concept which meant being pro-India without being anti-foreign. Swadeshi did not mean a retreat into protectionism or the raising of high-tariff walls. It meant calibrating globalization to suit national interest. I emphasized that India was back in business, indeed, it was a better business opportunity than ever before.

5

Preparing and Presenting
a Budget

The annual budget of the Government of India is one of the most complex, time-taking and detailed exercises involving the financial and economic issues facing the country. The finance minister is directly charged with the responsibility of preparing the budget and hence has to apply his mind to every detail.

How is the budget of the Government of India prepared? The prevailing economic situation is first reviewed and a broad strategy to deal with the problems devised. Then the budget numbers are examined. The additional secretary, budget, brings the projected budget figures typed on Blue Sheets—they contain details of the likely expenditure, receipts, fiscal deficit, revenue deficit and the amount of borrowing needed for the current year and the next. The team then proceeds to balance the budget as best it can by trying to cut expenditure and raise resources. This is the most difficult part of the budget exercise. While the finance minister holds wide-ranging discussions with all interests, including his colleagues in the cabinet, the only person he has to take fully into confidence and receive guidance from is the prime minister. In the normal course, the finance minister meets the prime minister at least four times before the budget is finalized. In these meetings every aspect of the budget is discussed in detail with the prime minister, including the budget speech.

It is up to the prime minister to decide which official from his office he would like to involve in the budget exercise. It was Brajesh Mishra in the first year. In later years, N.K. Singh was also involved in the budget exercise from the prime minister's office (PMO).

The process of budget preparation can be divided into four parts.

The first is the preparation of the expenditure budget. The expenditure proposals of the line ministries are scrutinized closely in the finance ministry. Important issues are brought to the notice of the finance minister, while the rest of the expenditure budget is finalized at the official level.

The second part of the budget exercise relates to the inclusion of new schemes in the budget. Every finance minister introduces a set of new schemes in his budget, which he identifies after discussions with his cabinet colleagues or on his own.

The third important part of the budget relates to taxation. This is the part which is of the greatest interest to trade and industrial circles, as well as to the middle class.

The fourth part is the budget speech, the last document to be prepared. Part A of the budget speech, dealing with the economic context, the various sectors of the economy, the new schemes and other general issues, is prepared by the chief economic adviser. Part B, which deals with the taxation proposals, is prepared by the revenue secretary. The finance minister then works on the speech personally, both in order to check the consistency and flow of the language and to ensure that it is of the right length. No finance minister would like to spend more than two hours reading the budget speech.

I used to work hard on my budget speeches, going through every sentence over and over again. I remember the many late nights that I spent in my North Block office alone, working on them. The poetry and the jokes, if any, were always the last to be added. I am fond of Hindi film songs, and often had a liberal dose in my speeches. Balmiki Prasad Singh, who was home secretary in 1998, had given me some rousing poetry from the works of the late Ramdhari Singh Dinkar, the famous Hindi poet, which I also used.

One of the most important aspects of budget-making is the balancing of the budget. The core group examines the Blue Sheets very closely and various permutations and combinations are experimented with so that the fiscal deficit is kept to the minimum. I remember poring over the Blue Sheets day after day, sometimes with the core team, sometimes with just the additional secretary, budget. Working on the Blue Sheets is a very painstaking exercise. The Blue Sheets are not kept for record. They are destroyed the moment they are done with.

The finance minister is required to share his thoughts on the budget with the prime minister. My interaction used to be in stages. My first meeting with the prime minister was as soon as I was ready with the broad framework of the budget. In this meeting, I discussed the economic situation, the fiscal scene, the budget strategy, the plans to reduce expenditure, including subsidies, and the proposals to raise revenues. This is the stage at which the prime minister used to convey to me his ideas about the budget. For instance, when I had my first meeting with Vajpayee regarding the 1998–99 budget, he asked me to give maximum attention to the rural areas, where the majority of our people live, and the farmers of India, because agriculture is the backbone of our economy and employs the largest workforce.

The second meeting with the prime minister was held after I had finalized my taxation proposals and those relating to the new schemes in the budget. This was a very important meeting, since the likely political implications of the budget are taken into account in this meeting. I held the third meeting with the prime minister when everything was finalized, and presented to him the final budget numbers and its final strategy. The fourth and last meeting was held after the budget speech had been prepared. Vajpayee used to go through the budget speech carefully and give useful directions. Once the prime minister approves the budget speech, substantive changes in it are ruled out. But I used to continue to work on the language until almost the last moment before the speech went for printing. Vajpayee used to set apart a lot of time for these meetings. He was never in a hurry, and paid great attention to the details and gave directions wherever necessary.

The budget is printed in the finance ministry's press located in the basement of North Block. This becomes a maximum security press during the budget exercise. In fact, North Block itself is under extra security during budget time, but the press has foolproof security. Everyone, including the finance minister, must have a pass to enter the press. A meticulous record is maintained of all entries and exits. The interesting part is that, as soon as the taxation proposals are finalized and work begins on the amendments to the finance bill, all those working on the budget in the press, including officials of the law ministry, are locked inside, and have to stay there for many days. They not only work, they also eat and sleep there. Telephone conversations with the outside world are banned. The only persons allowed to enter or walk out are the finance minister, the members of his core team and the additional secretary, budget. The finance minister's visits are both for work relating to the budget and for keeping up the morale of the people locked inside the press. It is an interesting and, at times, sobering experience.

THE BUDGET TEAM

During my tenure of four years in the Ministry of Finance, during which I presented five budgets, there were more changes in the core team than was desirable. In fact, for every budget I had a new finance secretary. I presented the 1998 budget with Montek Singh Ahluwalia as finance-secretary-cum-secretary, economic affairs; the 1999 budget with Vijay Kelkar, who held the same post; the 2000 budget with Piyush Mankad, who was finance-secretary-cum-revenue-secretary; the 2001 budget with Ajit Kumar, who was finance-secretary-cum-secretary, economic affairs; and the 2002 budget with C.M. Vasudev, who was just secretary, economic affairs. There was no finance secretary. I also had, during my tenure, three revenue secretaries in N.K. Singh, Javed Chowdhary and S. Narayan; and four expenditure secretaries in C. Ramachandran, E.A.S. Sarma, C.M. Vasudev and C.S. Rao. After Shankar Acharya left as chief economic adviser, I brought Rakesh Mohan in his place, though he could not get the designation of chief economic adviser owing to the long procedure for appointment to this post and continued as adviser to the finance minister. These rapid changes made my life very difficult. For instance, when Piyush Mankad became finance-secretary-cum-revenue-secretary and E.A.S. Sarma, secretary, economic affairs, we had avoidable problems between the two. As finance secretary, Mankad was the leader of the team. Sarma, however, zealously guarded his turf. Mankad did not like being left out of important decisions being made on the economic affairs side but there was no way of involving him directly in the decision-making process on a day-to-day basis. It was this experience which persuaded me not to repeat the mistake when Narayan was revenue secretary and Vasudev became the economic affairs secretary. Narayan might have felt unhappy at not being designated as finance secretary despite being the seniormost secretary in the ministry, but I knew that the flawed arrangement would not work.

We were not fair to Sarma. He was an extremely competent officer. The government did not do justice to him therefore when it transferred him from economic affairs to coal. He left the service in a huff. I would have, perhaps, done the same.

Not all changes are made by the finance minister, and not all officers deputed to the finance ministry are equally competent. While some are absolutely brilliant and outstanding, others are clearly pedestrian. Some of the problems I faced in the finance ministry could have been avoided if we had had more competent and experienced officers. Given my own civil service background, it was fairly easy for me to get along with the officers, even if they were not chosen by me.

BUDGET IN PARLIAMENT

Articles 112 to 116 of the Constitution of India deal with the presentation of the annual budget to Parliament and other matters connected with the budget. The Constitution, however, does not mention the word 'budget' in Article 112. It only lays down that the President shall in respect of every financial year cause to be laid before both the Houses of Parliament 'a statement of the estimated receipts and expenditure of the government of India for that year' and refers to it as the 'annual financial statement'. The Article also lays down that the estimates of the expenditure embodied in the annual financial statement shall show separately:

a) the sums required to meet expenditure described by the Constitution as expenditure charged upon the Consolidated Fund of India; and

b) the sums required to meet other expenditure proposed to be made from the Consolidated Fund of India and shall distinguish expenditure on revenue account from other expenditure.

Article 112 (3) defines the expenditure which shall be charged on the Consolidated Fund of India.

a) the emoluments and allowances of the President and other expenditure relating to his office;

b) the salaries and allowances of the Chairman and the Deputy Chairman of the Council of States and the Speaker and the Deputy Speaker of the House of the People;

c) debt charges for which the Government of India is liable including interest, sinking fund charges and redemption charges, and other expenditure relating to the raising of loans and the service and redemption of debt;

d) (i)   the salaries, allowances and pensions payable to or in respect of the Judges of the Supreme Court;

    (ii) the pensions payable to or in respect of Judges of the Federal Court;

(iii)   the pensions payable to or in respect of Judges of any High Court which exercises jurisdiction in relation to any area included in the territory of India or which at any time before the commencement of this Constitution exercised jurisdiction in relation to any area included in a Governor's Province of the Dominion of India;

e)   the salary, allowances and pension payable to or in respect of the Comptroller and Auditor General of India;

f)   any sums required to satisfy any judgment, decree or award of any court or arbitral tribunal;

g)   any other expenditure declared by this Constitution or by Parliament by law to be so charged.

Article 113 lays down that the expenditure charged from the Consolidated Fund of India shall not be submitted to the vote of Parliament, though Parliament may discuss any of those estimates. The Constitution goes on to define 'Demands for Grants', appropriation bills, supplementary, additional or excess grants, and votes on account, votes of credit and exceptional grants in the subsequent articles.

According to an old convention, again from the days of the British, the Railway budget is presented separately to Parliament.

All revenues received by the Government of India, all loans raised by it and all monies received by it by way of repayment of loans are credited to the Consolidated Fund. All other receipts are credited to the Public Account. The budget gives an account of three consecutive years. It contains the actuals of expenditure for the preceding year, the revised estimates for the current year and the budget estimates for the following year. It also gives separately the figures of revenue receipts and capital receipts and the figures of revenue expenditure and capital expenditure. It is also required to show separately the funds made available for the annual plan both for the central ministries and for the states.

The budget consists of a series of bulky documents, that is, the receipts budget, the expenditure budget in two volumes, the demands for grants, the appropriation bills, the finance bill, a document containing the budget at a glance, a document containing the key features of the budget, a document containing a report on the implementation of the budget announcement of the previous year and the budget speech of the finance minister, among others. The Fiscal Responsibility and Budget Management Act, 2003 enjoins upon the finance minister to submit further documents from time to time to Parliament within a financial year. The presentation of the annual budget is preceded by the presentation to Parliament by the finance minister of the Economic Survey, a detailed document on the state of the economy and its future outlook. It also contains a very large number of useful statistics on the economy.

Until 1998 and beginning with the days of the British, budgets were presented to Parliament at 5 p.m. on the last working day of February every year. The time for presentation of the budget in India was fixed according to the convenience of the British Parliament. The Secretary of State for India laid a copy of the budget of the Government of India on the table of the House of Commons in the afternoon, after it had been presented in India. This tradition continued even after independence. With the growing importance of the budget and the interest of the people and the media, presentation of the budget late in the day created its own problems. With the advent of television, it became even more necessary to explain the budget to the people immediately after it was presented. Late presentation of the budget reduced the time available for this purpose. I remember how, in 1998, all of us in the Ministry of Finance rushed from one interview to another, across the city, to various TV channels. We also had to find the time to give interviews to the print media. When I returned home from the last interview, it was near midnight, and I was completely exhausted. I made up my mind to change the time of budget presentation from the next year.

At the beginning of 1999, I suggested to the prime minister and the parliamentary affairs minister that I would like to present the budget at 11 a.m., instead of 5 p.m. I could go to the President for his approval of the budget at 9.30 a.m., the cabinet meeting to approve the budget could be held at 10 a.m. and the budget could be easily presented to the Lok Sabha at 11 a.m. The proposal was welcomed by everyone. In fact, I was surprised that a simple and easy-to-implement decision like this had not been taken by finance ministers before me for fifty years. The change of timing made life easier for everyone concerned with the evaluation and analysis of the budget.

In the year 2000, there was a slip-up on my part. I thought the change of timing had been settled once and for all in 1999 and did not take up this matter again with the Minister of Parliamentary Affairs. Once the summons for the session is issued and question hour fixed for each day, it is difficult to change the schedule. So, in 2000, we decided to present the budget at 2 p.m. It was at least better than presenting it at 5 p.m. From 2001 onwards, however, there was no confusion and the procedure is now firmly established that the budget will be presented to the Lok Sabha at 11 a.m. on the last working day of February.

After the budget presentation, there is a general discussion on it in both Houses of Parliament, but first in the Lok Sabha, on dates fixed by the presiding officers. This discussion could extend to three days in the Lok Sabha. At the end of this discussion, the House does not pass the budget as such, but only the appropriation bill relating to the vote on account for two months' (April and May) expenditure of the next financial year. A few days after the presentation of the budget, the finance minister also presents the final batch of supplementary demands for the current year.

The budget session of Parliament is held in two parts and could extend from the middle of February to the middle of May. During the recess, the various standing committees of Parliament hold their own meetings and prepare their comments on the budgets of the ministries under their charge. When Parliament reconvenes, the Lok Sabha takes up for detailed discussion the demands for grants of some selected ministries.

In the Rajya Sabha, which has limited powers in financial matters, the working of the ministries is discussed, not their demands for grant. The list of ministries is selected by the business advisory committees of the two Houses. It is at this stage in the Lok Sabha that members can move cut motions to reduce the demand of the ministry under discussion by a certain amount, generally one rupee. Cut motions cannot be moved on any other occasion and are limited to only those ministries which are taken up for discussion in the Lok Sabha. At the end of the discussion on the demands for grant of the selected ministries, the guillotine is applied, when the Speaker puts to the vote of the House the demands of all the ministries for its approval. The appropriation bill, which authorizes the government to incur expenditure as budgeted, is then passed by the House.

The third stage in Parliament is the discussion and passing of the finance bill. This is taken up after the passing of the appropriation bill. The finance bill contains the taxation proposals of the budget. This is also the occasion on which the finance minister moves amendments to the bill to change his budget proposals in the light of representations which he may have received in the meanwhile. The passing of the finance bill by the Lok Sabha and its return to the Lok Sabha by the Rajya Sabha after it too has discussed the finance bill mark the end of budget related work in Parliament during the budget session.

As the Rajya Sabha has limited jurisdiction in financial matters, it can hold discussions, like the Lok Sabha, on the appropriation and the finance bills, but it does not pass them; it only returns them to the Lok Sabha. It does not have powers to make amendments in these bills. No cut motion can be moved in the Rajya Sabha. Even if the Rajya Sabha fails to return a financial bill, its approval will be presumed after fifteen days of the passage of the bill in the Lok Sabha, and the President can be approached for his assent to the bill.

I have described the procedure in some detail based on my own experience because during my tenure I noticed that even veteran MPs are often unaware of the budgetary procedure.

So, when a general discussion on the budget takes place, they freely comment on the taxation proposals also, ignoring the fact that the appropriate time to discuss the taxation proposals is when the discussion on the finance bill is taken up. Similarly, when discussion on the finance bill takes place, they make general comments on the budget as a whole. Even the media is blissfully unaware of these details. I have been asked by senior journalists, for instance, whether a cut motion was being moved on the finance bill.

6

The Nuclear Tests

After my return from Washington in April 1998, I plunged myself into the preparation of the budget. There was no time to waste. I had decided to present the budget on 1 June so that we would miss only two months of the year, April and May, as far as new taxes were concerned. This is when I got hit, literally, by a bombshell.

One day some time in early May, I got a call from Vajpayee's office to meet him at his residence. Vajpayee was living at 7 Safdarjung Road; he had yet to shift to the official residence of the prime minister at Race Course Road. I was not told about the subject of the meeting, but assumed that it might be about the budget. Usually, our meetings took place in one of the living rooms of the house. On this occasion, I was taken to his bedroom. I was intrigued and a little apprehensive. What was so important and confidential that he had to take me to his bedroom to discuss it? As soon as we were alone, he gave me the earth-shaking news! He had decided to go ahead with a series of nuclear tests and had fixed 11 May as the date for the tests. He took me into confidence because he expected serious economic fallout from this action and wanted me to be prepared for any eventuality. I did not know how to react. I was totally dumbfounded.

Vajpayee was aware that we were facing enormous problems on the economic front. The nuclear tests would surely multiply them manifold. While I was grateful to him for taking me into confidence, there was not much comfort I could provide except to promise him that I would do my best. I came back a worried man, acutely aware of the sensitivity of the information that the prime minister had shared with me. He had not told me the names of the others he had taken into confidence, so I was not free to discuss the matter with my officers or colleagues. I could only roll over the consequences of this development and its impact on the economy in my mind, and work out steps to counter them. Even as my mind went into overdrive as I considered various permutations to counter the economic impact of the tests, I felt very lonely. I kept the secret to myself and thought furiously about the adverse impact and how to tackle it.

On 11 May, I waited with bated breath for news of the tests, which were scheduled to take place at 11 a.m. But there was no news in the forenoon.

Later, in the afternoon, Jaswant Singh rang up to invite me to an important meeting convened by Vajpayee at his residence (he had shifted to Race Course Road). Jaswant told me that a major development had taken place which we needed to discuss. I asked him if the event had already occurred. He replied with a short yes. I went to 5 Race Course Road. Those assembled for this historic meeting were L.K. Advani, the home minister, George Fernandes, the defence minister, Jaswant Singh, the deputy chairperson of the Planning Commission, Brajesh Mishra, the principal secretary to the prime minister, and I. We were informed that the tests had to be delayed a little because of the weather and that two more tests would be conducted on 13 May.

I was not much into military strategy and security issues then, but it was clear to me that we could take credit for the fact that nobody got wind of the plan to conduct the nuclear tests, especially the Americans. An earlier initiative, under Narasimha Rao, had to be abandoned as the Americans had detected the preparations and exerted pressure on Rao to dissuade him from going ahead.

The issue being discussed in the meeting was how the news should be broken to the world. We discussed the draft of the letter that Vajpayee was planning to write to the heads of state and governments. The draft was ready and quickly approved. A consensus was also reached that considering the importance of the event Vajpayee himself should meet the media and inform them about it. A very brief statement was prepared which Vajpayee read out to the media. The media was told that there would be no questions. More tests were carried out on 13 May, after which we declared a voluntary moratorium on further tests.

The nuclear tests created a diplomatic and political furore internationally and had an immediate economic impact. Share prices on both the Bombay Stock Exchange (BSE) and the National Stock Exchange (NSE) fell sharply, following selling by foreign institutional investors and speculators across the board. The BSE Sensex nosedived by 77 points while the NSE Nifty dropped by 28 points. With the follow-up tests of 13 May, the Sensex dipped further by 162 points. It was the biggest decline since the day the Deve Gowda government had fallen on 31 March 1997.

Apart from the sharp reaction in the stock markets, the nuclear tests also invited immediate economic sanctions from many western countries and Japan and Australia. Our worst experience was with Germany. Our joint secretary in the finance ministry, who had gone there for aid talks, was told that the meeting was off and he could go back home. This is just an example of the sharp reaction that took place throughout the world. Across the board, they imposed economic sanctions. All aid was stopped except for the current commitments. Restrictions were placed even on commercial credit flows. Many restrictions were also imposed on several items of trade, especially by the United States. Large loans which were being negotiated by the private sector, for instance, were put on hold. Under the influence of these countries an embargo was also imposed on new loans from the World Bank and the Asian Development Bank.

It was in the midst of these challenges that I had to formulate my budget proposals. It was not an easy task.

7

A Road Map for the Future

The budget of 1998–99 was the first budget of the Vajpayee government. I described it as a defining moment in history, also as an occasion fraught with expectation. In paragraph 3 of the speech I said:

> It has been just over ten weeks since this Government took office. But, we know already that a new India is rising. And as May 11 was surely the first step, today is yet another. Certainly, a long journey lies ahead, but as history will prove, we have now begun to build a new India. This will be a strong and prosperous India—a nation self-reliant, but not autarchic, rather a nation keen to deal with the world as an equal partner with other countries. As the saying goes, only the strong can be free. And only the productive can be strong. This is the new India we propose to build.

At the back of my mind was the traumatic experience of 1991. I was determined there would never be a repeat of that situation. Only a strong and productive India could achieve that goal. Only a strong and productive India could be self-reliant. On economic sanctions, I said:

> While the people of India have reacted with pride over the events of May 11, some of our friends abroad have

responded negatively. I am confident that these initial
negative responses will be moderated as our position
gets better understood, and will not have any significant
impact on our economic development. On our part,
our policies have to be clearly directed and firm.

After declaring that my budget was rooted in swadeshi, I
proceeded to define the term. 'Swadeshi does not mean isolation,
swadeshi means making India strong and self-reliant so that
we can compete with the world and win,' I explained. At the
end of the speech I emphasized my firm conviction: 'In the
days to come India will stand tall on the world's stage because
of our commitment to democracy and the pursuit of prosperity.'
    Nine years down the line and after ten budgets, five of
which were presented by me, I can say with a degree of
satisfaction that the target I set and the vision I unfolded on
that first day of June 1998 has largely been realized. India is
on a sustained growth path, its suppressed energy has been
finally unleashed and, barring an unprecedented catastrophe, it
is unstoppable.
    I also reflected Vajpayee's concern about the rural economy
and the farmers. 'As I stand here and address this august
House, my thoughts wander naturally to the remote villages of
India and to millions of our toiling farmers. I have no doubt
in my mind that the health and dynamism of the rural
economy is central to India's economic and social development.'
I introduced a number of schemes, including the Kisan Credit
Card for farmers. Ashok V. Desai, consulting editor of the
Telegraph and a renowned economist, was one of my most
trenchant critics when I was finance minister. I came across a
piece written by him in the 28 November 2005 issue of
Business World in which he says, 'Once, Yashwant Sinha was
so pained by my criticism of his actions that he was constrained
to protest. On reviewing my record, I found that I had really
bestowed more criticism than praise on him. The imbalance
cannot be rectified. But, I would like to acknowledge one of
his policy innovations that has paid handsome dividends.' He

goes on to mention the Kisan Credit Card and how it has changed the rural credit scenario.

Credit to the farming community has always been problematic. We had stipulated that it was the most important item in priority sector lending, and its share was fixed at 18 per cent out of the 40 per cent of total bank lending fixed for the priority sector. But there were many banks which could not meet the target. Chidambaram had devised the system of mopping up the unused funds and putting them at the disposal of NABARD, the National Bank for Agriculture and Rural Development, under a new window called the Rural Infrastructure Development Fund. But that was not quite a substitute for lending directly to the farmers. I therefore devised a scheme where a card which would offer rolling credit to farmers could be issued to them. The card had a limit and the farmer could borrow up to that limit whenever he needed money for insecticides, pesticides, fertilizers and seeds from listed retailers. It also enabled him to borrow in cash.

The limit on the card was to be fixed according to the earning capacity of the farmer, based on the land that he owned, the proportion of irrigated land, the kind of crops he grew, his annual income and his needs. He was required to repay the amounts he withdrew over a period of time from the money he earned after selling his produce.

We started the Kisan Credit Card scheme in late 1998. The RBI and NABARD together worked out the details. Instructions were sent out to the banks to issue the cards. I reviewed the progress of the scheme in each of my subsequent budgets and was encouraged to find that all our banks—the cooperative banks, the regional rural banks, the commercial banks, the public sector banks—were enthusiastic about it. I attended various functions across the country where the Kisan Credit Card was distributed to eligible farmers. The aim was to cover all the eligible farmers in the country with Kisan Credit Cards within the tenure of the Vajpayee government. We almost did it, issuing about 4.5 crore cards to the farmers by the end of our term.

The author (third from right) at a function to spread awareness about the Kisan Credit Card scheme.

At the time of preparation of the budgets, I invariably reviewed with the banks the progress of two projects that were of special interest to me—the Kisan Credit Card scheme, and the self-help groups, and the micro-credit advanced to them.

In subsequent years, we linked the card to insurance. Every farmer who had a Kisan Credit Card was automatically insured against death and disability. We separately improved the crop insurance system, the idea being that every farmer who had the card should also be covered by crop insurance. Thereby the card also became a social security scheme for the Indian farmer.

The credit card scheme was very well received in Parliament and outside, though I personally feel that we could not organize the kind of publicity that was needed to popularize it. As a result, a large numbers of farmers remained unaware about the scheme. Once, in my constituency, when I talked to farmers about Kisan Credit Cards, I was dismayed to notice that many did not know about the scheme. Others complained that, although they had applied for the card in the local bank branch, their applications were not entertained. On one occasion, I felt so angry that I walked into the bank myself, accosted the manager and demanded to know why he was not implementing the scheme properly. Mostly, however, the banks did get into stride and issued a large number of these cards. I once accompanied the prime minister on a visit to Patna. We organized an impressive function at the Sri Krishna Memorial Hall where Vajpayee distributed the cards. During my election campaign in 1999 (the details of why India had another election so soon are dealt with in a later chapter), I came across at least one farmer in my constituency who showed me the card given to him by the Prime Minister of India. In a TV interview when I replied that I would regard the Kisan Credit Card scheme as my most important achievement as finance minister, the anchor was quite surprised.

Housing is a major issue in India and shelter is something people want most of all. So, I paid a lot of attention to this sector in my budgets. In the rural areas, especially of Bihar and Jharkhand, one of the more persistent and vociferous demands, particularly from the women, was for a 'colony'—a house—from their elected representatives. The Indira Awas Yojna enabled them to get a small house worth Rs 20,000 free of cost. Unfortunately, the implementation of the Indira Awas Yojna was full of loopholes at the village and district levels. This led to great bitterness among the people. In the 1999 budget I thought of changing the concept of the scheme and making it more comprehensive: I introduced a new scheme called the Samagra Awas Yojna. It subsumed the Indira Awas Yojna. Under the new scheme, the existing grant scheme was to continue but with a few modifications. Accordingly, the beneficiary could also make a contribution of his labour, material or cash, to build a bigger, better house to suit his needs, rather than be restricted to a one-room house as under the Indira Awas Yojna.

While this was welcomed by many, others thought we

were indulging in politics by removing Indira Gandhi's name from the scheme. There were protests in Parliament from the Congress party members. We could have weathered the protest, but Vajpayee, being a very sensitive person, did not want any controversy. He asked me not to change the name of the scheme, and we did not. Many in the BJP did not appreciate this climbdown and protested against the decision. They quoted numerous examples where the Congress party had changed the names of existing schemes and retitled them after their leaders.

In 1998 I added a new document called 'Key Features of the Budget' to the list of budget documents presented to Parliament. It listed in one place the important features of the budget, including the new schemes and the changes in taxation. If a reader wished to have a bird's-eye view of the budget, all he had to do was refer to this document.

Unfortunately for me, as soon as it was presented to Parliament, the 1998 budget got mired in an unseemly controversy. One of my dreams, ever since my return from a posting in Germany in 1974, had been to develop highways, across the length and breadth of our own country, along the lines of the German autobahns. I now had the opportunity, in 1998, to give shape to my vision. The constraint was money, and I proposed an additional levy of Re 1 per litre on petrol with immediate effect. It would generate a sum of Rs 790 crore a year, which could go entirely to the corpus of the National Highways Authority of India for the development of roads. The duties on petrol were to be adjusted accordingly.

I do not know how and where the misunderstanding took place between the finance and the petroleum ministries. But, to my great shock the next morning I learnt that, from the midnight of 1 June, petrol prices had been raised by Rs 4 per litre! I felt terrible. The mistake was quickly corrected, but the damage was done. The opposition parties made much of it in Parliament the next day.

The other issue on which I was on the back foot in Parliament the next day was not a mistake but a carefully considered decision. It related to the raising of the price of urea by Rs 40 per bag of 100 kg. There was a big hue and cry in Parliament at the steep increase. MPs, even those of the ruling coalition, were up in arms on the issue. I rushed to the Lok Sabha and then to the Rajya Sabha to explain my position. On the petrol price issue I made an honest admission that it was a mistake and that I had issued instructions for it to be corrected immediately. But the members kept heckling me about the increase in the price of urea. On the spur of the moment, and even without consulting the prime minister, I announced that the hike of Rs 40 would be halved and the increase would be only Rs 20 per bag. Later, under pressure from my own party MPs, even this increase was undone.

The balanced use of fertilizers was, and still is, a very important issue facing the country. The excessive use of urea, since it is heavily subsidized, adversely affects the fertility of the soil. Farmers tend to use large quantities of urea to obtain quick results. In the long term, this is bound to play havoc with agricultural productivity in the country. My effort to correct the imbalance by raising urea prices met with complete failure in 1998. A reduction in fertilizer subsidy would have also enabled us to make more capital investment in agriculture, which was declining. But that also had to wait.

I felt extremely unhappy at these developments. If we had not made the mistake regarding the petrol price hike, I would perhaps have been on stronger ground to resist the demand for rolling back the urea price hike. It was these quick rollbacks the very next day after presentation of the budget that prompted some in the media to give me the nickname 'Roll-back Sinha'.

As a result of the controversy created by the two price hikes and their rollback, many important steps that I had announced in the budget got lost. For instance, in agriculture and rural development, apart from the Kisan Credit Card, I raised the allocation for the Watershed Development Programme and for the Accelerated Irrigation Benefit Programme to give a boost to irrigation projects. The Rural Infrastructure Development Fund was augmented by Rs 500 crore. NABARD was entrusted with the responsibility of extending the coverage of self-help groups to another forty lakh families over the next five years. Two lakh families were to be covered within 1998–99. The National Housing Bank was asked to finance one lakh rural dwelling units under the Swarn Jayanti Housing Finance scheme. Regional rural banks were strengthened. I said that no farmer would go to jail for loan repayment default or be compelled to commit suicide. The RBI was instructed to issue appropriate guidelines to banks for hassle-free settlement of old dues.

The problem of production, marketing and movement of agricultural commodities as a result of numerous central and state laws and regulations was to be tackled through a national agricultural policy. The Multi-State Cooperative Societies Act was to be replaced by a Model Cooperative Law. Farm implements and tools were removed from the list of items reserved for manufacture by the small-scale sector. I announced that futures trading in edible oilseeds, oils and oil cakes would also be allowed. Finally, I talked about the rationalization of the poverty alleviation and employment generation programmes in rural areas and their unification under the two broad categories of self-employment and wage-employment programmes.

The budget of 1998 did not go down well with many people. Trade and industry were unhappy, as also MPs for reasons of their own. One criticism was that the budget lacked vision and a philosophy.

But the budget definitely had a philosophy: that demand must be generated in order to give momentum to the economy, and that demand would come from rural India, where the largest number of our people live. If the rural areas did not generate demand, industrial India would not be able to move forward. I had therefore taken various important steps to improve the rural economy. It was not merely good social policy; it was good economics as well. Demand must be generated by the masses. Their purchasing power must increase; they must consume more. Only when that happens can the surplus capacity in industry be gainfully utilized, and in course of time more investment will be made to create new capacity. That was the approach in the 1998 budget, and indeed in all my subsequent budgets.

I may not have been happy with some of the post-budget developments. But I was extremely distressed at the motivated criticism that came from some well-informed political colleagues and sections of the media. The usual political criticism of a budget being anti-farmer, anti-labour and anti-people is understandable. But, when a person like Dr Manmohan Singh said that I had not factored in the full impact of the economic sanctions, that I had presented only half a budget and that sooner rather than later I would have to come back to Parliament with a full budget, I was definitely not amused.

But, there was appreciation as well. M.S. Swaminathan, the eminent agricultural expert, said, 'This budget will impart growth to the rural economy, to agriculture.' And one of my parliamentary colleagues said, 'If you sat back with your eyes closed during the early part of Mr Sinha's speech, it could well have been Mrs Gandhi holding forth.'

8

The Resurgent India Bond and the India Millennium Deposit

Having faced the 1991 crisis, I was determined not to have another balance of payments crisis on my hands. In 1998, soon after we came into office, I had to start worrying about our foreign exchange reserves. These reserves, though larger than before, were depleting fast as a result of the East Asian crisis and the economic sanctions following the nuclear tests. I knew that once the tolerance limit was crossed this slow bleeding could turn into a haemorrhage. In a modern, liberalized economy, which ours was by 1998, with large Non-Resident Indian (NRI) deposits and foreign institutional investment (FII) in the stock market, it is very easy to destabilize the economy. The absence of capital account convertibility would be of little comfort. If the FIIs wanted to take their money out, they could start selling in the stock market, which, apart from leading to a crash, could also destabilize the foreign exchange market and lead to a massive depreciation of the rupee. In the more liberalized tiger economies of East Asia, this is exactly what had happened. I wanted to avoid such a situation at all costs. It was a question of confidence. The confidence of the NRI investors and FIIs in India should not be shaken. The IMF option of a bailout to get over a balance of payments crisis, available to us in 1991, would not be available to us in 1998 since we had gone nuclear.

It was imperative that we shored up our foreign exchange reserves.

On my visits to London and New York in April 1998, investment bankers at both places had suggested that we bring out a sovereign bond issue. India had never issued sovereign bonds. I was not keen to depart from tradition. Instead, we decided to ask the State Bank of India to issue a bond abroad. When I disclosed my plan to issue such a bond to some of my cabinet colleagues, Advani suggested we call it the Resurgent India Bond (RIB). Our feedback was that the NRI community was very proud that India had stood up to the pressure of the rest of the world, including the sole superpower, the United States, and had gone ahead with the nuclear tests. We decided to offer these bonds only to NRIs and PIOs—persons of Indian origin. The details of the Resurgent India Bond scheme were worked out by the State Bank of India in consultation with the RBI and the finance ministry. It was to be a five-year bond, to be marketed in August 1998. We expected to collect around $2 billion through these bonds, which were to be open for sale for four weeks. The State Bank advertised the bonds widely and finally opened them for sale on 5 August 1998. In the normal course, the sale was supposed to come to a close on 4 September, with 17 August marked for the earliest closure. We ended up collecting $4.25 billion within about two weeks, which was well beyond our expectation. M.S. Verma, chairman of the State Bank, was an outstanding banker and did a wonderful job once again on this occasion. Since we had collected more than twice the amount that we had expected and did not want any more, we decided to close the sale of the bonds on 24 August 1998.

The criticism from some quarters was that we had raised expensive money from abroad. It was not true. In Parliament I met the criticism by quoting the interest rates being paid by some other developing countries on their sovereign bonds. Ours was not a sovereign bond and yet we had not paid a rate of interest which was out of line with comparable bonds from other countries. I was convinced that it was a very worthwhile step. It restored the confidence of foreign investors in our country and stopped the further depletion of our foreign exchange reserves. We never looked back again and in fact kept adding to our foreign exchange reserves after this.

We faced a similar situation in the year 2000. Global oil prices were trading at ten-year highs. The oil import bill was putting pressure on our reserves, which fell from $38 billion in April 2000 to $35 billion in November 2000. The rupee depreciated by 6 per cent during this period. Once again, we felt the need to augment our reserves and maintain the confidence of the people in our economy. We approached the State Bank of India and asked it to float the RIB type of bonds once again. This time, however, we decided to call it the India Millennium Deposit. This issue was once again a roaring success. We ended up collecting $5.5 billion.

The critics remained unfazed. They felt that when the day of reckoning came after five years, we would be hard put to find enough reserves to service the debt. I was always confident that repayment would be no problem. Today, nobody remembers when the RIBs were repaid and, as a result of the appreciation of the rupee vis-à-vis the US dollar, the State Bank of India has actually ended up with a profit of about Rs 800 crore on the redemption of the bonds. I must give full credit to Dr Bimal Jalan, governor of the RBI, for handling the two issues so efficiently at his end.

As far as the economy was concerned, however, we were passing through a very difficult time. Demand was not picking up. The economy was sluggish. Rural areas were in distress because agriculture had not done well. There was hardly any major infrastructure activity taking place in the economy. There was surplus capacity in industry as a result of excess capacity creation in past years. Interest rates were high. There was a global meltdown and, on top of it all, there was the impact of economic sanctions.

We also cannot ignore the role of sentiment in the economy.

In a globalized world it is not merely sentiment at home but global sentiment which affects an economy. I realized in 1998 itself that sentiment had come to play a very important role in determining the perception of the people about the performance of the economy. Consumption and investment in the economy were dependent on that perception. For instance, the immediate impact of sanctions imposed on us after the nuclear tests in May 1998 was not substantial. We were not critically dependent on aid. But the impact of sanctions on sentiment was huge. Similarly, the East Asian crisis had a very adverse impact on sentiment. The stock market and foreign exchange market move on the basis of sentiment which often may not be in keeping with the fundamentals of the economy. In 1998 we logged a growth rate of 6.5 per cent, not bad at all, but sentiment remained depressed. The feel-good factor was missing.

The World Economic Forum–Confederation of Indian Industry (CII) meeting was held in January 1999 in Delhi. The president of the forum, Claus Schwab, had come to India to participate in the meeting. I could not attend the opening ceremony since I was busy with the preparation of the annual budget for 1999–2000. In his opening remarks on the inaugural day, Schwab predicted that India was about to face a 1991 type of crisis. I felt very unhappy at this remark. So, when I went to address the closing session of the meeting I joined issue with Schwab. I told the audience that such prophets of gloom should keep their counsel to themselves and not come here and talk the economy down since such remarks become a self-fulfilling prophecy.

This was not all. Throughout 1998 I had to give plenty of pep talks to trade and industry to improve their morale. I remember, in particular, the speech I made at the twenty-fifth National Management Convention in Kolkata in September 1998. The All India Management Association had invited luminaries like Paul Krugman, the famous economist, Rajat Gupta, the head of McKinsey&Co., Vikram Gandhi, a famous investment banker, and others to address the convention. I spoke extempore and ended my speech with these words:

A great opportunity beckons India today; perhaps the greatest that has ever appeared before it. This is a moment in history India must seize. This is a moment in history India must not let pass. If all Indians create that will that India shall go out and take this opportunity, the country has a great future. I am often dispirited myself, disheartened when people make too much of that 'feel-good factor'. Somehow, somewhere, Indians are allowing themselves to be discouraged, to be weakened, to be diffident. I have met representatives of trade and industry in various parts of this country and do not see any reason why India should be despondent. I do not see why some problems in some sectors should make the whole nation so dispirited. The challenges are many. So are the opportunities. I do not have any prescriptions for the weak, for the diffident. For those who believe in themselves, who believe in India, the time to move forward is now. The time to forge ahead is now. I am confident that, with the combined commitment and determination of the people and the goodwill that the country has, India shall not fail its people. It shall not fail its friends. It shall be able to meet the challenges internally and the opportunities externally. It is into that kind of future that India must be prepared to move—a vibrant, buoyant, fast-growing economy, based on competition, based on fair competition, forward looking, modern and out to compete with the rest of the world and ready to win.

This is only a sample of the exhortation I used to give India Inc. to shore up its confidence in itself and in India and to assure it that its travails were only temporary. It took time, but it had the desired effect in the long run.

9

Lessons Learnt

The year 1998 was one of great economic turmoil globally. The East Asian financial crisis spread. Japan continued to be in recession and in August 1998 a severe balance of payments crisis afflicted Russia. World output growth dropped below 2 per cent, the growth of world trade decelerated, commodity prices fell steeply, currencies were savaged and capital flows to developing countries declined sharply. By January 1999 the contagion had spread to Brazil, triggering massive capital flight and a steep depreciation of the currency.

In India we had to contend with the additional challenge of economic sanctions imposed on us after the Pokhran nuclear tests. But, despite these adversities, we had reason to be satisfied with the way we withstood the impact of these challenges. Our GDP growth in 1998–99 had accelerated to 6.5 per cent compared to 4.8 per cent in the previous year. The agriculture sector put up a better performance and contributed to the healthy GDP growth. Our foreign exchange reserves were in better shape and we had successfully curbed undue volatility in the forex market. Although inflation had risen sharply during the year, it was successfully brought down to below 5 per cent.

I presented a better budget in 1999. I had learnt my lessons from the 1998 budget and was able to avoid the mistakes I had made then. This budget was also received much more favourably. In fact, when political developments forced an election, Advani said that we would go to the polls with the slogan of 'Three Bs'. The first was the good budget; the second was Bihar, because we had imposed President's rule there, though we could not carry it through the Rajya Sabha. The third B, of course, was the 'bomb'—the nuclear tests.

The first part of the budget session passed without any mishap. But, during the parliamentary recess Jayalalitha decided to withdraw her support to the government. This created a doubt about our majority in the Lok Sabha. The opposition parties started demanding that the government seek a vote of confidence, as soon as Parliament met. The President also suggested to the prime minister that he seek a vote of confidence. To ask a government to seek a vote of confidence in a budget session was a very unusual request to make, because during the budget session the government's majority is on test almost on a daily basis in the Lok Sabha through some financial business or the other. Under our system, if the government loses the vote on any financial business, it has to resign. As directed by the President, however, we sought a vote of confidence. There was a day-long debate followed by the vote. We lost that vote of confidence by just one vote. Giridhar Gomango, who was the chief minister of Orissa, was technically still a member of the Lok Sabha. He was asked by the Congress party to come to the House that day and vote against us. Many felt that it was morally not correct for him to do so. But politics and morality do not often go together. We had all worked hard to ensure our win but we did not succeed. In the annals of our democracy this loss by one vote will surely stand out as a memorable event, and as a sign of the maturity of our democracy.

There was dismay, disappointment and demoralization in our party on account of the loss. There was speculation after the fall of our government that the Congress party, led by Sonia Gandhi, would form the next government. In fact, she went to Rashtrapati Bhavan and staked her claim, but she could not muster a majority. Since no alternative government could be formed, the country had to face another general election within eighteen months.

This created a peculiar situation for the financial business pending before the Lok Sabha. A general discussion on the budget had taken place, but neither the appropriation bill nor the finance bill had been passed. We had to find a way out of it.

President Narayanan also felt concerned because, as the custodian of the Constitution, he had the ultimate responsibility. He invited me for a discussion to Rashtrapati Bhavan. I suggested that the best way would be for Parliament to meet and pass the budget without any discussion and without any amendments. It was my privilege as finance minister to move amendments. I would forgo that opportunity. But the opposition would also have to forgo the opportunity of discussing the budget and offering its suggestions. It was finally decided that we would pass the budget without discussion. There had been many rollbacks in the 1998 budget. This was going to be a budget which would be passed without any amendment, in fact, without any discussion. We had indeed made history of sorts.

Elections could have been held within a couple of months in June. But the Election Commission decided to hold elections during the months of September and October. My own election was to be held towards the end of September, which meant that the entire campaigning had to be done during the monsoon months. Unfortunately, due to political uncertainty, many of the initiatives of the budget could not be taken forward for six to seven months, until a new government was in place.

As the country prepared for the polls, news reached us about Pakistani troop incursions in the high mountains of the Kargil sector of the Himalaya. In May 1999 some shepherds spotted Pakistani troops on Jubbar Heights in Kargil. The whole country was agog when the Kargil incursions first came to light. Soon, there was a full-fledged conflict between India and Pakistan.

The war imposed a financial burden upon us both immediately and in the long term. We could not take any chances with defence preparedness. The end of the conflict could not be predicted and we had to be prepared to meet any contingency. We also discovered many operational and procedural problems in replenishing defence supplies during this period. The defence forces were therefore asked to work out their requirements in terms of equipment and supplies. In a meeting of the Cabinet Committee on Security, we decided to change the procedure for defence purchases. The defence minister was authorized to approve proposals of up to Rs 50 crore at his level, and up to Rs 300 crore in consultation with the finance minister. Any proposal beyond that amount had to go to the Cabinet Committee on Security for approval. This procedural improvement helped a great deal in securing quick supplies. The conflict came to an end in July 1999 when Indian troops threw out the last intruder and captured all the lost ground.

The conflict did create an uncertainty in the capital markets. The Sensex dipped by almost 200 points between 26 May and 27 May—day one and two of Operation Vijay that was launched to counter the intrusions—but it soon recovered. I tried to calm the fear of volatility in the capital markets by repeatedly reassuring that the economy would be able to withstand the effects of war.

In September 1999 I went to my constituency to start my election campaign formally.

10

The General Election of 1999

Since both 1998 and the early part of 1999 had been difficult from the point of view of the economy, I had remained busy in Delhi, and had thus not been able to give much time to my constituency. I had not even fully utilized the funds available to me as an MP for local area development. The few schemes which had been sanctioned had not taken off. So, when I went back for re-election, people told me quite bluntly that, while I might have been the finance minister of India, I had done nothing for them. Though it was highly demoralizing for me to hear comments of this kind, I decided to work hard to convince my voters that I meant well and deserved another chance. It had the desired result. I won the election even more convincingly than I had in 1998.

The election campaign brought home to me once again the pitiable state of rural roads, and the great need to improve them immediately. Most areas of Bihar do not have proper roads, and on numerous occasions my vehicle got stuck in the mud. People enjoyed my discomfiture on such occasions, hoping that I would thereby realize the difficulties they faced. Somehow they held us responsible for all their travails—even for long-standing problems which we certainly could not have solved in twelve months—since we were in power at that time.

On the campaign trail.

There was a general feeling that we would win the elections and the Vajpayee government would return to office. True to expectations we did, and the new government led by Vajpayee was sworn in on 13 October.

The ministers and their respective portfolios were again in the realm of uncertainty and speculation. I was sworn in as a cabinet minister. There was speculation in the media, however, that since the DMK, our coalition partner from Tamil Nadu, had a sizeable number of members in the Lok Sabha, its leader, M. Karunanidhi, might insist on the allocation of the finance portfolio to his representative in the government. The name being mentioned for the job was that of Murasoli Maran. He was the seniormost leader of the DMK after Karunanidhi. Later, there was a statement by Karunanidhi himself that, since I had been re-elected, he saw no reason for a change. Maran was ultimately given charge of the combined ministries of commerce and industry.

After the election results had been announced, but before the formation of the ministry, I got a call from Vajpayee's office asking me to come over for a meeting. The others present were L.K. Advani, Jaswant Singh, Brajesh Mishra and N.K. Singh. The meeting had been called to discuss the reorganization of ministries. Two ministries were to be split. The first was the Ministry of Home Affairs. The suggestion was that the Department of Internal Security could become a separate ministry. When this issue came up, Advani put his foot down and the proposal was nipped in the bud then and there.

The other ministry which was to be split was the Ministry of Finance. I was shocked to hear that the idea was to split the finance ministry into three—a Ministry of Finance which would consist of the Department of Economic Affairs, a Ministry of Expenditure and a Ministry of Revenue. When I was asked to offer my views, I said that, since a discussion on the issue was likely to take time, it would be better to discuss the other issues on the agenda first. My suggestion was accepted and we discussed other ministries that day.

When we met the next day, the matter was raised again. I opposed the proposal to split the ministry, as I had done in 1998. I told Vajpayee that, if he had reservations about me as finance minister, I should be moved out, but requested him not to permanently damage the structure of the ministry. The meeting ended without any decision being taken.

When I reached home, I got a call from Brajesh Mishra. He asked me if I was prepared to make a compromise on the issue and accept a two-way split. I told him that it was not a personal matter but a fundamental issue of governance. I repeated my suggestion that, if I could not be trusted with the whole ministry for any reason, the ministry must remain intact and I should be shifted elsewhere. Ultimately, I think, Vajpayee must have decided not to split the ministry because when the portfolios were announced I was again made the Minister of Finance in charge of the whole ministry, and not of a part of it. I did not care to find out who were the people behind this move.

When I returned to the finance ministry in October 1999,

it was the third government in which I came to hold that portfolio. On assuming charge, I tried to pick up the pieces as quickly as possible so that at least some of the budget initiatives could be implemented. We had already lost six months. Many schemes introduced in the 1999 budget had not been implemented. Even those that had been implemented were not to my satisfaction.

11

The Path to Sustained Growth

The budget of 2000–01 was the first budget of the new Vajpayee government which had won a clear mandate from the people. We therefore devoted a lot of time to formulating our response to the confidence the people had reposed in us. It was also the first budget of the new millennium. It was my good fortune that I was going to present it.

The previous year, 1999, had been a tough one for India with the fifty-day military operation in Kargil, the super-cyclone in Orissa, long months of political uncertainty before the general election, a somewhat weak monsoon, a near tripling of world oil prices and the continued fragility in world economic recovery. But the industrial sector in India had started recovering after a recession. The various schemes in the infrastructure sector like highways and ports and the housing sector had finally started propelling its growth. Efforts to control inflation were also paying off. Exports had achieved a remarkable turnaround from a negative growth in the previous year to nearly 13 per cent growth in dollar terms from April to December 1999.

I prepared my third budget with the avowed objective of putting India on a sustained, equitable and job-creating growth path of 7 to 8 per cent a year in order to banish poverty within a decade. While presenting the budget for the year 2000–01 I predicted that the next ten years would be India's decade of development and unfolded the strategy to achieve this objective.

(Photograph by S.N. Bhat)

The author and Minister of State for Finance, V. Dhananjay Kumar, entering Parliament to present the 2000–01 Union Budget on 29 February 2000.

Having once again personally experienced while campaigning the plight of the people in the rural areas during the rainy season, I introduced a new scheme called the Pradhan Mantri Gramodaya Yojana with the objective of undertaking timebound programmes to fulfil the critical needs of the rural people. It formed a package which included the development of rural roads and other infrastructural requirements. Out of the Rs 5000 crore set aside for this scheme, Rs 2500 crore was committed for the development of rural roads alone.

I introduced the Janashree Bima Yojana, an insurance scheme for the weaker sections, especially the rural people and agricultural workers, in consultation with the Life Insurance Corporation. Sarva Shiksha Abhiyan, a scheme for universalization of elementary education, was also introduced in the budget. There was also a review of the Kisan Credit

Card scheme. A new target was fixed for the cards as well as for the self-help groups.

The budget of 2000 also contained important suggestions for the management of the food economy. Orissa, Chhattisgarh, Madhya Pradesh, Gujarat and Rajasthan had been badly affected by drought. It was proposed to give to each state government 100,000 tonnes of food grains, wheat or rice, free of cost, to enable them to start food-for-work programmes. We also planned to extend the food-for-work programme to all those states which wanted to implement it in their areas.

I announced the reduction in interest rates on Employees' Provident Fund (EPF), and other savings schemes, by one percentage point, from 12 per cent to 11 per cent. This was a routine step in view of the falling inflation and falling interest rates. It was also a beneficial step for the economy. But it met with tremendous resistance. The labour ministry was up in arms. The EPF board rejected the suggestion of reducing interest rates, though we finally persuaded it to accept the proposal. This step made me very unpopular politically. Reducing interest rates was absolutely necessary because if the government, which was the biggest borrower, kept borrowing at higher interest rates there was no way in which the interest rates in the economy as a whole could be brought down and advantage taken of declining inflation. High interest rates had been the bane of the Indian economy for decades. All sectors of the economy suffered as a result of two major weaknesses. The first was the lack of proper physical infrastructure and the other was very high interest rates compared to other countries. Development of infrastructure was naturally a time-taking process but interest rates could certainly be brought down sooner if one tackled the problem of inflation. Even during the reform years this issue had largely remained unattended, partly because inflation was still high and partly because reducing interest rates is an unpopular move. Yet, the Indian economy could not become globally competitive without reducing interest rates. Domestic demand also could not be fully exploited without reducing interest rates.

This was therefore an area which needed drastic action despite the unpopularity it would earn for me personally. We also reduced the interest rates on the General Provident Fund of government employees and the Public Provident Fund and small savings schemes which were open to the general public. This too met with a great deal of opposition from senior citizens. I received many letters protesting against the move. I tried explaining the concept of real and nominal interest rates and how a fall in inflation protected the real interest rate despite a fall in nominal interest rate. But my explanation did not cut any ice with those who thought that their interest income had been reduced and that I was responsible for it. Nobody was willing to look at the upside of it for the economy. Nobody seemed to care about the relief it provided to the borrowers. They were concerned only with their perceived loss.

In the budget of 2000, I introduced many significant changes on the taxation front. I introduced the Central Vat (CENVAT) rate of 16 per cent and further cleaned up the excise duty structure. Customs duty rates were compressed into four rates, that is, 35 per cent, 25 per cent, 15 per cent and 5 per cent. On the direct taxes side, I offered concessions to senior citizens and to women. I also laid a great deal of stress on the use of PAN—permanent account number. In consultation with the states, I decided that the PAN itself could become the business identifier number (BIN) and this was proposed to be introduced along with VAT from 1 April 2002. The basic objective was to plug all possible leakages of revenue both at the state and at the national level and persuade people to pay what they owed to the state by way of taxes. The annual budget of 2000–01 was thus a major step forward in taxation reforms.

Subsidies on food and fertilizers and a host of other articles were an ever increasing burden on the Government of India's budget. Reducing subsidies therefore was a dire economic necessity but, as elsewhere, an economically necessary step is not always a popular step. I decided to tackle this problem, despite the setback on the urea front in 1998. I reduced the subsidy on food grains by raising the issue prices of wheat and rice. This anti-populist step raised a major controversy. The media speculated whether I would be able to stand my ground and not yield to the demand of the opposition and our own allies to roll back the increase in food grain prices. Nobody appreciated the fact that the blow had been softened by the increase in the quantity of food grains made available from the public distribution system. As it always is in life, everybody looks at what they have lost rather than what they have gained.

I had to face the ire of even those in government. Some of our allies too adopted a holier-than-thou attitude and regarded themselves as defenders of the faith. They raised the issue everywhere—in Parliament, on television and in meetings of the National Democratic Alliance (NDA). They also spoke against the government in the Lok Sabha, to my great embarrassment. The criticism was music to the opposition's ears, and they thumped the desks loudly at every such remark. A member of one of our allied parties made a speech in the Lok Sabha saying that I did not have any idea of how farmers toiled in this country because there were no farmers in my constituency. During the discussion on the finance bill, a member of the Rajya Sabha from Bihar said that since I was in the bureaucracy I did not have any idea of poverty. Such offensive statements were made by people who were supposed to be our supporters. Throughout the budget session of 2000, the media kept on speculating if 'Roll-back Sinha' would roll back the increase in food grain prices. I stood my ground, resisted the pressure and did not roll back. I received no kudos, however, for my courage. If I had succumbed to the pressure, surely I would have been the butt of ridicule in the media once again.

On the expenditure side, four items—salaries, wages and allowances of government employees; the gross budgetary support for the annual plan; defence; and interest payments—accounted for the bulk of the expenditure. After the Kargil conflict, the needs of the defence ministry had clearly gone up and more funds were urgently needed. I increased the defence budget by Rs 13,000 crore, even though it added to the fiscal deficit. I had the fullest sympathy for defence and in every budget I not only increased the defence allocation but also held out an assurance that I would meet its requirements whenever the need arose in the course of the year. There was much speculation that I would impose a Kargil tax in the budget. To the disappointment of those who predicted it, I imposed no such tax. In fact, in the budget of 2000 I was lenient as far as fresh taxes were concerned. There were no harsh elements in the budget even though we had substantially raised the defence allocation.

The year 2000 witnessed the crash of technology stocks. The dotcom boom came to an end. This led to depressed market conditions the world over. For instance, NASDAQ, which consists mainly of 'new' economy stocks, declined by about 59 per cent between March 2000 and March 2001. The BSE Sensex declined by 22 per cent in one year or so while technology stocks declined by about 63 per cent.

The Pradhan Mantri Gram Sadak Yojana initiated by me to improve rural roads was inaugurated online by the prime minister on 25 December 2000 from Delhi. The day also happens to be Vajpayee's birthday. I wished him a happy birthday in the morning before taking the service flight to Ranchi. I then went to my constituency. Babulal Marandi, the chief minister of Jharkhand, and I travelled to a remote area where we had fixed television monitors and watched the online inauguration of a road in my constituency.

Towards the end of 2000, we started working on the annual budget for 2001–02. The challenges we faced were awesome, made more so by the tragedy and devastation caused by the Gujarat earthquake in January 2001.

12

Continuing Reforms

The budget of 2001–02 was the second budget of the NDA government and the fourth under Vajpayee's prime ministership. Therefore I wanted the budget of 2001 to be a landmark budget which would deal with all the pending issues on the reform front which had not been tackled in the first three budgets. So, I suggested to the prime minister that we should have prior discussions with some of our important ministerial colleagues, including those from our major allies, on the reform initiatives I had in mind. The prime minister accepted the suggestion and in the weeks preceding the budget we had three meetings with a small group of our ministerial colleagues. Apart from the prime minister and me, the group included L.K. Advani, Jaswant Singh, George Fernandes, Murasoli Maran and a few others.

Among the areas that I was keen to tackle in this budget were reforms in the laws governing agriculture in our country, which included the Essential Commodities Act. I had already held discussions with the chief ministers because they had a major role in amending this law and it was important to take them into confidence. The other issues I discussed during these meetings were subsidies on food and fertilizers, dereservation of products reserved for the small-scale sector and labour market reforms. While the Labour Commission was still working on labour reforms, it was possible to take some initiatives in this area. Most of the reform measures that I wanted to include in the budget were discussed in this small group of ministers. I thought the consensus achieved in these meetings would help me to vigorously implement the second generation of economic reforms.

I presented the budget on 28 February 2001. One of the initiatives I took in the 2001 budget was to present a new document called 'Implementation of Budget Announcements', an action taken report on the promises made in the budget of the previous year. In 2001 I submitted a report for two years, 1999–2000 and 2000–01. I found that the preparation of this report kept not only the officials of the finance ministry but also the officials of the other ministries on their toes, since the progress was reviewed every quarter.

(Photograph by Mahesh Shankar)

Giving final touches to the 2001–02 Union Budget.

The 2001 budget was the NDA government's most important policy document on reforms. It continues to remain the agenda for reforms even today. It is sad that some of these important reforms could not go through because they were met with determined resistance from certain quarters, like trade unions on labour market reforms, or from elements within our own government which were against them.

There was another hurdle that we faced. Many of the reforms involved the state governments which had to actually implement the reforms and, if they did not do so, these reforms remained on paper. For instance, I wanted the states to play a larger role in both food procurement and distribution. We assured them that we would meet the entire cost of the work and there was no question of their losing money in these operations. I wanted the states to take up procurement so that the system was not dependent merely on the Food Corporation of India (FCI) or NAFED. The FCI concentrated only on a few states to procure its requirements—Punjab, Haryana, parts of western Uttar Pradesh and Andhra Pradesh. Many states complained that their farmers were not able to derive the benefit of support prices for various crops because the FCI did not have any infrastructure for procurement in those states. MPs from Bihar, Assam and Orissa always used to complain against the FCI's limited role. But, strangely enough, when I made this offer to the states to come forward and take up this responsibility, they were unwilling to do so.

Similarly, as far as the agricultural marketing laws of the state governments relating to the movement and sale of agricultural produce, and the Essential Commodities Act dealing with the storage and trade of a large number of products of mass consumption were concerned, I found that, though they were entirely restrictive in their operations, the states were not willing to help their farmers by abolishing these laws, or at least the restrictive clauses in these laws. Wherever we needed to work with the states, we faced problems in implementing the reforms.

There was hardly any sector which was not covered by the budget of 2001. The power sector, largely with the state governments, was in a total mess with outstanding dues of the central utilities alone on the state electricity boards at about

Rs 40,000 crore. I proposed MOUs with the states which included a timebound programme for installation of 100 per cent metering by December 2001, conducting energy audit at all levels, a specific programme for reduction and eventual elimination of power theft, tariff determination by state electricity regulatory commissions and compliance thereof, commercialization of distribution and the restructuring of the state electricity boards. The government's commitment towards an accelerated power development programme was demonstrated again through increased allocations. I submitted a report on the National Highway Development Programme, the telecom sector and the corporatization of ports. By March 2001, the overall tele-density in our country had reached 3.5 per hundred, about twice the density of two years ago.

Reforms in the financial sector and capital markets were continued with the launch of various schemes to strengthen the debt market, promote capital account liberalization and encourage foreign direct investment (FDI) and FII inflows. A major reform was made in the banking sector to provide autonomy to bank managements through the abolition of the Banking Services Recruitment Boards.

Dismantling of the administered price mechanism in the petroleum, fertilizer and sugar sectors and drug price control liberalization were highlighted. Social sector schemes like Ashraya Bima Yojana and students' educational loan schemes were launched. The year 2001 was declared as Women's Empowerment Year. A task force under the chairmanship of the deputy chairman of the Planning Commission was set up to review the programmes for women. The Khetihar Mazdoor Bima Yojana, a special scheme for landless agricultural labourers, a Journalists' Welfare Fund and Shiksha Sahyog Yojana to aid the education of those below the poverty line were also launched.

I took some harsh measures too, for instance, on expenditure management. One was reduction of interest rates by 150 basis points with effect from 1 March 2001 on all administered interest rates. I talked about pension reforms, implementation of the recommendations of the Expenditure Reforms Commission by first implementing these in my own ministry, fiscal reforms at the state level, restructuring and divestment in public sector enterprises and a special scheme to help the victims of the Gujarat earthquake.

I described the 2001 budget as a budget for carrying forward the second generation of economic reforms, a budget for growth and equity with efficiency.

All in all, the 2001 budget was well received. It appeared as though all the criticism that had been levelled against me in the earlier years had vanished, as if in one stroke. The media described it as my dream budget and I was projected as the 'Master of Feel-Good' by *India Today* on its cover. I have often wondered what a dream budget means. My experience of the 2001 budget led me to the conclusion that a dream budget is one which goes for tax reduction. People who belong to the tax-paying class, like the middle class, industrialists, journalists and high net worth individuals—those who are the opinion makers in our society—praise a finance minister who gives concessions, and criticize the one who imposes a burden on them. It is as simple as that.

13

The Misfortune of Terror

The year 2001 will forever remain etched in our memory for 9/11—11 September when the twin towers of the World Trade Center (WTC) in New York were pierced by hijacked passenger planes and brought down. I was in Mumbai that day to review the progress in collection of taxes, especially income tax, with the tax authorities. Mumbai is the most important centre of tax collection, and I believed that, by keeping up the pressure on tax officials through these personal reviews, Mumbai would perform better in 2001–02. I was staying at the Sahayadri guest house of the Maharashtra government where the review meetings were being held. It was almost 6 p.m. by the time the meetings were over. I went to another room where some visitors were waiting to meet me. As soon as I reached there I was told that an accident had taken place in New York at the WTC.

My younger son, Sumant, was living in New York those days. His office was near the twin towers. Anxious about his safety, I tried to find out what exactly had happened. We switched on the television. It showed frightening scenes of the attack, first on one tower and then on the second. As I saw the plane crash into the second tower, I realized immediately that it was not an accident but a deliberate attack. I rang up my wife in Delhi to inquire about Sumant. She said she had not been able to speak to him because the phones in New York were not working. After many anxious hours of waiting, we at last got a call. It was a great relief to hear his voice and learn that he was safe.

On 9/11, the whole world woke up to the threat of terrorism. I was told later that because of the attack, for the first time perhaps in its history, the New York Stock Exchange would remain closed. We had to decide about the functioning of our own stock exchanges the next day. The matter was discussed with SEBI—the Securities and Exchange Board of India—and the RBI. There were risks involved, but we decided to take the bull by its horns and remain open the next day. The BSE Sensex fell by 6.7 per cent that week but bounced back soon thereafter. There was no disaster in the markets.

The author at the New York Stock Exchange, 14 April 2000, being welcomed by Richard Grasso, CEO of the NYSE.

Gradually everything got back to normal, at least in the financial world. But the WTC attack had other ramifications. People were afraid to travel and tourism collapsed worldwide. In our case, the tourist season was just about to begin. The sector was badly hit, with most hotel bookings getting cancelled. Insurance companies raised the insurance premium for aircraft. Late one evening, one of my officers informed me that, since we had not paid the higher premium for our aircraft, their insurance cover was expiring in a few hours and thereafter they would not be allowed to operate on overseas routes. I immediately rang up the civil aviation minister, Shahnawaz Hussain, who appeared to be unaware of this development. I called him for a meeting, discussed the matter in detail with him and his officials and sorted out the problem. I made sure that it was resolved in time and our aircraft were not stopped from flying abroad.

The attack also left a huge negative impact on investment sentiment. The World Bank and IMF meetings were put off. The G-20 meeting, which was supposed to be held in India, was postponed. My assuming the chairmanship of the G-20 was also postponed as a result of this.

In October 2001 we had a major terrorist attack on the Jammu and Kashmir assembly in Srinagar while it was in session. Many people were killed, and Farooq Abdullah, the chief minister, had a narrow escape. It was an attack on a democratic institution of India. Our external affairs minister, Jaswant Singh, happened to be on a visit to the United States at that time. He had gone there to commiserate with the people of New York on behalf of the people of India. We held a meeting of the Cabinet Committee on Security, where it was decided that we should tell the Americans that enough was enough and India would not take such attacks lying down any more. Jaswant Singh was asked to convey this message in Washington. We were sure that the Americans would convey the message, in turn, to the Pakistanis. Even if they did, it had no impact, because two months later, on 13 December 2001, came the dastardly terrorist attack on Parliament.

Fortunately, the opposition was stalling Parliament those days and so both Houses of Parliament were not functioning. At the time of the attack, I was in my office in North Block and not in Parliament. I had an appointment with Sanjaya Baru, the editor of *Financial Express*. He had arrived and we had started the conversation when Pandey, the peon attached to me, rushed in to tell us that there had been a terrorist attack on Parliament. We ran to the window to look out. My office was a stone's throw from Parliament and we could hear the firing. Soon, a rumour spread in North Block that some ministers had been killed in the attack. The security forces cordoned off the whole area and it was hard to find out what was happening except through media reports.

We followed the events on television, which was providing live coverage. Later, after it was all over, many of my colleagues went to Parliament House to satisfy their curiosity. I did not join them because I detest the sight of blood and death. By the next day, everything had been brought back to normal. It was important to restore normalcy as quickly as possible to prove that democracy in India had the resilience and the strength to face such situations and function normally. Everyone in the government and the opposition joined in this effort.

I was a member of the Cabinet Committee on Security. It was a small committee consisting of the prime minister, the home minister, the external affairs minister, the defence minister, and me. Following a tradition which was established when Jaswant Singh was the deputy chairperson of the Planning Commission, K.C. Pant was also invited to these meetings. He had earlier served as the defence minister and made valuable contributions to the discussions. As finance minister my role was limited. I generally concerned myself with issues which had a financial angle.

After the attack on Parliament, I came across reports in the media about meetings of the Cabinet Committee on Security. I had not received any notice for these meetings. A few days later, when I went to meet the prime minister in connection with another matter, I mentioned that I was not being invited to these meetings. This resulted in me also being invited to these informal meetings of the committee. If I had attended the earlier meetings, I would have surely advocated a stronger line with Pakistan, where the attack was seen to have originated.

Ultimately, we decided to mobilize our troops on the India–Pakistan border. It was a massive exercise for which troops were drawn from all over the country and transported to the border. India had probably never seen such a mobilization earlier. Soon it became an eyeball-to-eyeball confrontation all along the border as Pakistan also began mobilizing its troops. But we stopped short of actual war. There was a major financial cost involved in this operation. The world too took notice of the attack on the Indian Parliament. I received words of sympathy from friends abroad.

14

In August Company

The events of 2001 played havoc with economic sentiment. The year had started on a tragic note with a devastating earthquake in Gujarat on 26 January—Republic Day. This was followed by the market crash and the UTI crisis, details of which are dealt with in a later chapter. In September the twin towers in New York were attacked, followed by the terrorist attack on the Jammu and Kashmir assembly and on our Parliament. For all these reasons, the dream budget of 2001 was not able to deliver the goods, especially on the revenue front. I was acutely conscious of the fact that the fiscal deficit was likely to go up and we would end up borrowing more money from the market. This was the background in which the budget of 2002–03 had to be prepared.

The 2002 budget was my fifth budget. As finance minister of the Chandra Shekhar government, I had not been able to present even a single budget. I was, until 1998, one of the very few finance ministers who had never presented an annual budget. After presenting the 2002 budget, I joined the ranks of three distinguished predecessors, C.D. Deshmukh, Morarji Desai and Manmohan Singh, who had presented five or more budgets. The 2002 budget also made me the first non-Congress finance minister to present five budgets. It was, thus, history of sorts, and also a personal landmark.

The global economy had slowed down with a growth rate

estimated at 2.4 per cent in 2001. The Indian economy had performed relatively well despite the terrorist attacks and the global economic slowdown. We had had a reasonably well distributed monsoon and the growth rate was 5.8 per cent. Industrial growth had actually declined, but the fundamentals of the economy remained strong, with inflation falling to a record low of 1.1 per cent. The year 2001 also saw a fall in petroleum prices, which provided some relief to the economy.

Budget day started on a wrong note. When I rose to present the budget on 28 February 2002, some of my own party members walked into the well of the Lok Sabha and started disturbing the proceedings. The reason for their anger was the Godhra carnage in Gujarat. I was taken aback. I looked helplessly at Advani and the prime minister. With the intervention of our senior members the agitating members were persuaded to go back to their seats and I proceeded with my budget speech. It was perhaps the first instance of the presentation of the budget being delayed by members of the ruling party themselves.

There were, of course, attempts in the past on the part of the opposition to disrupt the proceedings on some pretext or the other before or during the presentation of the budget. For instance, just as I began to present one of my previous budgets, Renuka Chowdhury, a Congress MP, waved some papers in the House and claimed that the budget had been leaked. Though she was wrong in her assertion, she did succeed in delaying me for a while. A budget leak is a serious matter and could force the resignation of the finance minister, irrespective of whether he is guilty or not. I was acutely aware of this during my tenure as finance minister, and always worried about it. But fortunately this did not happen during any of the five budgets that I presented.

I still wonder why a budget is kept such a highly guarded secret in our country. Except for some proposals on the indirect taxes front, there is nothing in the budget which needs to remain confidential. I think a time has come when we should do away with this secrecy, make the budget exercise more open and transparent and adopt the system that prevails in other democracies. The finance minister should present a draft budget which should then be discussed widely, including in Parliament, and only then be finalized.

In the 2001 budget, I laid out a comprehensive agenda for the second generation of economic reforms, and deepened tax reforms to provide a modern tax regime. In the 2002 budget, I aimed to consolidate and implement these policies at all levels. I wanted to take the process further at the state level through a strategy of reforms-linked devolution of a part of the Government of India funds. On the agriculture front, I took the important initiative to permit futures trading in all agricultural commodities for better price discovery, which would help the farmers.

I remember this budget for two important reasons. The first was that perhaps for the first time in the history of India the budget was not the main news the next day. That slot was taken by the Godhra train carnage in Gujarat. The budget was the second lead in many newspapers.

The second reason was that it helped my detractors intensify rumours that I was about to be shifted from the Ministry of Finance.

One of the many lessons I had learnt from the 1998 budget was that decisions not directly related to the budget should be taken outside the budget. This valuable advice was given by Vijay Kelkar, who suggested that all unpleasant decisions should be taken before the budget so that the budget itself appears to be soft. A budget's perception is made or marred, he felt, largely by decisions which are not required to be taken while presenting the budget, such as cutting subsidies or raising petroleum product prices, so why not do it before the budget? In 2002 I failed to follow this advice.

The budget of 2002 had several good measures for the economy. For instance, we had been experimenting with employment generation schemes in each successive budget previously. In 1999 I had decided to have only two kinds of employment generation schemes—one for self-employment and the other for wage employment—instead of a plethora of them. I had merged all the existing schemes within these two broad categories. But I still felt that this was not enough in a country like India where poverty and unemployment are widespread. We needed a two-pronged strategy to tackle the problem of unemployment. First, we needed a strategy for higher growth in the economy and, second, we needed special employment generating schemes, especially in rural areas. Higher growth in the economy would create employment opportunities, especially in the manufacturing and infrastructure sectors, while the special schemes could directly benefit the unemployed. In 2001 we had launched the Sampoorna Grameen Rozgar Yojana. In 2002 I went a step further and announced the launch of the Jaiprakash Narayan Rozgar Guarantee Yojana. A working group under the rural development minister was to work out the details of the scheme. Unfortunately, this initiative was not followed up after I left the finance ministry. A similar scheme has now been launched by the United Progressive Alliance (UPA) government with much fanfare as a flagship scheme.

Encouraged by the Kisan Credit Card scheme, I started the Laghu Udyami Credit Card scheme for providing simplified and borrower-friendly credit facilities by public sector banks to small businessmen, retail traders, artisans, small entrepreneurs, professionals and other self-employed persons.

A key initiative to promote exports was taken with the proposal to establish special economic zones (SEZs).

Most important of all, I brought back the dividend tax, which adversely affected high net worth individuals. The abolition of the dividend tax by Chidambaram had troubled me throughout my stay in the finance ministry. In my budget of 2000, I had clearly said that all income should be taxed irrespective of its nature or source. I had brought export income in the tax net on the basis of this principle. I felt that the same logic should apply to dividend income also. I was personally aware of people in industry who took a very small amount by way of salary but received large sums of money as dividends from their companies. A 10 per cent tax on dividends was paid by companies, but they were not taxed in the hands of the recipient at the rate on which they paid tax, on the plea that they could not be taxed twice. So, dividend income in the hands of individuals remained tax-free. These tax-free monies, running into crores of rupees, were then deposited in RBI bonds, which were also tax-free. So, these individuals paid no tax at all on a large portion of their personal income. Thus, while we taxed people who earned far less, we allowed individuals who were smart enough to take advantage of the loopholes in the law to go scot-free. I considered this unfair and unacceptable.

I finally decided to take the plunge in 2002. This is what I said in my budget speech on this issue:

> Under the present system of taxation of dividends and income from units, the company or the mutual fund pays a 10 per cent tax, and the income is exempt in the hands of the recipient. Such a system not only taxes income in the hands of a person to whom it does not belong; it also militates against the pass-through status which is the very essence of a mutual fund. There is also an inherent inequity in the present system, which allows persons in the high-income groups to be taxed at much lower rates than the rates applicable to them. These issues have been troubling me over the past four years, and I am now convinced that the existing system must go. I, therefore, propose to abolish the distribution tax of 10 per cent on companies and mutual funds on the dividends or income distributed by them. Such income will henceforth be taxed in the hands of the recipients at the rates applicable to them, and will be subject to tax deduction at source at the rate of 10 per cent. In order to avoid a cascading effect, companies receiving such income will be entitled to claim a deduction for the amount in turn distributed by them as dividends. To continue the support given by me to

equity-oriented funds of the UTI and other mutual funds, the income received during the financial year 2002–03 by unit holders of such funds will be taxed only at 10 per cent as at present.

I also tightened the rules and imposed a limit on the amount that could be invested in tax-free RBI bonds. The reimposition of dividend tax and the cap on deposits in RBI bonds hurt the high net worth individuals, who also happen to be the opinion makers in our society. They came together and deliberately created an impression that the budget was anti-middle-class. When I went to FICCI, CII and other chambers of commerce meetings to explain the budget, I found members there very unhappy with the reimposition of the dividend tax.

This was a major reason for the budget becoming unpopular in the media and with the chambers of commerce. The rich and the influential turned against me. The party, too, fell for the propaganda that I was alienating the middle class. This, no doubt, hastened my departure from the Ministry of Finance.

15

Strategy over the Five Budgets

In all the five budgets I presented, I had a clear and well-defined strategy in mind. I laid great emphasis on agricultural and rural growth, pushed for industrial growth, revival of exports and development of infrastructure. I did my best to encourage the services sector. I tried to control the fiscal deficit and the revenue deficit. I took a number of steps in all my budgets for the uplift of the weaker sections, women and the youth. I believed that the government should have enough resources at its disposal to spend on development, especially on physical and rural infrastructure and on improving the quality of life of the people. The expenditure incurred on these projects would have its own multiplier effect on the economy.

I was convinced that there was a huge suppressed demand in India. In fact, the economic policies which had been followed for decades were clearly anti-consumer. The consumer had no choice and had to buy whatever was available in the market irrespective of its quality and price. Monopolies were created in the public sector in the name of controlling 'the commanding heights of the economy'. A favoured few in the private sector also enjoyed the benefits of monopoly. Competition, the driving force of the market to ensure a better deal to the consumer, was totally at a discount. Entrepreneurship also became a casualty during the licence-permit-quota raj. So, along with unleashing consumer demand, I had to take steps to free the private sector from unnecessary controls and restrictions and allow their energy and talent free play. The public sector had to become lean, efficient and competitive.

Controlling inflation and moderating interest rates were necessary steps to encourage consumer demand. High inflation and high interest rates have been chronic problems of the Indian economy. They form a vicious cycle and impose an unacceptable burden on the economy. High interest rates were one of the reasons the Indian economy was uncompetitive globally. Before we came into office, interest rates were at 18 to 20 per cent. High interest rates also made government borrowings extremely expensive. The interest burden of the government was going up steeply. I realized immediately that sooner rather than later it would become unbearable.

Tackling inflation and softening interest rates therefore became an important objective of my policy. Since it spared the consumer the burden of high prices, it was a happy amalgam of good politics and good economics. At least, that is what I thought. I became wiser later.

Given the sluggishness of the economy, I was looking for triggers to give it momentum. During my visit to Washington in April 1998, my son Jayant introduced to me his friend from IIT Delhi, Raghuram Rajan, who had subsequently studied economics in the United States and was now a professor of economics in Chicago. He suggested to me that, as in the United States, if we encouraged housing in India it could become a major multiplier of economic activity. I took his suggestion seriously and in my budget of 1998 gave a number of concessions to the construction industry. One of the income tax concessions that I made available to housing was increase in deduction for interest on borrowed capital from Rs 15,000 to Rs 30,000 for self-occupied property. In subsequent years, I raised it to Rs 1,50,000. Separately, our policies were leading to a softening of interest rates.

Apart from the reduction in the rate of interest and income tax concessions, creation of a secondary mortgage market for the housing sector was a very important area which needed to be encouraged. This was the only step that could lead to the recycling of funds by making mortgages tradable. To address this issue, we amended the National Housing Bank (NHB) Act so that a secondary mortgage market could come into existence. We studied the systems in vogue in other countries and incorporated those into the amendments to the act. These steps led to a virtual explosion in housing construction. Banks and financial institutions vied with each other to advance loans, especially to the young, for constructing or buying houses and apartments. This boom had its expected multiplier effect on the economy as a whole.

Moderating interest rates became a very important plank of my policy. In January 1999 I decided to reduce the interest rates on small savings from 14.5 per cent to 14 per cent. With falling inflation, the rates were successively reduced to 13.5 per cent in April 1999, to 12.5 per cent in April 2000 and then to 11 per cent in April 2001. In my budget of 2002 I not only reduced administered interest rates by another 0.5 per cent but also announced the benchmarking of these rates to the average annual yields of government securities of equivalent maturities in the secondary market. The next year my successor, Jaswant Singh, reduced the rates further by 1 per cent. Thus, within a span of four years the Vajpayee government brought administered interest rates down from 14.5 per cent to 9.5 per cent, while at the same time fully protecting the real interest rate of the saver by keeping inflation under control.

The government was the biggest borrower in the market and if it continued to pay high interest on its loans there was no way in which the overall interest rates could go down. Administered interest rates therefore had to be brought down in order to soften interest rates generally. But I was wrong in my thinking that I was combining good economics with good politics. The reduction in interest rates led to a lot of protests, especially from senior citizens and employees. Nobody was prepared to understand the concept of real interest rates. Nobody was willing to look at the falling inflation rate. They just looked at the loss in their interest income, and that was enough to turn them against the government. Arguments were also advanced that domestic savings would decline, since people would not be keen on saving because of the reduction in interest rates. On the contrary, history shows that domestic savings went up from 23.5 per cent to 29.7 per cent of GDP during these years. This is a massive increase in domestic savings despite the continuous reduction of interest rates on all kinds of savings instruments.

The decisions to reduce interest rates on small savings and to raise fertilizer prices and the issue prices of food grains through the public distribution system, which were taken in January 1999 before the annual budget, were politically unpopular. Though I had the complete support of the prime minister in implementing these decisions, our own allies were very unhappy. Immediately after the announcement of these hikes, I had gone to Davos to attend the annual meeting of the World Economic Forum. When I returned to Delhi, I was informed at the airport itself that a very important meeting of the NDA Coordination Committee was taking place at 7 Race Course Road and the prime minister had desired that I should reach there directly. Most of our allies looked disapprovingly at me when I reached the meeting. As one newspaper reported, the meeting went on for four hours. At the end of it, we succumbed to pressure and were forced to withdraw the hike in the issue prices of rice and wheat for those living below the poverty line. I was happy that at least the rest of the decisions were left untouched. Economics in India has always been dominated by politics. My experience as finance minister proves this point beyond any doubt.

PART 2

POLICY AND REFORMS

16

Insurance Sector Reforms

M y four years in the finance ministry were marked by bold reforms on the economic front. I had made my intentions clear in my interim budget speech of 1998 itself, where I had talked of broadening and deepening the economic reforms process. Neither the party nor the rest of the government was ready for this. If it had not been for Vajpayee, economic reforms would not have moved forward at all. It was his perseverance and skilful handling of difficult situations which enabled me to achieve what I did on this front. My first test was the reform of the insurance sector.

*

The story of the reform of the insurance sector is interesting, as well as instructive. There were many lessons I learnt while moving the reform process forward in this sector. When we were in the opposition, P. Chidambaram had brought a bill for setting up the Insurance Regulatory and Development Authority (IRDA) which would have opened up the sector to private participation. Chidambaram claimed that the BJP had promised him support in passing this bill in the Lok Sabha. Ultimately, the BJP refused to support the bill for want of wider support for it in Parliament which the government failed to secure. Even those in government and those supporting it opposed it on the floor of the House. Chidambaram was very sore with the BJP for what he considered a breach of faith and he had to face the humiliation of withdrawing the bill from the Lok Sabha.

Even before we came to power, Advani had once asked me what our policy should be for the liberalization of the insurance sector. I was clear that public sector monopoly should end. But while we should open the sector for the Indian private sector, we need not allow foreign investment. When I became finance minister, my views underwent a further change. A non-statutory IRDA was already in existence. It was headed by N. Rangachari, an outstanding officer of the Indian Audit and Accounts Service. I had known him for a long time since both of us belonged to the same batch in service. When he came to see me soon after I assumed charge, he explained in detail what we needed to do to strengthen and liberalize the insurance industry. The first point he made was that a new company in this sector should start with a minimum capital of Rs 100 crore. As very few Indian companies had the capacity to make this kind of investment it was necessary to allow some FDI in this sector. The second point he made was about insurance products. We had a limited number of them in the country. Many more kinds of insurance products could come into the market through the foreign collaborator. Thirdly, we were spending a lot of money on reinsurance. The entire reinsurance business was abroad and we were thus paying large sums of money in foreign exchange every year to these reinsurers. India had the potential to emerge as a major reinsurance hub if we liberalized this sector. Fourthly, the coverage of insurance in our country, both life and general, was limited. India, with its huge population and a growing economy, ought to be doing much better in respect of coverage. Fifthly, the opening of the insurance sector would create considerable employment opportunities for our people. Sixthly, it would do no harm to our public sector companies. In fact, competition might do them a lot of good. Seventhly, the insurance sector was the only sector which generated long-term funds and the world over it was the richest source of long-term funds for investment in infrastructure projects which had a long gestation period.

I was convinced that the insurance sector should be opened up and liberalized. I was also convinced that if we did not want to restrict the field to just a few Indian players, and wanted to take advantage of new products and practices, some FDI was necessary. Accordingly, a cabinet note was prepared in which we suggested that FDI up to 26 per cent be allowed in this sector. I decided to be upfront about it rather than leave the issue of foreign investment vague. When the proposal finally came to the cabinet, I explained in detail the reasons that had prompted me to bring the proposal before it and the benefits that were likely to accrue by opening up this sector. My proposal, however, met with severe opposition from many of my colleagues. They felt that we were going back on all that we had stood for in the past, that the proposal involved a major departure from our philosophy and that it was anti-swadeshi. There was hardly any support for my proposal and the cabinet was about to reject it.

It was at this stage that I looked with silent appeal in my eyes at the prime minister and urged him not to summarily reject the proposal. I suggested to him that, instead of rejecting the proposal, it could be referred to a group of ministers. The prime minister accepted my suggestion and a group of ministers headed by Jaswant Singh was set up to examine this matter further and bring it back to the cabinet. The group met only once and decided to clear the bill. The only new condition incorporated was that while the foreign investor would be allowed to repatriate his dividends and profits, the funds collected by way of insurance premium could be invested only in India and not abroad. The cabinet subsequently approved the proposal with this additional condition and without much argument.

The introduction of the insurance bill in the Lok Sabha was met with strong resistance from the Left parties. They objected vehemently even to the introduction of the bill. There is a rule according to which the Speaker may not allow a bill to be introduced in the House if he is satisfied that a bill is against the Constitution. The Left party members argued on this point. But, while they could give vent to their feelings, they could not prove that the bill was against the Constitution. So, the bill was finally introduced and, since it was an important bill, it was referred to the standing committee. While the standing committee was still examining it, the government fell and the Lok Sabha was dissolved.

When we returned to power after the general election of 1999, the passing of the IRDA bill was taken up by us in right earnest once again. Murli Deora, an important MP of the Congress party, was the chairman of the Parliamentary Standing Committee on Finance. He was completely in sync with us on this bill. He overrode the objections of the Left party members in the committee and gave a favourable report supporting the bill. There were still some glitches. We could not have got the bill passed in the Rajya Sabha without the support of the Congress party. We could not therefore ignore their point of view even in the Lok Sabha, where we had a majority. The Congress party still had some points to make. Negotiations were held with the leaders of the Congress party and we showed readiness to accommodate their concerns. The issue was finally clinched at a breakfast meeting with them at the residence of Pramod Mahajan, the parliamentary affairs minister. I assured Parliament that all foreign investment, direct and institutional, would be within the limit of 26 per cent and that no financial engineering would be allowed to cross this limit under any circumstance. I also had no desire to leave any loophole in the law that the foreign investors could take advantage of, as they had done in the telecom sector.

The Left parties were not alone in their opposition to the bill. The socialists also opposed it, as did the proponents of swadeshi. Even the trade unions opposed it tooth and nail. They went on a nationwide general strike for one day.

The IRDA bill had also come to be regarded as the symbol of our will for economic reforms, especially by foreign investors. At the end of September 1999 I had gone to Washington for the annual meetings of the IMF and the World Bank. This was in the midst of the elections of 1999. Elections in my constituency were over; a few rounds were still being held elsewhere. Though we fully expected to be returned to power, a surprise verdict could not be ruled out. Yet, in all my meetings with investors in Washington and New York, the single most important question was whether the bill would be passed and whether the insurance sector would be opened up. I felt that such single tests of our resolve for economic reforms, from time to time, was undesirable and I was not happy with this attitude. Our resolve for reforms had to be judged over a range of issues and over a period of time. The foreign investor also had to understand the systems and procedures under which we worked. If that required a bill being sent to the concerned standing committee of Parliament for consideration, there was no way in which this procedure could be short-circuited. But the foreign investors were always impatient, always asking for more and always ready to jump to the wrong conclusions. Negotiating one's way through stout opposition at home and excessive expectation abroad was always a tricky business. The saga of insurance sector reform is ample proof of it.

17

Agricultural Reforms

The economic reforms that I initiated through my five budgets were mainly to give impetus to the growth of the Indian economy. Boosting growth was a major challenge during the years I was finance minister. Therefore, year after year, I tried to remove the constraints to growth and introduce structural changes in the economy but I was also acutely conscious that growth would not take place if agriculture did not grow at a satisfactory rate. The growth of agriculture is also necessary to ensure equity and social justice for the vast masses of our people, since two-thirds of them depend on agriculture and allied activities and live in rural areas.

Historical and empirical evidence has proved beyond doubt that availability of water is essential for prosperity in agriculture. When the farmer gets this facility, he races ahead. When water resources have been lacking, he has had to struggle. Yet, despite this obvious truth, not enough has been done to make water available to the farmer. By the late 1990s, only 37 per cent of our land was under assured irrigation. The rest depended on nature. 'Paani' (water) and 'paisa' (credit) were thus the two basic needs of the Indian farmer which had to be urgently met. I stated as much when I said in my budget speech of 1999, 'Water and credit must flow together for maximum impact.' The Kisan Credit Card and other measures tried to cover the latter need. Through a series of other measures I tried to provide for the former.

In my very first budget I decided to accord top priority to the development of rainfed areas on a watershed basis. Watershed development programmes which were spread across several ministries and departments were to be unified and the plan allocation raised by Rs 160 crore to Rs 677 crore. The provision for the Accelerated Irrigation Benefit Programme was raised by 58 per cent over the previous year.

In order to give further impetus to this programme, in my 1999 budget I launched a National Movement of Watershed Development. The aim was to develop implementation ability at the local level and create community infrastructure for micro watershed projects through the active involvement of gram panchayats, local self-help groups and NGOs. I asked NABARD to establish a Watershed Development Fund to cover a hundred priority districts within three years. The allocation for the Accelerated Irrigation Benefit Programme was raised to Rs 2800 crore from Rs 2000 crore for the completion of unfinished medium and major irrigation projects.

I also laid a great deal of emphasis in all my budgets on the setting up of water users' associations to manage and maintain village- or panchayat-level irrigation schemes and also to collect water charges from the users. This idea was based on my experience in the bureaucracy which was further confirmed when I roamed the villages of my constituency as a political worker. I was convinced that this task could not be left to the bureaucracy alone.

After losing the Lok Sabha election from the Hazaribagh parliamentary constituency in 1984, I did not give up. I doggedly kept going back to the people. In one of my padyatras I visited a village called Nawada in Bishnugarh block of the district. When the curious villagers gathered around me, I asked them what was the one thing they wanted the most. A villager came forward boldly and told me in chaste Urdu, '*Huzoor, hamare kheton me paani ka intezaam kar den, phir dekhiye ki hum is ilaake ko kaise Kashmir jaisa chaman bana dete hain.*' (Give us water for our fields and then see how we transform this area into a garden as green and beautiful as

Kashmir.) This remark from a simple old man in a remote village left a deep and permanent imprint on my mind. I sought to achieve the goal through the watershed development programme. Under it we could build a series of micro and small irrigation projects like check dams, tanks and baandhs, to trap rainwater, based on the scientific principle of watershed management. They could be built by the government or out of government funds and managed and maintained by the beneficiaries.

Did I succeed? Only partly. The reason was simple. As in many other areas, so in this, we were dependent on the state governments for implementation. The smarter states took advantage of the central government's schemes and funds; the less smart ones lagged behind. Even Nawada has remained without water in its fields despite all my efforts.

I wanted the Indian farmer to be freed from the multiplicity of laws and regulations which governed the disposal of his produce. I said in my 2002 budget speech that 'freedom to the farmer, *kissan ki azadi*, is the overarching goal of our policy'. I also talked about our readiness to launch a third revolution in agriculture after the success of the Green Revolution and the White Revolution. The third revolution was to consist of agricultural diversification and food processing. With this in mind I proposed the following steps:

1. Amendment of the Milk and Milk Products Order (MMPO) to remove restrictions on new milk processing capacity, while continuing to regulate health and safety conditions.
2. Removal of small-scale-industry reservations related to various agricultural equipment items.
3. Decanalization of the export of agricultural commodities and phasing out of remaining export controls.
4. Expansion of futures and forward trading to cover all agricultural commodities.
5. A multiplicity of regulations for food standards under the Prevention of Food Adulteration Act, the Food Products Order, the Meat Products Order, the Bureau of Industrial

Standards and the MMPO affected the food and food processing sectors. They needed to be modernized and converged together. The prime minister had decided to set up a Group of Ministers to propose legislative and other changes for preparing a modern integrated food law and related regulations.

6. This process of providing freedom to the farmers now needed to be carried forward by state governments. Amendment of the Agricultural Produce Marketing Acts to enable farmers to sell directly to potential processors would help them receive better prices and access potential new markets. In addition, the remaining State control orders which were acting as barriers to inter-state trade needed to be lifted. I proposed that additional allocations in respect of centrally sponsored schemes would be linked to decontrol and deregulation of the agricultural sector by the states.

The idea of freeing the farmer from the debilitating shackles of various laws and regulations did not occur to me for the first time in 2002. In my very first budget of 1998 I had said, 'The ingenuity and enterprise of our farmers is today hamstrung by numerous central and state laws and regulations relating to the production, marketing and movement of agricultural commodities. This is clearly unacceptable.' I expressed the hope that the new national agricultural policy, to be brought out soon, would address these constraints. I continued to work on these issues with my colleagues in the central government as well as with the state chief ministers through the sub-committees of the National Development Council and the Inter State Council. It was important to take the chief ministers on board, cutting across political party lines, since most of the laws and regulations are state laws and a consensus with them was essential for forward movement. As in the case of VAT, in this too I received the cooperation and understanding of the chief ministers and whatever we were able to achieve had their full support.

Other important reforms which I included in my five budgets related to:

1. A hassle-free settlement scheme by banks for the settlement of old dues of the farmers. In my 1998 budget I had stated, 'This government is determined to create conditions so that no farmer goes to jail for a loan repayment default or is forced to commit suicide.' I am convinced that despite this, if farmers committed suicide when we were in government—and the numbers have increased manifold now—it was largely on account of loans which they had taken from private moneylenders which they were unable to pay.

2. To revitalize the cooperative sector, we decided to bring a model cooperative law in 1998 to replace the existing Multi-State Cooperative Societies Act of 1984.

3. We decided to strengthen the Regional Rural Banks through a process of recapitalization.

4. To strengthen the post-harvest infrastructure, I introduced in my 1999 budget a new credit-linked capital subsidy scheme for construction of cold storages and godowns. I set a target of 12 lakh tonnes of cold storage capacity. Later, I was happy to report, in the 2002 budget speech, that sanction had already been given for the creation of 21 lakh tonnes capacity for cold storages.

5. To tackle the problem of fragmentation of agricultural landholdings, I announced in the 1999 budget a scheme to provide special financial assistance to states which undertook the task.

6. I was acutely aware of the problems which cropped up from time to time regarding land use. Prime agricultural land was often sacrificed at the altar of industrialization or urbanization. Forest cover was also declining. Therefore, in my 2000 budget speech I called for an urgent review and coordination of our long-term strategy at the national and the state levels on the pattern of land use in the country, development of agriculture in relation to the

agro-climatic conditions in the different regions and preservation of our forest resources. I said, 'We need to adopt an integrated approach to a number of related subjects such as preservation and development of the forest wealth, optimum utilization of the wasteland, watershed development, safeguarding bio-diversity etc. In view of the complexity of the issues involved, a National Commission on Land Use Policy comprising experts in the relevant fields will be set up to examine the various aspects and make appropriate recommendations to Government.'

This goal is still far from realized. My idea was to have the experts prepare a land use policy for the next fifty to hundred years covering every inch of our land. If such a policy is prepared and put in practice, we will be able to avoid controversies like Singur in West Bengal or the one relating to SEZs.

I identified five elements of social and economic infrastructure which were critical to the quality of life in rural areas: health, education, drinking water, housing and roads. 'Even after 52 years of Independence the provision of basic services in rural areas remains very unsatisfactory. Forty per cent of our villages are without proper roads; 1.8 lakh villages do not have a primary school within 1 km; 4.5 lakh villages have drinking water problems; some estimates indicate a shortage of 140 lakh rural dwelling units; rural health infrastructure suffers from large deficiencies.' Which is why, in order to impart greater momentum to the task of meeting these critical needs, I announced a new scheme called the Pradhan Mantri Gramodaya Yojana with an allocation of Rs 13,000 crore in the 2000 budget.

I tried to bring a comprehensive approach in my budgets in order to strengthen the agricultural sector and improve the lot of our farmers, working closely with the RBI, NABARD and public sector banks to ensure that the needs of our farmers were fully met and local bodies, NGOs, beneficiary groups and government departments were enabled to play their due role. Since agriculture is a state subject, the role of the states is crucial in the implementation of various schemes. The quality of governance at the state level thus became all important and remains so even now. A state will progress or lag behind depending on the leadership of the chief minister of that state.

I recall, in particular, the initiative which General (retd.) S.K. Sinha took as Governor of Assam with the full cooperation of the chief minister, P.K. Mohanta. He invited me to Assam to attend a seminar on agricultural development. He had warned me that he was going to demand the installation of one lakh shallow tubewells in Assam in order to give a boost to agriculture. I went prepared with my response. At the end of the day, we agreed that through tripartite participation of NABARD, the Assam government and the farmers we would undertake the task of sinking one lakh shallow tubewells in Assam. I went back to Assam a year later and saw for myself some of the tubewells which had been sunk and were functioning. Within two years, Assam became surplus in rice production from being a traditionally deficit state.

18

Taxation Reforms

Tax reform is necessarily a continuous process. Thus, though a lot of reform had taken place earlier in the area of taxation, it was still a minefield through which one had to negotiate one's way very carefully. There are powerful vested interests and even more powerful political lobbyists. Even a small change in the rate of tax can make a huge difference to some people. No wonder, then, that the response to a budget is largely determined by its tax proposals. Part B of the budget speech attracts the maximum attention of all those who take an interest in the budget exercise.

When budget time comes, the Ministry of Finance receives a very large number of representations and memoranda from various quarters including chambers of commerce, trade associations, tax practitioners, the general public and members of Parliament. The finance minister also holds pre-budget meetings with various groups like agriculturists, industrialists, representatives of small-scale industries, trade unions, consumer organizations and economists. In my time, I expanded this list to include representatives of the cooperative movement and economic journalists. In these meetings, many suggestions are made regarding taxes. The suggestions can often be in conflict with each other. Every section looks for concessions for itself and wants the burden to be placed somewhere else. For instance, an agriculturist may ask for small-scale industry to be taxed, the small-scale industry representative asks for big industries to be taxed more, the big industry, in turn, asks for agriculture and the small-scale sector to be taxed and all available exemptions to them be withdrawn. In short, everyone tries to place the tax burden on someone else but is not prepared to take it on themselves.

The second problem arises because of selfish interests. For instance, in the area of import duties, a manufacturer will say that there should be zero or negligible import duty on raw materials or components that he imports since this would make his product cheaper. However, the same producer will want the highest duty to be slapped against the import of products he is producing, to protect his interest. The producers of raw materials and components will, at the same time, ask for the highest duty to be imposed on what they produce so that they are not affected adversely. Thus, not only among sectors but even within the same sector of industry there is a conflict of interest with regard to tax rates. This makes the life of a finance minister difficult since the responsibility of resolving the conflict and establishing harmony devolves on him.

People hate to be brought within the tax net. I recall a very amusing experience. In 1998, while preparing the budget, we were, as usual, looking at ways to garner more resources. In the high-security Tax Research Unit of the CBEC we were going through the list of items which were exempt from excise duty. A description, under the head 'Branded edible preparations when produced in factories', attracted my attention. I thought this description would apply to high-end branded food products which would normally be consumed only by the elite. So, along with some other branded products, I brought this item also under 8 per cent excise duty. I was staying at Vithalbhai Patel House, a hostel for MPs on Rafi Marg, in those days. One morning, as I came down from my apartment to go to my office, I found an unusually large number of expensive Indian and foreign cars parked inside the premises. I wondered whether some big function was being held in the complex. I was told, to my surprise, that the people in those cars had come to see me. Since I could not meet them there, they came to see me in my Parliament House office along with some MPs. And who were they? They were producers of Indian sweets (mithai) from all over the country. They were also covered by the 8 per cent tax and had come to protest against it. That day I met the manufacturers of some of the most famous brand names of Indian sweets, saw the fancy cars in which they had come to see me and heard arguments from them and the MPs who were supporting their cause as to why they should not pay any tax.

A not so amusing incident occurred when the finance bill was due to come up for discussion in the Lok Sabha in 1998. I had already discussed the proposed amendments to it with the prime minister and finalized them. I was giving the final touches to the speech I was going to make in the House. It was lunchtime and the bill was to come up immediately after the lunch recess. I received a sudden and unexpected telephone call from a very senior colleague considered close to the prime minister. He told me that the prime minister had instructed him to tell me to reduce the rate of import duty on a certain product. I was surprised. The change, as suggested, would have exposed us to the criticism of favouring one industrial house. I was reluctant to do it. I immediately left my office in North Block and drove to the prime minister's office in Parliament. Fortunately, I was able to catch him alone, since he was just about to have lunch. I apprised him of the telephone call and asked whether he wanted me to make the change. To my surprise he told me that he had not authorized anyone to make such a suggestion. With great relief I thanked him and left for the Lok Sabha. The change, as suggested, never saw the light of day.

The plethora of excise duty rates encouraged vested interests to ask for concessions. I was determined to put an end to this by compressing the rates and limiting them to just a few. I had already set out my idea about excise duty reforms in my budget speech of 1998:

My proposals regarding other changes in excise duty are guided by the overall need to rationalize the rate structure so as to reduce the multiplicity of rates and ensure convergence towards a mean rate of 18 per cent ad valorem. An ideal tax structure would be one where, barring the mean rate, there is one lower rate for items deserving concession and a higher rate for what may be described as demerit goods. This would minimize the oscillations in rates and call for compression of intermediate rates.

The various representations I received after the budget of 1998 convinced me that we had to implement this intent without losing time. Therefore in my budget of 1999 I decided to streamline the tax structure. I reduced the existing eleven major ad valorem rates to three, namely, a central rate of 16 per cent (instead of 18 per cent which I had mentioned earlier), a merit rate of 8 per cent and a demerit rate of 24 per cent. Of course, for revenue considerations I had to levy special duty of excise on some products. Later, however, I decided to have only one rate, a central rate of 16 per cent, and converge all rates to this one rate. In my subsequent budgets, I continued the streamlining by reducing the number of rates until I had brought most items under the mean rate of 16 per cent. Some items, which were in the merit rate, did continue at 8 per cent but the number was very limited. Since I was also against exemptions, I introduced the escalator clause, under which exempted items were to be brought within the tax net gradually, starting at 4 per cent and going up to 16 per cent.

I also made considerable procedural changes in the central excise laws for the benefit of taxpayers.

Many MPs have either a constituency interest or general interest in some trade or industry. After every budget, any finance minister will receive a large number of representations from them, mostly regarding taxation. They also bring delegations or come separately to suggest the changes they would like. These representations cannot be ignored and have to be carefully considered by the finance minister.

The story of the major revamp of central excise duties carried out during my tenure would be incomplete if I did not recognize the contribution of T.R. Rustagi, joint secretary, Tax Research Unit, and his team in this effort. TR was an extremely efficient officer and an expert in taxation matters, with most of the information at his fingertips. He used to make PowerPoint presentations in his room, where we assembled to discuss and take decisions on excise and customs matters. I had once asked TR what he would do in the area of indirect tax reforms if he was finance minister. He had responded with some really valuable suggestions which I incorporated in my budget.

Tax reforms during my ministership were not confined to central excise. They covered customs duty as well. Both Manmohan Singh and Chidambaram had already announced that India should move to ASEAN levels of customs duties, though no deadline had been fixed for it. Here, my effort was threefold. The first was to reduce the number of rates. This I did through my budgets and ultimately settled for two basic rates, one of 10 per cent covering generally raw materials, intermediates and components, and the other of 20 per cent for the rest. The second objective was to reduce the peak duty every year. I did that by bringing the peak duty down to 30 per cent from 35 per cent in my 2002 budget with a clear road map of reducing it by 5 per cent every year in order to eventually align it with ASEAN rates. The third objective was to streamline procedures, which also was attended to in budget after budget.

By setting this predictable path of rationalization of indirect taxes, life became less tense after the presentation of my budgets. Whenever someone approached me for any special concession, I always highlighted the already laid-down principles and avoided making individual exceptions which would have meant undoing the whole system. The proposal to do away with ad hoc exemptions was made to me by M.R. Sivaraman, who had earlier served as revenue secretary, and during my time was India's director on the IMF board. He told me that if I could do away with the system of ad hoc exemptions it would bring about a great improvement in revenue administration. Ad hoc exemptions empowered the finance minister to grant exemption from customs duty for specific imports; for example, the import of a car won as a prize abroad by a cricketer could be allowed without payment of tax. Sivaraman alerted me to the fact that a lot of revenue was being lost and a lot of corruption was taking place as a result of ad hoc exemptions. I accepted his suggestion and in my budget of 1999 announced the abolition of the government's power to grant such exemptions. In the next budget I was able to report to Parliament that this step alone had saved the government revenue of Rs 500 crore in one year. What I did not report was that it had liberated me as well! Here again, I could give a simple answer to people who came to me to ask for remission of import duty on a particular item of import— that I did not have the power any more. I strongly believe that the system of granting ad hoc exemptions is wrong and we can do without it.

On the direct taxes side, I continued with the three rates of personal income tax that Chidambaram had introduced in his budget of 1997–98 and also with the same rate of corporate tax. I did rationalize the procedures and exemptions. I also tried to give relief to low-paid employees, women and senior citizens. I made project- and business-related exemptions more rational. I also brought within the tax net, on a gradual basis, income from exports, which was hitherto completely exempt. In my last budget, I brought dividend income within the tax net, once again on the same logic that all income, irrespective of its source, must be taxed. I also introduced the Saral form for income tax returns in my budget of 1998, and the Samman scheme for honouring honest taxpayers. I changed Chidambaram's two-by-four formula to a one-by-six formula. He had introduced a scheme under which if someone fulfilled two of four criteria, namely, possession of a house, a phone, a car or expenditure on foreign travel, he/she would be obliged to file an income tax return. I added two additional criteria to this, namely, holding a credit card and membership of an expensive club. I also removed the requirement of matching two out of four criteria. One was enough to oblige a person to file a return. I also extended the application of this scheme from twelve to thirty-five cities. This, plus a series of other measures, enabled us to raise the number of assessees under income tax almost threefold in four years. It also improved the contribution of direct taxes in our overall tax collection. At the beginning of the previous decade, the contribution of direct taxes to total tax was only 20 per cent. Indirect taxes contributed the rest. By 2002 the contribution of direct taxes had gone up to 40 per cent and the contribution of indirect taxes had declined to less than 60 per cent.

TAX RAIDS

I am not a supporter of the 'raid raj'. I strongly believe in voluntary compliance. We need to inculcate the spirit of tax compliance in our people; they should take pride in being honest taxpayers. The propensity in India is to not pay taxes. People want everyone else to be taxed but them. If one is doing business honestly, there is nothing to fear. The problem is that many do not comply strictly with the law in their business dealings and that is why they submit to the blackmail of tax officials. And it was this belief that led me to announce a new scheme called Samman in my very first budget, a scheme in which honest taxpayers would be recognized and honoured by the government.

There was often political *sifarish* (pressure) when raids were conducted and requests for help either to let off the person or to reduce the rigour of punishment. These requests came from political colleagues and even members of the cabinet. I have always found it disagreeable to interfere with the work of tax officials, doing so only in cases of any unbecoming behaviour on the part of my officials or unfair demands made on those raided. There were occasions when I did feel that the department had crossed the line and harassed people during the raids, like treating the women of the household rudely and confiscating jewellery even when not required. In one case, when the son-in-law of a cabinet colleague was raided, I received a complaint that the concerned official had asked for a bribe. I immediately transferred the officer and ordered an inquiry. The inquiry revealed that the allegation was indeed true, and I placed the officer under suspension.

I was prepared to be strict and take stern action against my officials if they committed any wrong. But I also encouraged them to perform their duty without fear of political interference. One had to maintain a fine balance and I think it is up to every finance minister to determine what that fine balance should be. We live in a society where clearly it is quite common to try to influence those in authority by whatever means one can. This attitude is wrong and needs to be curbed. The spirit of fair play needs to be inculcated so that the system functions better than it does at the moment.

CADRE MANAGEMENT

The Ministry of Finance is the cadre-controlling authority of the Indian Economic Service and the Indian Revenue Service (customs and excise, and income tax). These are very large cadres and at the time of every annual transfer I used to be inundated with requests from all and sundry to transfer officers to desired posts. Sometimes these requests came from people so close to me that it became acutely embarrassing. Whenever I interacted with the officers, I used to take up this issue with them, emphasizing that we had well laid-out norms for transfers and that I was very keen that those norms be observed. I used to exhort them to desist from influencing decisions for personal gain. But the requests still continued to pour in. The Indian Economic Service was a comparatively quiet service. The worst was customs and excise.

In fact, the minister of state for revenue and I dealt only with the transfers of chief commissioners and not of officers below that rank. All other transfers were done by the two boards. But I received requests even with regard to transfers of officers at junior levels. I used to prepare a list of such requests and, when the proposal came to me from the ministry, compare my list with the proposals put up by the ministry. If they matched, it was fine; if not, I ignored the request. If I was convinced that the request was genuine, I called the chairman of the concerned board and asked him what could be done to accommodate the request. In most cases, we found a common approach. Having served in the civil service myself, I felt that as long as the officers were working according to rules there should be no interference. The sad part was that even at the bureaucratic level all kinds of pressures and extra-departmental considerations prevailed, and sometimes proposals were put up which were clearly in violation of the norms. I always asked searching questions in such cases and often turned them down. But, by and large, I did not interfere and also prevented my ministers of state from interfering in transfers and postings.

Intra-cadre rivalry was at its worst in the Central Board of Excise and Customs. The officers here did not mind cutting each other's throats to reach senior positions. They filed anonymous petitions against each other (unfortunately many were often also true). In many cases, the careers of promising officers were spoilt or brought to an abrupt end as a result of these internecine wars. Even the appointment to the post of chairman, CBEC was not spared, as in the (infamous) case of B.P. Verma.

The post was falling vacant in 2001 and we had to find a replacement. Verma was the seniormost member of the CBEC. There had to be a very strong case to supersede him. If he went for a legal redress we would have had to justify our decision before a court of law. We looked into his record and found that there was nothing in it that would debar him from being promoted to the post, although his reputation was tarred. He was member (budget), which was a very sensitive assignment. A.M. Prasad, also under consideration for the post, happened to be related to me—my elder brother was married to his sister. Prasad was naturally keen on the promotion. He knew that Verma did not enjoy a good reputation. I was equally aware that if we promoted Prasad the immediate allegation would have been that Verma had been superseded in order to promote a relative of mine. So, from the ministry we recommended Verma for the post, and the Cabinet Committee on Appointments approved the proposal. Prasad was so unhappy that he even went to court. It is another matter that he did not get any relief there. Verma's functioning as chairman left much to be desired. I was not happy with his performance. There were adverse reports about his integrity though there was no concrete proof of it. After watching him for some months, I decided that he should not continue as chairman. I then sent a proposal to the prime minister that he be shifted and the next person in line for the job be made chairman of the CBEC.

This proposal remained pending in the PMO for a few weeks. In the meanwhile Verma was raided by the CBI and arrested in April 2001. I was not alerted about the CBI raid beforehand and did not know about his arrest until it took place. The arrest of the chairman of the CBEC on charges of corruption did not add to the reputation of the finance ministry. Naturally, he had to be put under suspension. I was unhappy, because if my proposal to shift him had been accepted in time, and he had actually been shifted from the post he was holding, the action of the CBI would not have appeared so stark. In the Flex company case, details of which I shall mention later, the chief commissioner of excise of Delhi was arrested by the CBI, again on corruption charges, though nothing came of the case. I was told that even charges were not framed in this case. I later learnt that the whole episode was the result of rivalry among the senior officers of the CBEC.

We also had the scandalous incident of large quantities of Chinese silk being smuggled into the country. In August 2000 an Uzbek woman was intercepted at the Indira Gandhi International Airport while attempting to clear a large consignment of Chinese silk without declaring it to the customs authorities. This woman had made fifty-four trips to India between July 1999 and August 2000. This incident exposed the loopholes in the functioning of our customs service because the woman had made repeated trips and brought large quantities of silk from Uzbekistan, which was a known point of origin for smuggled silk. Obviously, our officers were being less than vigilant, which left a bad taste in my mouth about the functioning of the department.

There are certain wet (lucrative) postings even at juniormost levels like inspectors. One such place is Raxaul, a checkpoint on Bihar's border with Nepal. The checkpoint is much sought after because of the money one can make there checking goods vehicles plying between the two countries. I used to get numerous requests for postings in Raxaul. I did not interfere and generally made sure that nobody else did either, and told the board that it should prepare guidelines for such postings which everyone should follow. I soon realized that as the minister in charge of a ministry that dealt with large cadres, it is almost a full-time job just to resist pressures for such postings.

Postings, however, were not the only problem. There were occasions when people approached me to help them get bank loans or loans from financial institutions. I refused to make such requests to the banks; it is inappropriate to tell a bank chairman to suspend his judgement and go by mine. There was a very important individual in my party at one time who regularly put unreasonable requests for loans. I was determined not to give in to such requests. One day he lost his cool and complained to me that I never accommodated any of his requests. He even held out a veiled threat. I decided to tell the prime minister the entire story before he could do me any harm.

One of my basic objectives of tax reforms was to minimize the discretionary powers of officers both on the direct and indirect tax fronts and reduce the role of inspectors. With less discretionary powers, the chances of corruption would also get minimized. My effort to reduce the number of rates and make the procedure as simple and transparent as possible was meant to achieve this objective. It is interesting to note that, when I announced my intention to end inspector raj, the inspectors in the department protested vociferously.

I also met the long-standing demand of the officers and staff of the two boards by restructuring the various cadres to provide for more efficiency, speedier disposal of cases and better chances of promotion.

VALUE ADDED TAX

Even though I had clearly expressed my intention to move towards a Central Value Added Tax in my budget speech of 1998, I knew that reform of indirect taxes, especially central excise, would remain incomplete if it was not accompanied by simultaneous reforms in state sales tax. There was already a long-pending demand from traders that sales tax be abolished and replaced with a simpler tax which would enable them to avoid paying tax on tax. My predecessors had taken some tentative steps in this direction but nothing concrete had materialized so far. I was keen to attend to this issue without losing time and called a meeting of chief ministers to discuss the issue in 1998 itself.

Since it was a subject entirely within the jurisdiction of the states, the initiative for reform had to come from them, with the Government of India playing the role of a facilitator. I was also aware that there was a new-found zeal for federalism in our polity and the states were very conscious of their rights and privileges. As such, any false step on my part could jeopardize the whole initiative. Combining caution with keenness, I worked out a clear plan of action in my mind. My plea for tax reforms at the state level found support from many chief ministers, cutting across political party lines. Some states had already experimented with VAT, but could not sustain the experiment because other states had not fallen in line. Since I was keen that the initiative for reforms should come from the states themselves, I suggested that a committee of chief ministers, led by the seniormost chief minister in the country, Jyoti Basu, be formed. This committee could examine the issue and submit a report to the conference of chief ministers in about three months. My suggestion was accepted, as they say, with acclaim.

The committee submitted its report and, fortunately, it was a favourable one. I then called another meeting of chief ministers to discuss the report where I suggested that, in order to ensure follow-up action on a systematic and sustained basis, we should set up a group of state finance ministers. I recommended that the finance minister of West Bengal, Dr Asim Dasgupta, one of the longest-serving finance ministers in the country, head the group. These suggestions were accepted unanimously. In a subsequent meeting of chief ministers, I suggested that, since it may not be practical to call the chief ministers every time a decision had to be taken, it would be better to empower the state finance ministers to take decisions. This was accepted and the group became an empowered group of state finance ministers.

This group, led by Dasgupta, started work in earnest and did a wonderful job of the task assigned to it. I participated in their meetings as a partner and friend and encouraged Dasgupta to take full charge, including briefing the media. I was unhappy therefore when I found that the minister of state in my ministry was trying to unnecessarily hog the limelight by speaking to the media out of turn. I was quite clear that we had to remain in the background and such media adventurism on our part would upset the delicately balanced apple cart between the centre and the states. Many non-NDA chief ministers looked at our honest intentions with suspicion and were ready to withdraw cooperation at the slightest pretext. Pushing VAT called for handling the issue with the greatest caution. It took some effort on my part to dissuade my colleague from seeking personal publicity and jeopardizing this important venture.

Ironically, one of the early obstacles that I faced in the task came from BJP leaders in Delhi who, like some traders, were opposed to VAT tooth and nail. Their opposition was not based on reason but on fear of the unknown. They joined the traders in protests and demonstrations. There was a Congress party government in Delhi which was keen to implement VAT. But the opposition from the BJP leaders caused me acute embarrassment. I had to take the help of our seniormost leaders like Vajpayee and Advani to make them fall in line.

As facilitators, we had provided the services of the National Institute of Public Finance and Policy to the state finance ministers. Professor Ashok Lahiri and Dr B.C. Purohit of this institute rendered yeoman service in the pursuit of the task. As the work of the group of state finance ministers increased, the Delhi government agreed to provide secretariat support to it.

One of the early harvests we reaped in the process was the harmonization of state sales tax rates. Over time, the states had evolved varying rates for the same products. A rate war among the states was not unknown. States were also in the habit of giving sales tax concessions to attract industries. This was more often than not a race to the bottom. The states therefore agreed that pending the introduction of VAT they would agree to have only four rates of sales tax and do away with the practice of offering sales tax concessions to attract industries. This agreement was a major achievement and paved the way for the introduction of VAT.

As always, this agreement did not come our way easily. We had to overcome resistance from some states, for instance, the union territory of Pondicherry. The Pondicherry chief minister and other politicians from there met me a number of times to explain why they should not be compelled to implement the uniform sales tax rates. They even told me of some assurance given by Pandit Nehru that Pondicherry would be treated differently. I held firm—there was no question of leaving out any state or union territory because even a single exception could unravel the whole exercise. If Pondicherry did not implement the scheme, Tamil Nadu would not either, and before long there would be a domino effect that would affect all the states.

The empowered group of state finance ministers finished most of its preparatory work by the end of December 2001. Draft legislations were ready. From the centre, I made the offer to compensate the states for any loss of revenue they might suffer in the first three years according to a graded formula. I also agreed to move a constitutional amendment to authorize the states to levy service tax on certain specified services to compensate them for the loss of revenue when central sales tax would be abolished. It was agreed that all the states would introduce VAT with effect from 1 April 2002. The empowered group of finance ministers, I was assured, had already held a number of meetings to discuss the implementation of VAT with the representatives of trade and industry. Though I could not participate in any of these meetings for want of time, I had assumed that the state finance ministers would have explained the new system of taxation to the traders in their respective states.

I was in for a rude shock. In a meeting which was held in the Delhi government secretariat, one of my own party MPs, Shyam Behari Mishra, who was also the head of an all-India body of traders, not only opposed the introduction of VAT but even threatened violent agitations throughout the country if we persisted with our plans. Greatly upset, I discussed the matter with Dasgupta. Clearly, we needed to do more homework with the trading community. VAT could not be successfully introduced in the teeth of their opposition. We decided by consensus to postpone the implementation of VAT by a year, and use the intervening period to educate the traders and finish all the other pending work at the state level.

It is a matter of considerable personal regret to me that VAT, for which I had worked so hard, could not be introduced during my tenure as finance minister. In fact, it could not be introduced during our tenure in government. It was left to the succeeding UPA government to introduce it from 1 April 2005. The BJP-ruled states, along with Uttar Pradesh and Tamil Nadu, did not join the national mainstream on that day and further postponed its introduction. This is hardly the kind of postscript I had expected for the Herculean effort made to introduce the most fundamental and long-lasting tax reform in independent India. The BJP-ruled states joined the mainstream the next year, which was some consolation.

19

Banking Sector Reforms

When I assumed office, one of the most important problems of the banking sector was the large quantum of non-performing assets (NPAs), or loans advanced earlier which were not being repaid to the banks. The second most important problem was the weak condition of three banks—Indian Bank, UCO Bank and the United Bank of India—where reckless lending in the past had eroded the capital base, as a result of which they could not meet the capital adequacy norms. I had already taken a policy decision that we would not infuse more capital into them from the budget but change their management and charge the new team with the responsibility of improving their functioning. The third problem area was the genuine need for the recapitalization of public sector banks. The banks, in order to meet the Basel II norms (an internationally accepted set of norms for capital adequacy of banks), needed infusion of fresh capital to shore up their equity base. But, where was the money to come from? One option was for the government to increase its shareholding in the banks. But we were not financially in a position to spare that money from our budget for the weaker banks. The other option was for the banks to go to the market and raise funds. In the case of many banks, where disinvestment had already taken place, the government's shareholding was already close to 51 per cent, and there was hardly any headroom left to raise fresh equity from the market as this would have brought the government's shareholding to below 51 per cent. The issue of recapitalization of banks could not be postponed any further. Hence, we took the politically difficult decision to reduce the government's stake in the banks to less than 50 per cent and, if needed, go down to 33 per cent. I knew there would be opposition to the move. Many politicians and parties would be against diluting government's control over these banks. I prepared my case carefully. Public sector banks are regulated by the RBI, not by the government. Norms like priority sector lending are fixed by the RBI and enforced by it. But as owners we had a special management responsibility for them, and I needed to be careful that reduction of the government's equity to 33 per cent would not lead to any dilution of our management control over these banks. The solution I sought was one where we would retain our right to appoint the chairmen, the executive directors and the boards of these banks despite our share reducing to less than 50 per cent. Thereby, without diluting control, the banks would be enabled to raise fresh capital. I went with this legislation to Parliament.

As in the case of the insurance bill, when I rose to introduce the banking bill in the Lok Sabha, there was a great deal of protest. Representatives of the Left parties refused to allow me to introduce the bill. They were supported by the socialists. Even Chandra Shekhar criticized me for the move. He had played an important role in the nationalization of banks and felt that I was now denationalizing them. In my reply I pointed out that we were protecting the social purpose of the banks and retaining government control over them and assured the House that things would only be better and not worse after this amendment. I added that we also had to conform to international norms and the banks needed this headroom to raise capital. The bill was introduced in the face of great opposition. Generally, I used to keep quiet when Chandra Shekhar criticized me, but in this particular case I did reply to his criticism, which was personally difficult for me to do. It was perhaps the only occasion where I had to contest what he said in Parliament. The bill went to the standing committee of Parliament and was never returned. The whole exercise thus turned out to be infructuous.

As owners the government should always have a fairly good idea of how the banks are doing. I encouraged meetings with trade union leaders from time to time to keep them on my side without conceding those demands that I felt were unreasonable. My individual interactions with the chairmen and executive directors of the banks also helped. It is equally the government's responsibility to select the best people to head public sector banks. I remember, in particular, the case of Indian Bank. In consultation with the RBI governor, we selected Ranjana Kumar to head the bank. She did an excellent job and turned the bank around. She went on to become the chairman of NABARD. I lent my support to such chairmen publicly and encouraged them to do their duty effectively.

I especially respected the opinion of Dr Bimal Jalan, particularly when pressure was brought to bear on me with regard to certain appointments. Bimal Jalan is an economist of repute, and a very pleasant and positive person. He was the RBI governor when the BJP came to power in 1998. He had been appointed by the previous United Front (UF) government, and I had personally called to wish him on that occasion. We got along well and had a very close working relationship. Because of his vast experience I often consulted him informally on various issues, including budget proposals. On his part, he not only kept me informed but consulted me with regard to some of the problems he faced as RBI governor, such as exchange rate volatility and its management, which had a direct bearing on the value of the rupee. He was a great asset to our team, and a source of strength to us in the finance ministry with his experience and knowledge.

NPAs IN BANKS

The question of the NPAs of public sector banks was the most difficult one I faced in the finance ministry from almost the very first day. This issue was discussed in practically every session of Parliament. The Left parties insisted that the list of defaulters be made public. They believed that the big industrialists alone were responsible for the NPAs. They were only partly correct as there was a substantial percentage of NPAs in the priority sector as well. At the start of every Parliament session, the finance ministry prepares comprehensive notes on issues which could come up in Parliament, including the latest figures on NPAs. I would go through them carefully even before the session commenced so that I could be ready with the latest information. I also gathered information on NPAs from the banks directly on the sectors which were responsible for them. I always went to Parliament armed with these figures. With bigger loans advanced to the large industrial houses, their proportion in NPAs was naturally higher than those of others.

The Left parties demanded that the government abolish the secrecy clause in the banking law and publish the list of defaulters, especially large defaulters. The demand to expose the defaulters became a big issue towards the end of 1999. The CII appointed a task force on NPAs under the chairmanship of K.V. Kamath, chief executive officer of ICICI Bank. This group submitted its report in December 1999. The report recommended closure of the three weak banks, among its many recommendations.

The trade unions protested vehemently against the Kamath committee report and they were strongly supported in Parliament by the Left parties, even though the committee had not been appointed by the government and the report was not binding on us. They persisted with their demand for making public the list of defaulters. The All India Bank Employees Association (AIBEA) controlled by the Left parties went a step further and published its own list of defaulters. My position was difficult as I could neither confirm nor deny the veracity of the list.

Politics apart, I was very keen that the NPAs, which were averaging around 9 per cent in 1996–97, be brought down. We were moving towards Basel II norms and there was a deadline before which our banks had to adopt these norms. Therefore, the issue of NPAs had to be attended to on a priority basis. One way of reducing NPAs was to strengthen the Debt Recovery Tribunals (DRTs) and set up more tribunals to cover all the states. The DRT Act had been challenged in the Supreme Court and remained pending for long. Later, when it was decided by the Supreme Court that the DRT Act was valid and constitutional, we tried to strengthen the tribunals by amending the act with a view to facilitating expeditious recovery of bank dues. The law needed to be changed to make it possible for the banks to take punitive action against the defaulters, especially wilful defaulters. A settlement scheme for small borrowers was also needed.

We adopted a comprehensive scheme which included all the three elements—a settlement scheme for small borrowers, specially agriculturists, amendments of the law to strengthen the DRTs and further changes in the law to enable the banks to take punitive action against wilful defaulters. We amended the law in order to enable the banks to appropriate the assets which had been hypothecated against the loan.

In subsequent years, we introduced one more measure in our effort to deal with NPAs—we set up asset reconstruction companies which could buy the bad loans at a discount, pursue the defaulters to recover the loans and help the banks clean up their balance sheets. I initiated regular meetings with the chairmen of the public sector banks where I constantly reviewed the NPAs and urged the banks to liquidate them at the earliest.

Bringing down the level of NPAs also involved a much greater application of the mind by bank officials to borrowings under the scheme of government-directed lending for the priority sector.

BANK RECRUITMENTS

The Banking Services Recruitment Boards (BSRBs) had been in existence for many years. All public sector banks were required to recruit their personnel through the BSRBs. The post of chairmen of these boards fell vacant from time to time and we had to find suitable people to man them—another set of appointments for which a finance minister is under continuous pressure from friends and colleagues. I have always felt that the whole system of recruitment through these boards was defective. Firstly, it impinged on the autonomy of the banks. The banks had to go through a centralized system of recruitment. Secondly, I constantly received reports from various places that everything was not above board, and complaints of corruption and irregularities in these recruitments were not uncommon. A bank job has always been regarded as a prize post and people were prepared to pay large sums of money for it. In view of these factors, I decided in 2001 to do away with the BSRBs. I proposed to abolish them by the end of July 2001 and hand over the recruitment process to the banks themselves, enabling them to devise their own procedures and recruit their own people. Some people were disappointed at this move but we abolished these boards by the due date, nonetheless.

20

Electricity Sector Reforms

The concept of Fast Track Power Projects with special concessions was developed during the Narasimha Rao regime. The promoters were assured of a guaranteed net return of 16 per cent on their capital by the state governments, backed by a sovereign counter-guarantee of the Government of India. The most well-known example of this was the Dabhol power project of Enron. Though the country needed power, the concept itself was flawed. I did not like the idea of a guaranteed return to the promoters only because we needed electricity in the country. The promoters had to take business risk. The guarantee freed them completely from it. I was also against the counter-guarantee by the central government. When we came to power in 1998, many of these schemes were still pending. Rangarajan Kumaramangalam, the minister for power in our government, was very keen to implement the pending projects. We had innumerable meetings in the finance ministry to work out the details. Gajendra Haldea, the joint secretary dealing with this matter in my ministry, was an extremely efficient officer with a flair for detail. He was also a hard nut to crack. Ranga often complained to me about Haldea's tough and uncompromising attitude. Ultimately, we did work out an implementation plan for these projects, but I do not think any of them actually took off. Ranga and I had, in the meanwhile, worked out a new scheme of mega power projects to be located at pitheads or along the coast, with customs duty concessions. We also pushed forward the major hydroelectric schemes, especially in Himachal Pradesh and Jammu and Kashmir.

The power sector in the country was, and is, in a mess. State electricity boards have huge accumulated liabilities and most of them have become bywords for inefficiency and corruption. Since they had monopoly of power distribution in their states and did not collect their dues honestly, there was no way they could become viable. Financial institutions in India and abroad were not willing to lend them money, which meant no new projects could come up in the state sector. The situation was truly grim.

Apart from collecting dues, the states had three other main problems to tackle. The first was to reduce T&D—transmission and distribution—losses, which the prime minister described as theft and dacoity losses. Technical reasons did contribute in a small and acceptable way to these losses, but the major reason was electricity theft by unscrupulous consumers in collusion with the staff of the electricity boards. The second was to revamp the system of collection, which was so bad in some states that the consumers were not even given their bills. The third was to reduce the excessive subsidies which had created financial problems for the boards. This was the crux of the problem in the power sector. The independent power producers also had to be paid. They could not be paid if the dues were not collected by the state electricity boards. In my own state of Jharkhand, we depended on supplies from the Damodar Valley Corporation (DVC), a Government of India undertaking. On a visit to my constituency in December 2003, I was told that load shedding, the duration of which used to be three and a half hours, had been extended to seven hours. The situation in Jharkhand was that if the DVC supplied power worth Rs 50 crore every month to the state government, the state government paid only Rs 25 crore. The balance Rs 25 crore accumulated every month as overdues. The state government expected the DVC to continue supplying power without receiving full payment. I told the chief minister that a Government of India utility like the DVC was not going to bear the losses of the state government in perpetuity. The only alternative was for the state government to start collecting its dues from the consumers in order to pay the DVC fully, or the DVC should be paid from the state's own coffers.

In March 1999 the prime minister convened a meeting of chief ministers to discuss the issue of reforms in the power sector. The amount owed by the state electricity boards to the central government undertakings was a whopping Rs 40,000 crore and growing. The states were not in a position to pay these dues. The central government undertakings were thus indirectly subsidizing the state governments. Several state electricity boards had accumulated these dues over many years. They were in no position to pay the amount in one go. To get around this, I devised a scheme under which the dues could be securitized, and bonds issued by the boards in favour of the central undertakings which could be traded in the market. The only condition which I insisted on with all the force at my command was that the states start collecting their current dues from consumers and become up-to-date in their payments to our undertakings.

My idea of securitization of the outstanding dues of the electricity boards was accepted in principle in the chief ministers' conference, and a group of central and state government representatives under the chairmanship of the deputy chairman of the Planning Commission was set up to examine it further. We worked hard and soon evolved a scheme of securitization that was acceptable to all. As per the scheme, the state governments were to enter into an agreement with the central government along with their electricity boards. The agreement enjoined upon the state governments to be up-to-date in the payment of their current dues to the central PSUs and not burden the state electricity boards with their decision to supply free electricity. If there was still a shortfall, the central government retained the right to deduct the dues from the plan allocation of the state. Many states willingly entered into this tripartite agreement. Even Jharkhand did so after my intervention.

The energy sector has remained a problem area despite the many policy initiatives we undertook, like special treatment to mega power plants, setting up these plants where raw materials were easily available, cleaning up the financial mess of the state electricity boards and reorganizing them, opening up the sector for private players and the passing of the electricity act. All these initiatives needed a great deal of cooperation from the states. Some states did take unpleasant decisions, like raising tariffs in the teeth of opposition from consumers and reorganizing the boards despite protests by employees. Many, however, succumbed to political pressure and could not overcome the bane of our system, namely, free supply of power to farmers with the boards bearing the burden rather than the state governments.

I feel that the burden of any subsidy determined by the government should not be passed on to a commercial undertaking of the government. If the government wants to subsidize anything it should be through the budget. This, of course, would not apply to social sectors like education and health.

There are many infrastructure projects which could be financed by loans from the market on the strength of their financial viability. But much would depend on our approach to the collection of proper user charges, which is of critical importance. If additional steps are needed to establish the viability of a project, the government could consider giving tax concessions or reducing the interest burden on its loans.

21

Controlling Fiscal Deficit

Controlling fiscal deficit, the gap between the total receipts of the government and its total expenditure, is a major challenge for every finance minister. Manmohan Singh had ended the practice of government borrowing from the RBI, as this amounted to monetizing the government's deficit year after year. In other words, the RBI used to print that many additional currency notes which, once in circulation, created pressure on prices. Under the new arrangement the government borrowed its requirements from the market. This was not without risks. Since the government borrowed large sums of money every year from the market, it crowded out other borrowers. It also added to the interest burden of the government, because it had to borrow at market rates of interest.

No one can afford to live beyond their means year after year. This includes governments. Reining in fiscal deficit was therefore a major priority. As I have mentioned earlier, when we came into office in March 1998, the economy was in sharp decline and the growth rate had plummeted to 4.8 per cent from 7.8 per cent in the previous year. The fiscal deficit that year had also moved up to 4.8 per cent, compared to 4.1 per cent in the previous year.

The other challenge that we faced on the fiscal front was on account of the pay package given by the UF government in

1997 to government employees after the Fifth Pay Commission report. The UF government had gone beyond the recommendations of the Fifth Pay Commission and decided to give to the employees a deal which was more generous than what the commission had recommended. Fiscal deficit had ceased to matter. Other recommendations to promote efficiency in the government were just ignored. We were thus faced with the huge burden of a sudden increase in the establishment expenditure of the Government of India. Soon, the states, local bodies, schools, universities, in fact, everyone everywhere, adopted the same or similar pay scales as the central government, resulting in a national liability of staggering proportions. This led to a cascading effect across the economy. There was a sharp decline in public savings—by almost 200 basis points—during the period. The sharp fall in the domestic savings rate was not because of the fall in the household savings rate but because public savings turned negative.

The impact of the pay commission continued to be a challenge for me in all the five budgets I presented. State finances were also completely ruined as a result of the implementation of these recommendations. It was a major folly on the part of the UF government, in which the Communist Party of India was a partner and which had the support of the Communist Party of India (Marxist) and other Left parties. The irony is that the same people who were responsible for this indefensible decision blamed me for fiscal mismanagement during my tenure.

Fiscal deficit, apart from the economic malaise that it represents, also raises the serious question of inter-generational equity. It is morally wrong for one generation to indulge in excesses in order to make its present comfortable and create problems for future generations. We have no right to do so. The political class in general, and governments in particular, need to show a sense of responsibility. If we do not have the courage to show that sense of responsibility, we should not be in the business of government. I think it is the bounden duty of every government, and especially of the finance minister and the prime minister, to ensure that we rein in fiscal deficit, despite populist pressures.

I agree that fiscal deficit by itself may not be as dangerous as revenue deficit. We run a revenue deficit when we borrow to meet our current expenditure, as opposed to investment expenditure. Therefore, revenue deficit has to be eliminated on a top priority basis. There was a time when we used to have a revenue surplus which was utilized to finance the plans. But we had allowed ourselves to lapse into a situation where we had started incurring huge revenue deficits, which further added to fiscal deficit. I always explain this point—why government cannot afford to spend beyond its means—to the people in my constituency and elsewhere in simple terms, by quoting an example they can understand easily. If someone borrows money from a bank to set up a business but spends it on his daughter's marriage instead, he would be hard put to repay his debt when the time came. Instead, if he had invested the money in the business as expected, he could be making profits, and he would be better able to repay the bank loan as well as become self-reliant in due course. So, when we cannot earn as much as we need, we should control our expenditure, especially our current expenditure. We must cut our coat according to our cloth.

Jaipal Reddy once called me a 'fiscal terrorist' in the Lok Sabha. I did not mind, for I am prepared to accept any amount of criticism, but I am not prepared to give up the principle of eliminating revenue deficit completely and running a government preferably without fiscal deficit. Other countries have done it and there is no reason why India cannot. In fact, we are in the unenviable company of only a couple of African states as far as fiscal deficit is concerned and it definitely does not add to our prestige. I must also clarify that I am not a slave of the Washington Consensus, but if putting our own house in order means following the Washington Consensus, then so be it.

I took steps in budget after budget to reduce the interest burden, curtail subsidies, both explicit and hidden, and reduce the expenditure of the government. I initiated legislative steps to ensure that the fiscal and revenue deficits of the government were controlled and ultimately eliminated. I talked of expenditure restructuring and rationalization of the central sector and centrally sponsored schemes right from the start.

In the 1999 budget, I expressed my concern at the high rate of growth in non-developmental expenditure and proposed the following steps to control expenditure:

1. The most effective and lasting solution to this problem is to begin the process of downsizing the government. We are making an immediate beginning by abolishing four secretary-level posts through a process of merger and rationalization of central government departments. This will take effect on 1 April 1999.

2. To carry this process forward in a systematic way towards reducing the role and the administrative structure of the government, we will constitute an Expenditure Reforms Commission headed by an eminent and experienced person.

3. In preparation for the next budget, I propose to initiate a system of zero-base budgeting.

4. To promote transparency and curb the growth of contingent government liabilities, the government has decided to establish a Guarantee Redemption Fund with an initial corpus of Rs 50 crore. I encourage all state governments to set up similar funds.

In the 2000 budget, I asked Parliament to squarely confront and overcome the critical challenge posed by a weakening fiscal situation. I proposed the following initiatives:

1. All ongoing schemes would be subjected to rigorous zero-base budgeting scrutiny. I had announced this initiative last year and I am glad that this exercise has been completed in eight departments. As a result sixty-nine schemes are to be discontinued or merged. This process will be completed in a time bound manner in the remaining departments.

2. The manpower requirements of government departments will be reassessed by reviewing the norms for creation of posts.

3. Fresh recruitment in government departments and institutions will be limited to minimum essential needs.

4. The scheme for redeployment of surplus staff will be made more effective and will provide facilities for retraining. A VRS scheme will also be introduced for staff in the surplus pool.

5. All subsidies will be reviewed with a view to bringing in cost-based user charges wherever feasible.

6. No new autonomous institutions will be created without approval of cabinet. Budgetary support to autonomous institutions will be reviewed and they will be encouraged to maximize generation of internal resources.

7. In order to align with the overall interest rate structure, the interest rate on General Provident Funds is being reduced by 1 per cent to 11 per cent from 1 April 2000.

8. Excessive domestic borrowings to finance current expenditure has resulted in debt service payments approaching unsustainable levels. To reduce expenditure on this account, a portion of the disinvestment proceeds will be earmarked for retiring government debt. An initial provision of Rs 1000 crore has been made in the budget for this purpose.

In the 2001 budget, I carried forward the process of bringing about structural changes in the composition of central government expenditure by taking the following steps:

1. User charges for services provided by the government and its agencies would be revised keeping in view the increased cost of these services. A portion of this increase will be provided to enhance the maintenance and quality of these services.

2. Similarly, postal rates will be revised moderately to contain the rising postal deficit.

3. All requirements of recruitment will be scrutinized to

ensure that fresh recruitment is limited to 1 per cent of total civilian staff strength. As about 3 per cent of staff retire every year, this will reduce the manpower by 2 per cent per annum, achieving a reduction of 10 per cent in five years as announced by the prime minister.

4. The surplus pool under the Department of Personnel will be streamlined and equipped to redeploy and retrain surplus staff. Employees in the surplus pool will also be offered an attractive VRS package.

5. Standard licence fee (rent) on government accommodation will be enhanced by 50 per cent for Group A, 25 per cent for Group B and 15 per cent for other categories of staff with effect from 1 April 2001.

6. The facility of LTC to central government employees will be suspended for two years for the remaining part of the four-year block period, except for employees who are entitled to the last LTC before retirement.

7. The use of information technology in government activities with large public interface will be maximized to promote efficiency. For this purpose, operations like GPF, pension, pay and accounts offices, passports, income tax, customs, central excise will be fully computerized by 31 March 2002. Public sector banks and insurance companies are also being asked to complete computerization of their operations within this period.

I also announced plans to downsize various ministries and departments based on the report of the Expenditure Reforms Commission.

Setting up the Expenditure Reforms Commission was not an easy task. I succeeded only because of the complete support of the prime minister. Chidambaram had talked about setting up an expenditure commission in his budget of 1997–98 but could not actually do so. The most important task was to find a suitable chairman to head the commission, since much of the success of the commission would depend on his personality and style of functioning. I requested K.P. Geethakrishnan to take on this responsibility. A 1958 batch IAS officer from the

Tamil Nadu cadre, he had worked with me as expenditure secretary in 1991. I thought very highly of him and, true to expectations, Geethakrishnan did commendable work at the commission.

On the legislative side, my intention was to bring before Parliament a Fiscal Responsibility and Budget Management (FRBM) bill announced in the 1999 budget. Soon thereafter, I set up a committee to work out the details of this legislation. The committee, under expenditure secretary Sarma, prepared an excellent report. A draft legislation was prepared, based on the committee's recommendations. I had expected opposition to this move in the cabinet but, surprisingly, it went through without much discussion. I used to make such a fuss about the fiscal deficit in cabinet meetings that I suppose my colleagues decided to spare themselves further agony of having to listen to me one more time.

(Photograph by Sanjiv Misra)

The Expenditure Reforms Commission report presented to the author (right) by K.P. Geethakrishnan (centre), chairman of the commission, on 23 December 2000.

The FRBM bill, after its introduction in the Lok Sabha, was referred to the Standing Committee on Finance. Shivraj Patil was the chairman of the committee. The committee deliberated on the draft bill seriously and for long and then gave its report. I was not happy with some of the recommendations of the committee because they diluted the provisions of the bill and took away its teeth. However, since we were dependent on the Congress party's support in the Rajya Sabha to get legislations passed, I had no option but to accept the committee's recommendations and incorporate its suggestions in the revised bill. The bill was finally passed during the tenure of Jaswant Singh as finance minister and was notified when the UPA government came to power.

I also started the practice of meeting the financial advisers of various ministries periodically, where I reviewed their performance against the quarterly targets of expenditure. The idea was to ensure financial discipline and do away with the bunching of expenditure towards the end of the financial year.

In the interim budget of 1991, I had talked about setting up a Rashtriya Bachat Bank and putting all the small savings receipts in it so that these savings did not form part of the budget. The Rashtriya Bachat Bank would operate these savings schemes under the guarantee of the Government of India. This proposal was not followed up by my successors. On my return to the finance ministry in 1998, I looked at the whole system of small savings afresh. Under the existing system, the government borrowed money on its account first through these savings schemes and then transferred them to the states. A small portion of the money was kept by the government by way of collection charges and in order to meet contingencies. Thus, though we were borrowing for the state governments, the entire amount got reflected in our budget as part of the fiscal deficit of the Government of India. It was nothing but a statistical mirage because we were not borrowing it for ourselves but for the states. I therefore suggested that we should put this account outside the budget into the public account, though we would continue to operate it. The public account is an account through which the government performs a large number of banking functions, and is outside the budget. This obviated the need to set up a Rashtriya Bachat Bank. I implemented this idea in the 1999 budget. I knew that there would be criticism of this move. I would be accused of artificially reducing the fiscal deficit. I therefore asked the finance ministry to work out the figures of fiscal deficit for all the years from 1991–92 on the same basis for easy comparison. The criticism was indeed levelled in Parliament, but I was ready with my reply.

Many of the steps that I took—reduction of interest rates, downsizing of ministries and departments, increase in user charges, lowering of subsidies and the raising of the prices of food, fertilizers and sugar, and, above all, my continued emphasis on reducing government expenditure—did not go down well with various sections of people who were adversely affected by these decisions.

22

Gross Budgetary Support

Every year the government determines the gross budgetary support (GBS) for the annual plan. Usually a large sum of money is set aside for financing the plan, which adds to the fiscal problem of the government. A large part of the plan allocation goes to the states. But once the allocations are made to the states, the government is left with very little control over the expenditure of these funds. There are instances galore of states misusing plan funds. Instead of spending the funds for the purpose for which they are allocated, they are spent on wages and salaries of the staff, or just kept in some ledger account. The efficient and purposeful utilization of plan funds, especially by the state governments, is always a problem. The audit reports of the state governments go to the state assembly and they are examined by their Public Accounts Committee. Mamata Banerjee, the fiery Trinamul Congress Party leader from West Bengal, who was also our cabinet colleague, often used to raise the issue of her state's government misusing these funds. She expected me to discipline the West Bengal government. I tried to explain to her that our role and powers were limited in this respect but this did not satisfy her.

Every year there was a tussle between the Planning Commission and the finance ministry regarding the amount of the GBS. The finance ministry, in order to keep the fiscal deficit down, wanted to keep the annual incremental amount as small as possible. There is no doubt that the unrealistic manner in which our five-year plans are prepared casts an onerous burden on the budget. I was not opposed to increasing the GBS for the plan. Equity has always been an important issue in our economic policy and the plan size generally determines what will be spent on agriculture and social sectors like health and education. As such, I did not want to reduce the GBS and give overriding priority to fiscal adjustment, but the issue was of keeping the plan size at a reasonable level in order to establish a balance between the fiscal deficit and the plan size.

The Planning Commission always fixed a very ambitious target for the GBS. In instances when the finance minister and the deputy chairperson of the Planning Commission could not reach an agreement over the amount of GBS, the issue was taken to the prime minister, who played the role of an arbiter. During the discussions, the prime minister always ended up giving more to the Planning Commission than what the finance minister was willing to spare.

During 1998 and 1999, Jaswant Singh was the deputy chairman of the Planning Commission. We did not have any serious difference of opinion, though, naturally, each of us pushed our case hard. We were able to arrive at a settlement before the matter went to the prime minister. But later, whenever the issue went to the prime minister, I always lost the battle on this front.

Once the size of the support is decided, it is the Planning Commission which makes the allocations to various ministries. The finance ministry has no role in it. When the budget is debated in Parliament, these allocations come up for scrutiny. And the finance minister, who has played no role in allocating the funds, has to defend them to agitated MPs unhappy with the amount of funds allocated to various sectors like agriculture, health, education, rural development and irrigation, especially if they have not been increased substantially.

We face amusing situations when finance secretaries get transferred to the Planning Commission. For instance, Montek

Singh Ahluwalia, N.K. Singh and Ajit Kumar were transferred to the Planning Commission after serving in the finance ministry and soon started speaking the language of the commission. In 2002, when I was holding discussions with the Planning Commission, it was Ajit Kumar who was arguing why the finance ministry should give more funds to the commission. Ironical, considering it was he who had opposed increasing budgetary support in 2001, when he was working in the finance ministry. This is part of a civil servant's life. He has to shift his loyalty not only from government to government, but also from ministry to ministry.

There is a major flaw in our planning process. The line ministries of the Government of India and the state governments tend to include schemes and projects in their plans, the details of which have not been worked out properly. Often large and ambitious schemes are included in the plan and allocations made for them without even a feasibility study or preliminary estimates of expenditure. Time and cost overruns are therefore a routine phenomenon. I know of an irrigation project in my constituency which was started in 1978 at an estimated total cost of Rs 12 crore. It involved the construction of an underground tunnel, a few kilometres long, and a canal, to take water from the Konar dam to another area. The project was abandoned after a few years because the estimated amount had already been exhausted; the contractor of the project had left the project midway. When the project was restarted, the cost had gone up by a few hundred crore rupees.

Time and cost overruns in the implementation of projects is a serious issue for governments. I had dealt with this problem as a civil servant. While reviewing ship-building projects, for instance, I used to tell my interlocutors that I could understand the cost of labour, steel and other consumables going up, but I could not understand how the quantity of steel required could go up over the years. A financial overrun can be explained, but how can anyone explain a materials overrun? We prepare our schemes so unprofessionally that at the end there is not merely an expenditure but also a materials overrun in most cases.

When the NDA was in power, we did set up a system under which the concerned ministry had to explain why there had been a cost overrun. The matter was then examined by both the Planning Commission and the finance ministry and we offered our comments for the cabinet's consideration. But this lapsed into routine since hardly anything could be done to fix responsibility in the case of projects which had been delayed for decades. Those who had prepared the feasibility report and the detailed project report were all long gone by then. So, no one ever gets punished. This is a major weakness of our system and leads to a lot of wastage.

23

Disinvestment and Privatization

I firmly believe that the government has no need any more to be in business except in a limited number of strategic areas, and was thereby fully committed to disinvestment and privatization. In the heyday of socialism, the government had entered practically every sector of industry. This had led to the creation of a plethora of public sector undertakings (PSUs) in the country, many of them loss-making. Though subsequent governments had followed the policy of disinvestment mentioned in my interim budget of March 1991, the policy as it had evolved left much to be desired. I felt that the policy should be transparent and holistic, deal with the whole issue of PSU reforms and not limit itself to disinvestment alone. Privatization was to be part of this process. But considering the highly sensitive and politically volatile nature of the issue, I had to proceed with the greatest caution if I wanted to succeed even partially. This is what I proceeded to do, step by step, through my annual budgets.

In my very first budget of 1998 I had said, 'Government has also decided that in the generality of cases, the government shareholding in public sector enterprises will be brought down to 26 per cent. In cases of public sector enterprises involving strategic considerations, government will continue to retain majority holding. The interest of workers shall be protected in all cases.' The Vajpayee government's intention was thus announced clearly, transparently and forthrightly and the approval of Parliament secured for the policy.

While presenting the budget for 1999, I had this to say on disinvestment: 'Government's strategy towards public sector enterprises will continue to encompass a judicious mix of strengthening strategic units, privatizing non-strategic ones through gradual disinvestment or strategic sale, and devising viable rehabilitation strategies for weak units.' Incidentally, this was the first time the word 'privatization' was used in a government policy document.

I set out the government's policy regarding PSUs and their disinvestment even more clearly in my budget speech of 2000 when I said:

> Government's policy towards the public sector is clear and unambiguous. Its main elements are:
>
> 1. Restructure and revive potentially viable PSUs.
> 2. Close down PSUs which cannot be revived.
> 3. Bring down Government equity in all non-strategic PSUs to 26 per cent or lower, if necessary, and
> 4. Fully protect the interests of workers.

In my budget speech of 2000 I also said:

> In line with this policy during the last two years, financial restructuring of twenty PSUs has been approved by Government. As a result, many PSUs have been able to restructure their operations, improve productivity and achieve a turnaround in performance. Hon'ble members are aware that Government have recently approved a comprehensive package for restructuring of SAIL, one of our Navratna PSUs (selected PSUs with greater autonomy).

SAIL is today one of the more profitable PSUs. This would not have been possible if we had not spent thousands of crores of rupees on its restructuring.

On disinvestment I went on to say the following:

Government has recently established a new Department of Disinvestment to establish a systematic policy approach to disinvestment and privatization and to give a fresh impetus to this programme, which will emphasise increasingly on strategic sales of identified PSUs. Government equity in all non-strategic sales of identified PSUs will be reduced to 26 per cent or less and the interests of the workers will be fully protected. The entire receipt from disinvestment and privatization will be used for meeting expenditure in social sectors, restructuring of PSUs and retiring public debt.

While presenting my budget for 2001 I once again stated the government's stand clearly:

The procedure for privatization of public sector enterprises has now been considerably streamlined. The Department of Disinvestment has been set up to accelerate the privatization process. To maximize returns to government, our approach has shifted from the disinvestment of small lots of shares to strategic sales of blocks of shares to strategic investors.

In my 2002 budget I reiterated the same point when I said that 'the change in approach from the disinvestment of small lots of shares to strategic sales of blocks of shares to strategic investors has improved the price earning ratios obtained'.

In view of the increased workload relating to disinvestment, a new and separate Department of Disinvestment was created in August 1999. Until then disinvestment was a small part of the finance minister's job. Arun Jaitley became the first Minister for Disinvestment. The strategic sale of Modern Foods, a company which made bread, was done during his tenure. Arun Shourie soon succeeded Jaitley as disinvestment minister. The entire methodology of strategic sales was built assiduously, meticulously and in a fully transparent manner first by Jaitley and subsequently and largely by Shourie. The Cabinet Committee on Disinvestment, headed by the prime minister, gave final approval to all proposals.

Privatizing PSUs through the strategic sale route was not an easy task. A majority of our alliance partners, small and big and of different political ideologies, were united in opposing it. Many of the BJP ministers also did not have their heart in it. Each transaction therefore was a closely fought battle. Non-cooperation by the line ministry made the task of the disinvestment minister even more difficult. There were long and often heated arguments in the meetings of the Cabinet Committee on Disinvestment. Fortunately, the prime minister supported the pro-privatization group. My arguments often helped clinch a proposal. But line ministers treated each PSU as their personal and private fiefdom. The simple truth that they were concerned with the PSU only until they were in charge of that ministry and would have nothing to do with it after their departure did not dawn upon them.

I remember how once a colleague rang me up and said that we should not privatize a particular PSU since it was the only PSU under his charge. I was not surprised at all. On one occasion, when I was joint secretary in the Government of India, a colleague of mine, who was joint secretary in another ministry, entertained us to a lavish breakfast in a five-star hotel when our flight was delayed, and coolly passed on the bill to a PSU under his charge. PSUs of the Government of India have long been milch cows for politicians, trade union leaders and bureaucrats. They must be privatized for this reason alone, if for no other reason.

24

Other Reforms

TEXTILE SECTOR

The textile sector is the second largest employer in India with thirty-eight million workers, next only to agriculture. The phasing out of the multi-fibre agreement and the removal of all quantitative restrictions on export of textiles by 1 January 2004 was a huge challenge facing the industry. We needed to prepare ourselves to meet this challenge.

The industry's structure is most complicated. The khadi sector manufactures only hand-spun yarn and hand-woven cloth. The handloom sector uses mill yarn to produce fabrics on handlooms. The power loom sector uses mill yarn to produce greys and fabrics on power looms of various capacities. Finally, we have the integrated textile mills which manufacture their own yarn and fabrics. Some produce only yarn, while others produce only grey cloth. Some process it. Processing may be entirely manual, entirely by machine, or a mix of both. Then we have cotton, man-made and mixed fabrics. The textile industry is also geographically spread throughout the country. The complicated nature of the textile industry had, over a period of time, led to a very complex taxation structure for it which did not permit a straightforward solution.

I wrestled with the problems of the textile industry, trying to rationalize the tax structure, so as to modernize the sector and prepare it for the challenges ahead. I cannot say I succeeded fully. The textile minister in our government, Kashiram Rana, an MP from Surat, was very knowledgeable about the industry. He and I had some initial differences of opinion. He even complained to the prime minister once that I was insensitive to the needs of the industry. But subsequently we got along well and worked together for the development of the industry.

At Rana's suggestion, I set up a Technology Upgradation Fund which became operational from April 1999. The scheme provided a substantial interest incentive of 5 per cent on loans from financial institutions and banks availed of by textile units for modernization and upgradation. It covered all segments of the textile industry, such as weaving, knitting, processing and finishing units, garment manufacturing, cotton ginning and processing, the jute industry and the spinning industry.

In November 2000 a national textile policy was announced, aimed at preparing the industry for global competition. Integrated apparel parks were set up to help the industry establish modern units with world-class infrastructure. The customs duty on imports of specified textile machines was brought down.

I also met representatives of the industry from time to time to exhort them to modernize to meet the emerging competition at home and abroad. The performance of the industry, especially on the export front, after March 2004, shows that our efforts were not in vain.

TELECOM SECTOR

In May 1994 the Narasimha Rao government had announced a National Telecom Policy (NTP '94), which sought to make telephone connections widely available by throwing the industry open to private enterprise. This policy did not work effectively and efficiently primarily due to one reason—it was based on licensing and the licence fees were quite steep. A large number of players had entered the field and taken licences for various areas by paying or promising to pay very hefty licence fees. The majority of these operators could not fulfil their commitment to pay the government due to the huge amounts they had bid for the licences, and pleaded their inability to create the necessary infrastructure.

The obvious course of action for the government was to cancel their licences and invite fresh bids, but doing so was messy, since in many cases the operators had set up part of the infrastructure. When the issue of a new telecom policy came up in December 1998, Jagmohan, who was the telecom minister, had already shifted to another ministry. The Department of Telecommunications was under the direct charge of the prime minister.

After long discussions on the telecom policy and its associated problems in the Department of Telecommunications and in the PMO, it was decided to move from the system of licence fees to revenue sharing. The telecom department proposals then came for examination to the finance ministry. I did not have any objection to moving to a revenue-sharing system, but I had a problem with the percentage of revenue an operator had to share. There was clearly a moral hazard problem here. The operators, who came into the business with their eyes open, had not been forced by the government to bid the large amounts they had. When the business did not work out to their satisfaction, they came back to the government pleading for a complete overhaul of the system. The bidding process in which they had cornered the licences was open and transparent. As such, it was not morally right for them to come back to the government with a plea that the system needed to be changed. This was a basic objection raised by many, including the finance ministry.

While it was essential to promote telecom and let the operators migrate to a revenue-sharing regime, it was also our duty to ensure that the government did not end up losing a major share of its revenue in the process. The new system needed to be as clear and transparent as possible. In our advice, we emphasized these points.

The department took the case to the attorney general, who gave an opinion that it was legally valid to change the existing system. The cabinet approved the proposal and the New Telecom Policy (NTP '99) was announced in March 1999. The operators were required to give 15 per cent of their revenue to the government instead of the fixed licence fee.

The decision to shift to the revenue-sharing system led to hue and cry, especially from the Left parties, who felt that it was not a fair deal. They alleged that the treasury would lose a lot of money, estimated at Rs 48,000 crore over a period of ten years.

In July 1999 the Delhi Science Forum, a group of scientists and activists, moved the Supreme Court seeking a stay on the policy. But the Supreme Court decided it was not the court's job to lay down policy. The court ruled that the government should allow Parliament to discuss the policy after the elections and secure Parliament's approval.

When we were retuned to power in October 1999, the matter was taken to Parliament. There was heated debate in both Houses. We were ready with our replies to all the points the opposition made and the policy went through. There is no doubt that the new policy has been responsible for the recent phenomenal growth of the telecom sector in our country. But whether we should have got more in terms of revenue for the government's treasury in 1999 remains an issue. I now feel that it was a question of judgement and the government of the day made a judgement which has worked out well for all concerned.

REMOVAL OF QUANTITATIVE RESTRICTIONS

During the second half of the 1990s, Indian industry faced many new challenges. The first was of excess capacity as demand had not kept pace with the capacity created in the earlier years. The second was posed by the general global slowdown compounded by the East Asian crisis. The third was on account of the opening up of the Indian market under our commitment to the WTO made in 1995. In the initial years we opened up areas where the damage was likely to be limited. But we had to keep removing these restrictions on imports progressively every year. The moment of truth came in 2001, when by 1 April we had to remove all the remaining non-tariff restrictions and freely allow imports into India of everything from everywhere. The only instrument we had in our hands to protect domestic industry from the impact of imports was tariff. We could increase our tariffs up to the ceiling of the WTO-bound rates. As 1 April approached, a great fear gripped India. Wild stories started circulating about how import of milk was destroying the dairy industry in Punjab, the import of apples was affecting the apple economy of Himachal Pradesh and Jammu and Kashmir, the import of toys from China was killing the industry in India and how everything was coming cheap from China, including wristwatches, pens, shoes and dozens of other items. There was much hype created in the media about a second Chinese invasion. Many Indian industrialists were paralysed with fear.

There were two prominent industries in India which were most scared—the two-wheeler industry and the poultry industry. The representatives of the two-wheeler industry told me that the Chinese had kept large numbers of two-wheelers in ports like Dubai and were waiting for the Indian market to open up in order to flood it with their products. They predicted that the import of Chinese two-wheelers, which were much cheaper, would ruin the Indian industry. The poultry industry felt threatened not by the Chinese but by the Americans. A delegation led by Sharad Pawar came to see me and told me that the United States was sitting on mountains of frozen chicken legs. Since chicken legs were considered red meat, which was not a preferred meat in the United States, they had accumulated all the chicken legs for export to other countries. The fear was that once we opened up, the United States would inundate our market with frozen chicken legs. The poultry industry in India would be destroyed, since people in India preferred chicken legs. I raised the customs duty to the

WTO-bound rates on both these products to brace us for the coming onslaught.

The commerce ministry prepared a list of sensitive items whose imports were to be monitored carefully and regularly and the figures published for the information of all concerned. It was also meant to help us take appropriate steps as and when necessary to curb such imports.

The last of the quantitative restrictions were finally removed on 1 April 2001. But we were not overwhelmed by imports from any country, not even from China. Subsequent events showed that Indian industry had the strength to meet the Chinese challenge and all our fears were completely misplaced. Even after the complete opening up of the Indian economy, there was no flood of imports from China and we were able to hold our own against them. We can be proud of the fact that while our trade with China has increased rapidly, the balance of trade had been in our favour until recently. At a meeting between our prime minister and President Bush in New York in 2003, when I told the President that we had a favourable balance of trade with China, he sighed and said how he wished he could say the same about the United States. I believe that Indian industry faced the challenges during this period admirably. Often, like Hanuman, we are not aware of our own strength. During this period of adjustment, Indian industry restructured and retooled to become lean, mean and more efficient. It readied itself to meet global challenges on Indian soil, as indeed at the global level.

ABOLITION OF FERA

Reform of the foreign exchange laws was long overdue. In my budget of 1998–99, I had mentioned that the Foreign Exchange Regulation Act (FERA), a draconian legislation, had to be replaced by a more civilized legislation, the Foreign Exchange Management Act (FEMA), and a separate Money Laundering Act. Both the legislations were supposed to go together. I introduced both the bills in the Lok Sabha, where they were duly passed. When the bills went to the Rajya Sabha, where we did not have a majority, while the foreign exchange management bill was passed without difficulty, many reservations were expressed regarding the money laundering bill. Some reservations were genuine—certain provisions of the bill could be misused for political purposes by a less scrupulous government. I did not want to leave those loopholes. It was suggested by some members that the bill be referred to a select committee of the Rajya Sabha. I agreed with this proposal, and the bill was passed by the Rajya Sabha after the select committee had examined the bill and given its report.

PETROLEUM SECTOR

The UF government had, in November 1997, notified the details for dismantling the administered pricing mechanism (APM) for petroleum products by March 2002. In the budget of 2001, I announced my intention to adhere to this deadline. The petroleum minister, Ram Naik, and I, along with our senior officials, spent many hours in meetings to prepare the road map for this purpose. Perhaps, creating the APM was easier than dismantling it. There were pitfalls to be avoided, mindsets to be tackled, resistance to dismantling, especially among the bureaucracy, to be overcome and popular sentiment to be kept in mind. At the end of the long hours of very detailed work, we took the road map to the cabinet, which gave its approval for me to include this in the budget of 2002. In my budget speech, I spoke about the measure as follows:

1. The pricing of petroleum products will become market-determined.
2. The Oil Pool Account will be dismantled on 1 April 2002 and the outstanding balances will be liquidated by issue of oil bonds to the concerned oil companies.
3. Private companies will be permitted in distribution subject to specified guidelines.
4. A Petroleum Regulatory Board will be set up to oversee the sector.

5. Subsidies to refineries in the north-east will continue on a rationalized basis.

6. Freight subsidies will continue to be provided for LPG and kerosene supplies to far-flung areas.

7. As a result of the dismantling of APM, the price of diesel will come down by around 50 paise per litre and of petrol by around Re 1 per litre. These changes in prices will come into effect from 1 March 2002, initially as part of the Oil Pool Account.

8. The 1997 government decision on the dismantling of APM mandated the subsidy on LPG and kerosene oil to be reduced to 15 and 33 per cent respectively by 1 April 2002. Accordingly, the price of LPG is being raised by about Rs 40 per cylinder and of kerosene oil for PDS by about Rs 1.50 per litre from 1 March 2002. These subsidies will be borne by the consolidated fund from 1 April 2002.

9. The subsidies on LPG and kerosene will be on a specified flat rate basis from 1 April 2002. The retail prices will then vary as the price of crude oil changes in international markets.

10. These subsidies will be phased out in the next three to five years.

11. The post-APM excise and customs duty changes will be spelt out in Part B of the speech. Since the subsidy burden will be borne by the Union budget from next year, the taxation measures have been designed to raise the required resources.

It is a pity that the hard work which went into this exercise has all been wasted. The reason I mentioned that the decision to dismantle the APM was taken by the UF government in November 1997 was to emphasize that there was a national consensus behind it. It is a matter of great pity therefore that under the UPA government the notification of 2002 dismantling the APM has been cancelled and we have reverted to the old system. A part of the burden of the present subsidy is being passed on to future generations through the issue of oil bonds to the public sector oil companies.

INFORMATION TECHNOLOGY SECTOR

Prime Minister Vajpayee was very keen to promote information technology (IT). I was in full agreement with him on this. A national task force on Information Technology and Software Development headed by Jaswant Singh was appointed in May 1998. This task force had a mandate to formulate the draft of a National Informatics Policy. The group submitted its report in which it suggested a number of changes in the tax laws. But the report was submitted after the presentation of the 1998 budget; hence the recommendations relating to taxes could not be incorporated in that budget. I accepted almost all the suggestions of the report when I moved the finance bill for consideration in the Lok Sabha later. The whole process of examining and implementing the recommendations was done speedily and efficiently. In fact, a newspaper commented in an editorial that it had rarely seen any government act as fast as we did in this case.

Information technology continued to be a much-valued sector for the Vajpayee government. A Group on Telecom and IT Convergence (GOT-IT) was constituted by the prime minister in December 1999 under my chairmanship. It was a mixed group and had government officials, representatives of the IT industry, the then chief vigilance commissioner, N. Vittal, and Fali Nariman, the eminent jurist and MP, apart from the concerned ministers. This group resolved all the outstanding problems of the IT and telecom sectors and worked on a new and path-breaking convergence law covering the IT, telecom and broadcasting sectors. We also prepared amendments for the Telecom Regulatory Authority Act which led to the separation of the regulatory and judicial functions of the authority and the setting up of the appellate body of TRAI, the Telecom Regulatory Authority of India.

DERESERVATION OF PRODUCTS IN THE SMALL-SCALE INDUSTRY SECTOR

Dereservation of products reserved for the small-scale industry (SSI) sector was a very sensitive issue. We started with the dereservation of some products in 1998 and continued it progressively in subsequent budgets. There are many holy cows in the Indian economy. The issue of reservation of products for the SSI sector was one such. I was firmly of the view, however, that what the small-scale sector needed was more financial assistance, better technology, higher taxation benefits and less inspector raj, rather than reservation of products. With this objective in mind, I raised the limit of excise duty exemption for the SSI sector from Rs 30 lakh to Rs 50 lakh in the 1998 budget. Subsequently, I raised it to Rs 1 crore. I also started a new credit insurance scheme to help export-oriented SSI units and tiny sector enterprises which could not provide adequate security to banks. Alongside all these measures, I also continued with my policy of dereservation.

NATIONAL STATISTICAL COMMISSION

An important initiative which I took in the 1999 budget was the setting up of the National Statistical Commission (NSC). I have worked at the field level as an IAS officer. As a sub-divisional officer and later as district magistrate, I was required to collect and submit statistics on various subjects to the Department of Statistics of the state government. The states collated the figures received from the districts and sent them to the Government of India. The system has many weaknesses. We depended largely on eye estimates to collect statistics. The task was performed by junior functionaries of the government. For instance, the village level worker or the karamchari at the village level usually made an eye estimate of a particular crop. The rough estimate was not merely confined to agriculture and food production, but also applied to national income, inflation and growth rates. I became more acutely aware of this inadequacy when I started dealing closely with national statistics in the Ministry of Finance. Sometimes I had great doubts about the figures which were put up to me. I decided that the whole system of collection, collation, retrieval and usage of statistics should be looked at afresh. This led to the setting up of a National Statistical Commission with Dr C. Rangarajan as its chairman. The commission was assigned the responsibility of submitting a report to the government about ways and means of improving the system. Departments of statistics, including those in the states, were to be revamped based on the recommendations of the commission, so that the figures could be more reliable.

ZERO-BASED BUDGETING

Zero-based budgeting is an old concept, but not much had been done to make it operational in our budgets. My experience as a civil servant proved very useful in tackling this issue when I became finance minister. I had served as the animal husbandry commissioner of Bihar in the 1970s on my return from Germany. The department ran a sheep farm in one of the districts. During an inspection of the farm, I was surprised to find that there were hardly any sheep there. No worthwhile work was being done at the farm. The place was overstaffed and the money allotted to the farm was spent on salaries and allowances of the staff. I found that this had gone on from plan to plan and continued mainly because of lethargy and lack of initiative.

The same was true of the various reports and returns we were required to send. During my tenure as a sub-divisional magistrate in Bihar in the early 1960s, I came across a report that was being sent every month to the state government. It related to the status of Afghan refugees. Curious, I made inquiries and discovered that it originated from the time of the Anglo-Afghan wars of the nineteenth and early twentieth centuries. The report continued to be sent over the years. Obviously there was a need to review the utility of ongoing schemes every year. It could be achieved by introducing the concept of zero-based budgeting—that is, all expenditure had to be justified anew every year. If the justification was not convincing, the project could be scrapped altogether. This would force every ministry to review each scheme annually to decide whether it served a useful purpose or not, and it could then abolish those that were not useful.

Though the system was begun in consultation with the Planning Commission in the 1999 budget, it could not be fully implemented. There were two major problems in its implementation. Firstly, the addition of new schemes every year by ministries led to a plethora of development and welfare schemes and, secondly, there was strong resistance by the line ministries to the reduction in the number of schemes. Even as an IAS officer I could not have named all the development schemes in existence in my district—there were so many. The rationalization of schemes did reduce the number of schemes. But because of the resistance of the ministries, a large number of schemes still continue, many without adequate justification.

The concept of zero-based budgeting can play an important role in reducing the number of central and centrally sponsored schemes. It is a very important part of the overall expenditure reforms programme of any government. But there are entrenched vested interests. This resistance has to be met frontally, though it is not always easy.

FOREIGN INVESTMENT
IMPLEMENTATION AUTHORITY

I announced the setting up of the Foreign Investment Implementation Authority (FIIA) in the budget of 1999. In some way or the other, I have always been connected with the question of FDI—as an IAS officer when I worked in the Ministry of Commerce and later when I worked in Germany. As a director in the Ministry of Industry I handled the desk which dealt with foreign investment and collaborations. Whenever I talked to foreign companies about investing in

India, they complained bitterly about the bureaucracy in India and how it was impossible to do business in India while it was so easy to do business in China and other East Asian countries. It was, according to them, the most important reason why FDI was not flowing into our country. From time to time, we experimented with new models and new systems. When I was in the industry ministry, we had the Secretariat for Industrial Approvals. A time limit of ninety days was fixed for approving a proposal. A simple way out for the bureaucracy to deal with the time limit was to raise a query at the end of it and put the onus on the applicant. So, a system in which the government gave approval for each proposal was flawed and could never work properly. I was convinced that government should not involve itself in this process and it should be made as automatic as possible. This was exactly what we did subsequently by putting FDI in most sectors on the automatic route after clearly defining our policy.

But the problem of implementation remained. The project had to be physically located in one state or the other, and so the state government was directly involved. The state government had to provide land, water, electricity and administrative back-up. It was concerned with the implementation of various laws in that state. So it was actually a partnership between the Government of India, the state government and the foreign investor. But our system did not have any role for the states. Naturally, many investment decisions never saw the light of day. Consequently, I felt that there must be an implementation authority. It could consist of a representative of the administrative ministry, the industry ministry and a high-level representative of the concerned state. This group would be in constant touch with the foreign investor, identify the problems, ensure that the obstacles were removed and the implementation of the project speeded up. I am glad that this body has played a useful role.

We also enlarged the automatic route from time to time. It was for the government to lay down its foreign investment policy for the various sectors and the permissible levels of FDI in those sectors. The percentage of foreign investment could be decided on the basis of national consensus and national interest. Barring a few areas, there would be no problem in this approach. The foreign investor is looking for clarity in policy, speedy disposal of his application and speedy implementation of his project. As long as we are prepared to ensure that these expectations are met he will be attracted towards India. Otherwise, he will go elsewhere.

REVIVAL OF SAIL

The steel industry was in trouble during the earlier years of my tenure. Lack of domestic and export demand, overcapacity and falling prices had taken their toll. Our plans for the housing and infrastructure sectors were on their own not sufficient to boost the demand for steel immediately. SAIL— Steel Authority of India Ltd—was in dire distress and its losses were mounting. It was overstaffed and some of its units were clearly unviable. SAIL had appointed McKinsey&Co. to prepare a revival plan. Representatives of McKinsey came to present the report to me, when it was ready, and explain how SAIL could be revived. It was a good report. We worked closely with the steel ministry and prepared a bail-out package for SAIL. Contrary to the common impression that we were only interested in selling public sector undertakings, this proved that we were also interested in reviving those PSUs which could be revived. SAIL was one of the largest PSUs and it could not be allowed to sink. But I wanted to revive SAIL in a manner that would ensure it became viable in the long term. I knew of PSUs which came back with revival proposals repeatedly, even up to four times. The general rule of thumb that I followed was to examine the revival package of the PSU closely. If it could be revived, I would agree to make funds available for the purpose. Otherwise, I insisted on their closure.

Not all proposals were viable. In the finance ministry we asked searching questions and insisted on detailed replies. We studied the SAIL package carefully. It was a difficult package in two ways. Firstly, it involved a large financial outgo from the government, the largest perhaps for the revival of any unit till date. Secondly, it meant closing down some units which were considered unviable, and separating a large number of surplus employees. A package of Rs 8454 crore was prepared. The finance ministry agreed to it and it got the approval of the cabinet. The process of the revival of SAIL was set in motion in the year 2000. I am happy that SAIL is not only fully revived, it is also making large profits now. I believe that since SAIL was one of the most overstaffed PSUs, it ultimately had to voluntarily retire some 40,000 to 50,000 employees.

In this connection, I would like to point out that a separation package was in existence in the Government of India but, in the meanwhile, Gujarat had worked out a very good one for its employees. We looked at Gujarat's separation package and decided to adopt it at the centre too. This made separation of personnel easier. The banks, for instance, prepared their own separation package for their employees. It proved to be a very popular package and created a rather peculiar situation. A large number of employees in the banking sector decided to take advantage of the package and leave their jobs for better opportunities elsewhere. More than one lakh employees left the public sector banks, taking advantage of the separation package. I used to get requests from friends, acquaintances and even strangers that I should intervene with a particular bank's management to let an employee leave, not for his retention!

A NEW COMPETITION POLICY

The Monopolies and Restrictive Trade Practices (MRTP) Act had been in existence in India from the days of the socialist era, that is, from 1970. The basic thrust of the MRTP policy was to control unfair or restrictive business practices by controlling size, through an elaborate system of measures which could only be described as anti-growth. The country lacked a proper competition policy and a new law to implement that policy.

I emphasized the need for a new competition policy in my budget of 1999. Subsequently, we appointed an expert committee headed by S.V.S. Raghavan, an eminent management expert with long experience in industry, to examine the issue in detail. The committee submitted its report in August 2000. The prime minister appointed a Group of Ministers under my chairmanship to work out a new competition law and examine the feasibility of setting up a competition commission which would enforce the law. The group worked meticulously on all issues. We submitted our recommendations to the prime minister, which were later approved by the cabinet. A new competition bill was brought before Parliament, passed by it and became an act. The Competition Act was notified in January 2003 and the Competition Commission set up in October 2003.

The composition of the Competition Commission was challenged in the Supreme Court on the ground that an IAS officer had been appointed to head the commission, which had semi-judicial functions. The Supreme Court felt that the commission could not be headed by an administrator. The government promised to amend the law and make it mandatory for a judge to head the commission. I am mentioning this to show how slowly things move in our democracy. We must always keep in mind the time needed between the birth of an idea and its implementation in our system.

LIBERALIZATION OF THE FOREIGN EXCHANGE REGIME

As I have already mentioned, among the problems that I faced in 1998 was depleting foreign exchange reserves. I did not allow this development to deter me from liberalizing the foreign exchange regime. I announced my intention to replace the outdated Foreign Exchange Regulation Act, 1973 with a new Foreign Exchange Management Act and supplement it with an Anti Money Laundering bill. I also allowed FIIs who could until then invest only in listed debt securities to invest in unlisted domestic debt securities. For NRIs, I announced the following concessions in the 1998 budget:

1. NRIs were allowed to purchase shares in Indian companies in the secondary market subject to a limit of 1 per cent of the company's total equity for individual NRIs and NRI Overseas Corporate bodies, with a 5 per cent limit for aggregate NRI/OCB investments in the company. I raised this to 5 per cent and the aggregate limit to 10 per cent.
2. The UTI was encouraged to launch a new India Millennium Scheme only for NRIs. The money collected under this scheme was to be invested in shares of Indian companies and in debt stocks.
3. The Resurgent India Bond was launched in August 1998 only for NRIs.

In the 1999 budget, I announced:

1. The existing scheme of export credit in foreign currency was to be revamped to make available pre-shipment and post-shipment credit at internationally competitive rates.
2. We extended the facility of automatic approval for investment up to 100 per cent by NRIs/OCBs for all items, except those which attracted notified FDI equity caps, or compulsory licensing or public sector reservation under the industrial policy or those reserved for the SSI sector.
3. I asked the RBI to simplify the approval mechanism for NRI investment in Indian mutual funds.

In view of the success of the Resurgent India Bond and the India Millennium Deposit scheme, and the comfortable foreign exchange reserve position, I became bolder in the budget of 2000, and in my speech I said:

> In earlier millennia, India led the world on the basis of knowledge. Today history is repeating itself. Young Indian entrepreneurs are at the forefront of the infotech

revolution, whether in Silicon Valley, Bangalore or Hyderabad. They have shown us how ideas, knowledge, entrepreneurship and technology can combine to yield unprecedented growth of incomes, employment and wealth. Companies unknown five years ago have become world leaders. We must do everything possible to promote this flowering of knowledge-based enterprise and job creation.

A key ingredient for future success lies in venture capital finance. After a thorough review, I am proposing a major liberalisation of the tax treatment for venture capital funds. To simplify the procedures, SEBI will be the single point nodal agency for registration and regulation of both domestic and overseas venture capital funds. Venture activity is not limited to dotcom companies! Ideas and entrepreneurship, which merit venture finance, can be found in all sectors of the economy. The tax laws and SEBI guidelines are being formulated accordingly. I should add that this liberalisation will give a strong boost for Non Resident Indians in Silicon Valley and elsewhere to invest some of their capital, knowledge and enterprise in ventures in their motherland.

Thanks to our prudent macro-economic management and calibrated approach to currency convertibility, we have successfully weathered the East Asian crisis of the past two years. But we must not confuse caution with timidity. We must encourage Indian firms and businesses to grow into strong, India-based multinationals. To promote this trend, it is necessary to accord our firms increasing flexibility to undertake capital account transactions, especially for acquisitions of businesses abroad. Last month, Government had announced a policy to allow Indian companies to raise funds for investments through issue of ADRs/GDRs without prior Government approval. Up to 50 per cent of these proceeds can be used by them to acquire companies in overseas market. We had also announced on 27 December 1999, a liberalised mechanism for acquisition of software companies in the overseas market through stock swap options up to US$100 million on an automatic basis. I plan to further liberalise this policy for acquisition of companies abroad to enable Indian corporates in knowledge-based sectors to grow rapidly and lay the foundation for Indian multinationals in areas where we have comparative economic advantage. For acquisition in other sectors too, I propose to increase the ceiling under the automatic route from existing US$15 million to US$50 million for Indian corporates and beyond this, through approval by the Committee on Overseas Investment.

Under existing policy on portfolio investment, Foreign Institutional Investors (FIIs) are permitted to invest in a company, up to an aggregate of 24 per cent of equity shares, which can be increased to 30 per cent subject to approval by the Board of Directors and a Special Resolution of the General Body of the Company. To give our best companies greater access to foreign portfolio investment, I am increasing this limit from 30 per cent to 40 per cent.

Under my policy of gradual and phased liberalization of the capital account, I announced the following steps in the budget of 2001–02:

1. Indian companies wishing to invest abroad may now invest up to US$50 million on an annual basis through the automatic route without being subject to the three year profitability condition.
2. Companies which have issued ADRs/GDRs may henceforth make foreign investments up to 100 per cent of these proceeds; up from the current ceiling of 50 per cent.
3. Companies with proven track record wishing to invest

larger amounts may now get a block allocation in advance from the RBI for investments overseas.

4. Indian companies that have issued ADRs/GDRs may acquire shares of foreign companies up to an amount of US$100 million or an amount equivalent to ten times of their exports in a year, whichever is higher.

5. ADRs/GDRs will be provided two-way fungibility. Converted local shares may be reconverted to ADRs/GDRs while being subject to sectoral caps, wherever applicable.

6. Indian companies will now be permitted to list in foreign stock exchanges by sponsoring ADR/GDR issues against block share holding. This facility would have to be offered to all categories of shareholders.

I also announced that registered partnership firms and companies providing professional services which had so far not been permitted to make overseas investments would be allowed to do so. Similarly, Indian employees who enjoyed the benefit of ESOP schemes in foreign companies could now make investments abroad up to US$20,000 annually instead of in a block of five years.

It was, however, my budget of 2002–03 that contained a series of bold steps to further liberalize the capital account. I announced:

1. Full convertibility of deposit schemes for Non-Resident Indians. The existing Foreign Currency Non-Resident (FCNR) scheme and the Non-Resident External rupee (NRE) scheme will continue to be repatriable.

2. Schemes which do not offer full convertibility to NRIs will be discontinued from 1 April 2002. The existing balances in the non-resident (non-repatriable) rupee accounts will be allowed to be credited on maturity to the convertible NRE account.

3. NRIs will be free to repatriate in foreign currency their current earnings in India such as rent, dividend, pension, interest and the like based on appropriate certification.

4. Indian companies wishing to invest abroad may now invest up to US$100 million on an annual basis through the automatic route, up from the existing limit of US$50 million.

5. Indian companies making overseas investment in joint ventures abroad by market purchases may now do so without prior approval up to 50 per cent of their net worth, up from the current limit of 25 per cent.

6. Corporates with proven track record will be allowed to contribute funds from their foreign exchange earnings for setting up chairs in educational institutions abroad and for other welfare measures, likely to benefit the community abroad, on a case by case basis by the RBI.

7. Indian mutual funds will now be allowed to invest in rated securities in countries with fully convertible currencies, within the existing limits. Earlier such investment was only permitted in ADRs/GDRs issued by Indian companies in overseas markets.

8. Pre-payment of ECBs is permissible to the extent of balances available in EEFC accounts, which are currently restricted to 50 per cent of export proceeds. To enable ECB holders to benefit from lower interest rates, utilisation of higher amounts from export proceeds will be considered by RBI.

9. With a view to further liberalising the capital account transactions it is proposed to put the Foreign Currency Convertible Bond (FCCB) scheme under the automatic route up to US$50 million.

It gladdens me that my dream that Indian companies should become multinational companies in their own right through the liberalization of the capital account is now being realized.

PART 3

CONFESSIONS OF A SWADESHI REFORMER

25

Swadeshi and Globalization

I am a strong nationalist, and a staunch believer in swadeshi.
Therefore, I associated myself happily and wholeheartedly
with the swadeshi movement after joining the BJP. In fact, I
had gone round the country in 1994 propagating swadeshi on
behalf of the Swadeshi Jagran Manch, a body set up by the
RSS to promote swadeshi. Before we came into government,
RSS and BJP leaders used to meet regularly to discuss economic
issues. While we had a wide area of convergence, there were
some issues on which we differed even then.

I consulted RSS leaders before I finalized the 1998 budget.
They expected me to prepare a swadeshi budget. So did the
media. When I presented the budget, the media thought that
the 8 per cent surcharge on import duty (later reduced to 4 per
cent) which I had introduced was a swadeshi step. But the
8 per cent surcharge had been imposed more as a revenue
measure.

What is my vision of swadeshi, on which I tried to develop
my strategy over the five budgets? I do not believe in the
simplistic view which defines swadeshi according to which
product a person uses, that is, if I use locally made products
like Vicco Vajradanti or Babool toothpaste instead of an MNC
brand such as Colgate, I qualify as a votary of swadeshi. Use
of indigenous products is clearly an important element of
swadeshi. I do not dispute that. Every country should show

more loyalty towards its own products rather than to those from other countries. But this should not be carried to ridiculous lengths, as the mediaperson did in Lucknow when he asked me why I was not wearing a dhoti since I had come to talk about swadeshi, or as in Nagpur when someone wanted to examine whether the watch I was wearing was an Indian brand or a foreign one.

My understanding of swadeshi goes far beyond such narrow considerations. To me, swadeshi means making India economically self-reliant and strong, making India economically secure. We should not lurch from one crisis to another as we have done in the past four to five decades, which made us dependent on aid from foreign governments and international financial institutions. Freedom from such dependence is to me the essence of swadeshi. It is a concept which can only be practised by the strong, not the weak. I therefore felt that we needed to take steps to make India economically strong, especially after the nuclear tests and the East Asian crisis.

Self-reliance does not mean that we should produce everything ourselves. Instead, we should produce as many things as possible on an economically competitive basis, and possess the strength to import what we cannot produce competitively, so that our consumers get the best deal. This is the whole basis of the international division of labour and international trade. I think the best definition of swadeshi came from Gandhiji when he said that, while we should keep our doors and windows open to allow fresh air to come in, we should not allow the breeze to sweep us off our feet. So, to me swadeshi is neither being against imports nor against foreign investment. It is not autarkical. It does not mean hiding from the world outside. It means going out and dealing with the world, competing with it on equal terms and winning. Let me illustrate.

In May 1998 I went to Geneva to attend the annual meeting of the Asian Development Bank. Representatives of all the countries which had been affected by the East Asian crisis were present. Each one of us was given five minutes to present our views. Generally preferring to speak extempore, I set aside the prepared text. In my talk, I emphasized the need to examine in greater detail the genesis of the East Asian crisis. The crisis and its resolution had raised many ethical issues. The assistance which these countries were getting was not so much to bail them out as to bail out foreign lenders and investors. I inquired why multilateral financial institutions like the IMF and the Asian Development Bank had adopted different approaches to deal with Thailand, Malaysia, Indonesia and South Korea; why they had assisted South Korea far more than the other countries. Clearly, the Americans had more at stake in South Korea than elsewhere. I was against blaming the affected countries alone; we also had to lay some blame at the door of those who had manipulated these markets and created the problems. I was surprised to find that the representatives of these countries spoke meekly, in a tone which was pleading rather than assertive. They could not bring themselves to say that the crisis had also been caused by those who had played havoc with their economies. They looked beseechingly at the American representative present in the meeting, as if begging him to bail them out. I was disappointed by their attitude of helplessness. This was clearly not swadeshi. Between 1998 and 2000, when discussions on international financial architecture took place in various international forums, I steadfastly held on to my point of view.

My experience as finance minister during the 1991 crisis had steeled my resolve to avoid such a crisis in India at all cost. I realized that it was equally easy to destabilize our economy in a similar manner as had happened with the East Asian economies, even if we did not have complete capital account convertibility. I personally feel that the Indian economy did not get destabilized at that time because we managed the external sector, especially the balance of payments situation, far more cautiously than the other countries did. We were also able to retain the trust of the foreign investor in India during this crisis.

It is clear in my mind that an economically strong and

secure India is a sine qua non for swadeshi. Unfortunately, my views were not appreciated by many other proponents of swadeshi, despite my repeated efforts to explain it to them. An impression gathered ground that, while I started as a staunch supporter of swadeshi, I changed course and became an advocate of liberalization, privatization and globalization.

In this context, it is important to explain my views on globalization. I have not become a supporter of globalization today merely because India is now poised to join the big league. Technology has led to the death of distance in every sense of the word and has made globalization inevitable. Countries are coming closer economically and culturally. We can take what is beneficial and discard what is not. Each country, according to its own circumstances and wisdom, has to manage the process so that it benefits the most from globalization and minimizes the adverse impacts. That is the challenge we faced in the latter part of the 1990s. The arrival of information technology, IT-enabled services (ITES) and business process outsourcing (BPO) on the global scene had placed India in a very advantageous position vis-à-vis other countries. To take maximum advantage of our IT talent, we had to secure a liberal international regime for the movement of skilled workers. Already, a great deal of resistance was building up in other countries against employing skilled Indian personnel in those countries and against BPO, because both meant loss of jobs for their local people. If we wanted to take advantage of this resource, we had to moderate our opposition to foreign investment and imports. We were careful in our negotiations at the WTO so that our vital interests were not sacrificed. The challenge was to find the golden mean between the concept of swadeshi and the inevitability of globalization. In the six years when the NDA was at the helm, we were able to walk our way through this maze and establish that balance.

Today, Indian companies are freely investing abroad. They are buying foreign companies. They are setting up their subsidiaries on foreign soil. Indian professionals are found all over, employed by well-known multinational companies. As external affairs minister, I visited Brazil in 2003. I was taken to see Iguazu Falls, one of the largest waterfalls in the world, situated at the tri-junction of Brazil, Paraguay and Argentina. As my wife and I came down to the lobby of the hotel we were staying in to go to the falls, I suddenly heard someone greet us with a namaste. I looked back, and, to my surprise, saw an Indian couple standing behind me. What were they doing in Iguazu, I asked. They were from Ghaziabad, and were visiting their son, whom they introduced to us. He was the head of Nokia in Argentina and had brought them to see the waterfall. India and Indians are present in every country. How can India then reject the concept of benign globalization?

Our interaction on the global stage is not limited to economic exchanges alone. Indian food, fashion, films, literature, art, music and most of all yoga and meditation are deeply influencing people all over the world. Globalization is increasingly acquiring an Asian, if not a distinctly Indian, flavour.

Our interaction though must be in keeping with our historical tradition. We should deal with the rest of the world with understanding, compassion and goodwill and not with a view to exploiting it. Our interaction with others must be for their benefit as well, to improve the quality of life of all people. It cannot be for profit alone. This has been the message of India throughout history; this must be the message of modern-day India as well. If we fall prey to the western concept of globalization (equated with greed and consumption), our global forays will be unwelcome and short-lived.

26

Presenting India to the World

A very special feature of the finance minister's job is to relate, on the one hand, to the conditions prevailing at the grass-roots level at home and, on the other, to represent India at high-level international meetings. A finance minister can therefore one moment be looking at the sky to see whether the rains will arrive on time or not, and the next moment be dealing with such complex issues as the new international financial architecture. The variety and versatility of his responsibilities are unmatched by any other ministerial responsibility in the Government of India. I greatly enjoyed my forays abroad and tried my best to bring India to the centre stage of deliberations in international forums.

My first trip abroad as finance minister was in April 1998. In October 1998 I went to Washington to attend the annual meetings of the IMF and the World Bank. The Commonwealth finance ministers were meeting in Ottawa from 29 September to 1 October 1998, just before the IMF and World Bank meetings. When I decided to attend this meeting, and the meeting of the Commonwealth Business Forum, en route to Washington, I realized that the Finance Minister of India had not attended these meeting for some years. The meeting was held in the refurbished Ottawa railway station, which had been converted into a convention centre. The Canadian finance minister, Paul Martin, who went on to become prime minister, presided over the meeting. The main issue under discussion was the East Asian crisis. The discussion itself was of a routine nature. On the last day we assembled to adopt the communiqué of the meeting. This also should have been a routine affair. However, I noticed that there was a sentence in the draft communiqué which was critical of the Malaysian government for reimposing exchange controls. When we came to this part, I told Paul Martin that we were not being fair to the Malaysians. We were passing a value judgement on their action without discussing the matter in detail. Malaysia was represented by the deputy governor of Bank Negara, Malaysia's equivalent of the RBI. Their delegation had failed to notice this sentence, and was grateful to me for having raised it. I suggested the sentence be deleted. My suggestion received support from many others. The British delegation, however, was opposed to it. As Gordon Brown, the Chancellor of the Exchequer, was not present in the meeting when I raised the issue, the British delegation suggested that it be taken up a little later to enable Brown to join the discussions.

When Brown joined us, he explained his reasons for including the sentence. I disagreed with him. There was a stalemate. Many alternative formulations were suggested. Finally, our suggestion prevailed and was ultimately incorporated in the communiqué. I mention this episode in some detail because it establishes that India is capable of taking up the cause of other developing countries and fighting for them in global forums.

Chief Emeka Anyaoku, the then Commonwealth secretary-general, also invited me to join a select group of finance ministers, including Paul Martin and Gordon Brown, to meet and brief the media in Washington on the deliberation in Ottawa, which I accepted.

I did not have any bilateral meetings in Ottawa with the Canadian government. The Canadians were still sore with us about the nuclear tests and were not encouraging bilateral contact. I did not ask for any meetings either. Herb Dhaliwal, a cabinet minister of Indian origin, was keen to meet me and invited me home. His father, a first generation immigrant, was also there. We were served samosas, sweets and tea, and entertained in typical Indian fashion. Even though the minister regretted the fact that we could not meet officially, I told him in my opinion meeting socially was more important than meeting officially.

FORMATION OF THE G-20

The East Asian crisis had raised some serious questions about the effective functioning of the international financial system. The subject was discussed in the meetings of the IMF and the Asian Development Bank in 1998. The issue was not merely confined to bailing out these countries. The crisis had brought in sharp focus the whole question of international capital flows. The scale of the crisis was such that the entire resources of the IMF were stretched to the limit. When we approached the IMF, both at the beginning of the 1980s and the 1990s, we had asked for an assistance of $5 to $6 billion. But in these cases, the assistance required was as large as $40 to $50 billion. It was not a crisis of a temporary current account deficit, but of a huge capital account deficit.

The issue of global capital flows and the international financial architecture continued to be discussed at other forums. During the 1999 IMF/World Bank meetings, Paul Martin made a suggestion. The G-7, a powerful group of the world's industrialized countries, was equally concerned at these developments and felt that there should a more focused discussion about the international financial architecture in a somewhat larger group of systemically important countries. The idea was to form a new group, called the G-20. It would include members of the G-7, Russia, which was an associate member of G-7, India, China, Indonesia, Saudi Arabia, Mexico, Brazil, Argentina, Australia, South Africa and Turkey. The IMF and the World Bank would also be part of the group. I welcomed the idea and told Martin that India would be happy to join the group. Martin became the first chairman of the group, and its first meeting was held in Berlin in December 1999. The finance ministers and chairmen of the central banks of the member countries attended. It was a good, compact group for deliberating on the complex subject of international finance.

Martin was supposed to hand over charge as chairman of the G-20 in 2001 at the end of his two-year term. I had, during the course of meetings, built up a very good rapport with the finance ministers of these countries, especially with Hans Eichel, the finance minister of Germany. I suggested that the chairmanship of the group should alternate between members of the G-7 and the others. I also let it be known that India would be happy to be the next chairman. There were many who supported the idea and felt that, as one of the largest emerging market economies, we had a good claim. There were other claimants too.

(Photograph by P.D. Sombuwar)

Hans Eichel, finance minister of Germany, and the author, meeting in New Delhi, 2001.

In the second meeting of the G-20, in Montreal in October 2000, we succeeded in our objective and it was decided that India would take over the chairmanship of the group in 2001. The group also accepted my invitation to hold the next meeting in New Delhi. I had plans to hold the meeting in November 2001, but it had to be postponed due to 9/11 as people were scared to travel to our part of the world because of the terror threat. Many countries had issued advisories against travel to South Asia. It was finally decided that the G-20 meeting would be held, along with the World Bank and IMF meetings, in Ottawa. My assuming the chairmanship of the group also got postponed as a result of this development and Martin continued as chairman for another year. We finally met in Ottawa on 16 and 17 November 2001. The G-20 convened in New Delhi in November 2002 under India's chairmanship, but by then I had moved on from the finance ministry.

THE DEVELOPMENT COMMITTEE OF THE WORLD BANK

The IMF and the World Bank primarily operate through two main committees—the International Monetary and Finance Committee (IMFC) of the IMF and the Development Committee of the World Bank. These committees meet twice a year. When I attended my first meeting of the Development Committee in April 1998, the chairman of the committee was the finance minister of Malaysia, Anwar Ibrahim. He impressed me as a very competent person. Anwar was later sacked and arrested because of differences with Prime Minister Mahathir Mohamed. Anwar's sacking shocked all of us. When we met in the Development Committee in the spring of 1999, it was suggested that the committee should pass a resolution deploring his arrest. After some discussion we decided against it since this could be construed as interference in the internal affairs of Malaysia. After Anwar, the chairmanship of the Development Committee passed on to the finance minister of Thailand. He resigned some time later, throwing open the question of chairmanship once again.

The chair of the Development Committee is held by rotation among regions. Each region holds the chair for a duration of three years. When the finance minister of Thailand resigned from the chairmanship of the Development Committee, it was still Asia's turn to head the committee. But we had already had a turnover of two. I was visiting the United States for medical treatment in June 2001 and was staying at my son Jayant's house in Boston. I got a call from James Wolfensohn, president of the World Bank, informing me that they were looking for a new chairman for the Development Committee and all the members had unanimously suggested my name. He wanted to know if I would be willing to accept the responsibility, and I told him I was happy to accept if the election would be unanimous. He assured me that there was no difference of opinion. And so it was. I was unanimously elected the chairman of the committee a few days later. I was the first Indian to be bestowed this honour.

In the IMF and the World Bank meetings held in Prague in 2000 we had a joint meeting of the Development Committee and the IMFC, which was headed by Gordon Brown. The duty of presiding over the joint meeting was shared by both of us. The IMFC and the Development Committee continued to meet separately as well. I presided over the meetings of the committee held in April 2001 in Washington, the annual meeting in October 2001 in Ottawa and the spring meeting in April 2002 in Washington. This position gave India a very high profile in the international financial institutions. One Government of India official, a veteran of these meetings, once told me that he had never seen India have such a high profile in these forums.

When we met after 9/11 in Canada, Kofi Annan came to meet us for dinner. Paul Martin, Gordon Brown and I were the chairpersons of the G-20, IMFC and the Development Committee respectively. We had mutually agreed that I would preside over the first half of the dinner meeting and Brown the second half. I started the proceedings with a welcome to Kofi

Annan and then midway through the meeting, as agreed, invited Brown to take over the chairmanship. Brown declined the offer saying since I was doing such a fine job I should carry on. I said, 'Gordon was supposed to take over the chairmanship of the meeting at this stage from me. I requested him to do so. But he has refused. This is how the British have always exploited the Indians!'

At the meeting of the Development Committee of the World Bank, under the chairmanship of the author, with (from left to right) Paul Martin, Finance Minister, Canada, Paul O'Neill, Treasury Secretary, USA and Gordon Brown, Chancellor of the Exchequer of Britain.

At the WTO meeting in Seattle in 1999 there were massive demonstrations against the WTO. It became the trend thereafter to hold demonstrations wherever and whenever the meetings of international financial institutions took place. In the annual meetings of the IMF/World Bank held in Prague on

25 September 2000, the demonstrations became violent and the police had a tough time. Many of us watched the mobs battle the police in the streets of Prague from the roof of the building where our meeting was being held. It was not an edifying sight. This prompted me to start my speech with these words: 'I stand here on behalf of India, the land of Mahatma Gandhi, who espoused the cause of non-violence. I condemn the violence which was unleashed here yesterday. Whether the IMF or the World Bank exist or do not exist is a matter which will be decided by the will of the 182 countries represented here, not by a handful of hoodlums in the streets of Prague.' Little did I know then that this would become a quotable quote in *Newsweek*.

In the 2001 Ottawa meeting, Paul Martin decided that he, Gordon Brown and I, representing the international community, should have a meeting with the representatives of some of the protesting NGOs. In the meeting, a lady of Indian origin spoke on behalf of the NGOs and impressed all of us greatly. She put forth her case cogently and powerfully. The WTO meeting in Doha had just ended and India's stand at the WTO had pleased them. She said as much. All of us communicated that we were quite willing to talk and there was no need to hold demonstrations against us. Our assurances, however, fell on deaf ears.

Ironically though, in one meeting of the Development Committee, I myself threatened to join the protesters outside if the developed countries persisted with their obdurate attitude towards the developing countries in trade and aid.

In 2002 the chairmanship of the Development Committee was to pass on to a representative from Africa. Trevor Manuel, the finance minister of South Africa, was a very able and dynamic finance minister and I recommended his name. We found many takers for this proposal and in April 2002 Manuel took over as chairman of the committee from me.

DAVOS

I regularly attended the World Economic Forum meetings at Davos. In January 2001 I was invited to address the inaugural plenary of the meeting titled 'How can globalization deliver the goods: The view from the South'. It was a great honour, rarely bestowed on an Indian until then. My son Jayant, who used to help me from time to time on such occasions, gave me many ideas. Speaking extempore, I talked about a more equitable global economic order and listed the three important areas where I felt the North was hindering the economic growth of the South by its policies. These were (i) the North continued to keep many of its markets off-limits for the South; (ii) the North insisted that the South curb its growth to protect the environment; and (iii) the North tailored its immigration programmes to lure talent away from the South. I spoke about how the developed countries, enjoying high levels of consumption themselves, were, in the name of the environment, trying to put limits on the already limited consumption levels in developing countries. I described the lifestyle of the middle-class American and the vast quantities of energy and other exhaustible resources he consumed, in order to show how far behind we were in the South in our consumption levels. I ended by emphasizing that the South was not looking for charity, but for equal opportunity.

The applause at the end of my speech seemed to indicate it had been well received by the delegates at Davos. But my words definitely did not please everyone. At least one irate American wrote an angry letter to our embassy in Berne protesting in particular my comments about the consumption levels of middle-class Americans. He wrote to say that they had inherited their prosperity from their forefathers, who had worked hard for it and therefore they had every right to enjoy their high standard of living.

A conference on 'Financing for Development' was held in Monterrey, Mexico, in March 2002 under the aegis of the United Nations. Earlier, a meeting was held in New York at the UN to prepare for the conference. I was among the select group of people invited by the UN to participate in this meeting. I was supposed to lead the Indian delegation to this conference and play an important role on behalf of the developing countries. Unfortunately, my budgetary duties in Parliament came in the way and at the last moment I had to opt out of it.

STANFORD UNIVERSITY

In May 2000 I received an invitation from Stanford University to inaugurate their seminar on India, organized by the Stanford India Association, which I accepted. I decided to use the opportunity to interact with investors, IT entrepreneurs and the Indian community in Silicon Valley, Chicago and San Francisco. The Americans present in these meetings showed a great deal of interest in India.

The seminar at Stanford was very well organized with a number of Indian economists from various US universities attending the sessions. There was a strong presence from India. President Clinton was at the end of his second term, and most people felt that the Republicans led by George Bush Jr. would win the next presidential election. Stanford is the intellectual centre of the Republicans. This was visible throughout the seminar, with George P. Shultz, the former secretary of state, playing an important role during the conference. In my inaugural speech, I talked about the importance of global social stability and emphasized that it was at least as important as global financial stability. Later, I gave a lecture on Indian economic policy reform at a 'Town hall' meeting organized by the university and presided over by George Shultz. Many students attended, and the Q&A session which followed turned out to be very interesting.

GERMANY

Having spent four marvellous years of my life in Germany in the early 1970s, I have a special attachment to that country. It

might explain why I never missed an opportunity to go there.
My first official visit to Germany as finance minister was in
1999 for a meeting of the Indo-German Joint Commission. I
went back the next year for the meeting of the G-20, and again
in 2001 to promote investments from Germany into India and
strengthen relations between the two countries in the economic
field. I also took with me on this visit a large delegation of
businessmen from the CII and many senior officials of the
government so that we could make a comprehensive
presentation about the opportunities for investment in India to
German businessmen in Frankfurt and Berlin.

Between my first and second trips to Germany, I found
that the image of India had undergone a welcome change.
Chancellor Gerhard Schroeder had announced in the meanwhile
that he would give 20,000 green cards (visas) to non-European
IT specialists so that they could come to Germany and help
build its IT industry. One of the German provinces was going
to the polls post Schroeder's announcement. A candidate for
the chief minister's post (land president) coined a slogan which
he thought would help him win the election, given German
sensitivity about foreigners working in their country. The
slogan was 'Kinder stadt Inder' (Children, instead of Indians).
This led to a huge controversy. The candidate in question lost
the election but in the process did a lot of good to India's
image in Germany. When I visited Germany, many people
asked me what I thought of the slogan. I told them that
Indians were not desperate to come to Germany, that we were
a self-respecting people and went where we were welcome. If
the Germans wanted us to help them with their IT industry, we
would be happy to do so, but they should not think that we
were going to beg for green cards. The German point of view
was understandable. They are a proud people, proud of their
technology, proud of their progress. It was, perhaps, for the
first time they felt they were at the receiving end.

I again visited Germany in January 2002 at the invitation
of the German finance minister, Hans Eichel. The ministry of
finance in Berlin is housed in a very historic building. It was

the headquarters of the Luftwaffe during the Second World War. In my talks with Hans Eichel, we discussed, among other things, how the Germans were implementing VAT, since India was in the process of introducing it. It turned out to be a very fruitful and interesting exchange. I was delighted to see that India and Germany were coming closer. That was my last visit to Germany as finance minister, though I would visit it twice more as external affairs minister.

CHINA

The 2002 annual meeting of the Asian Development Bank was held in Shanghai in May. Since I had missed the annual meeting held in Hawaii in 2001, I decided to attend the Shanghai meeting. I was also keen to see the economic progress made by China, a country I had not visited for many years. I had gone there on a private visit in 1983 when my son-in-law was posted in the Indian embassy in Beijing.

In 2002 I stayed in a hotel in the Pudong area in Shanghai. Once green with paddy fields, it had undergone a complete transformation into a new city centre, with many five-star hotels. Shanghai itself had become a city of skyscrapers. The miracle of Shanghai showed how the infrastructure of a city and its skyline can be completely transformed, even in a developing country, within a very short time.

I was invited to talk to a group of Chinese businessmen. I began my talk by stating that I had visited China thousands of years ago, in 1983. This was to emphasize the point that so much had changed in China between my two visits. During the same visit, I also attended a seminar on 'Asia 2015: Thinking through Mega Trends' organized by the Asian Development Bank. The finance minister of Pakistan, Shaukat Aziz—now prime minister—was also one of the speakers at the seminar. In my address, I talked about the conflicts in various parts of Asia, including South Asia, without specifically referring to India and Pakistan. I envisaged that the conflicts would become history in times to come, and that by 2015 Asia would have coalesced together much more strongly than was evident now. The twenty-first century would be an Asian century.

When I visited the SEZ at Shanghai, I was amazed to see the massive infrastructure which had been built by the Chinese. It was a similar story all over China. I wondered where the money for all the roads, parks, buildings and SEZs came from. The answer was quite simple. The Chinese had created special purpose vehicles (SPVs) for each of these projects and provided them with seed money. The SPVs were expected to borrow the rest of the money needed from the banks. In most countries, including India, when any bank is approached for a large loan, hundreds of queries regarding the economic viability of the project are raised by the bank. They are generally reluctant to lend money for a project which is not economically viable and does not assure a certain minimum rate of return. Even for government and PSU projects in India, which are entirely financed by the government, there is the requirement of meeting a minimum rate of return. Accordingly, unviable projects are not allowed to be taken up. This requirement operates even more strictly in the case of private sector projects. The Chinese obviously have no such concerns. This may explain the large NPAs of the Chinese banks. We could perhaps do the same in India and change the landscape by creating highways, buildings, ports and airports, but we would not be able to live with those NPAs. The Chinese manage to survive with such NPAs mainly because of the high domestic savings rate and strong government support for the SPVs and the banks. The strong backing of the Chinese government ensures that the banks do not collapse. The Chinese in any case have only four major banks which do most of the lending. The Chinese system of developing infrastructure through SPVs takes the entire funding process outside the budget.

After my visit to China, I came to the conclusion that in India too we could take economically viable projects out of the budget, set up SPVs for them and finance them through banks. I suggested this to Nitish Kumar, the railway minister, when he approached me to replicate the National Highway Development

Programme for the railways. We could create a separate organization to take up the construction of the additional railway tracks to connect the four metros. With a lot of traffic expected to move through these routes, it would be an economically viable project. We could borrow money from domestic financial institutions, from multilateral financial institutions and even list the SPV in the market and raise money for it.

Nitish Kumar accepted my suggestion. This is the model I had in mind with regard to many public–private partnership projects in the infrastructure sector, where the government could provide the seed capital and the rest could be raised from financial institutions. With the opening up of the insurance sector and availability of large funds through them for long-term projects, this would be an ideal model for us to adopt for economically viable projects. I did not remain long enough in the finance ministry after my visit to China to translate these ideas into practice. But I am glad that the seeds of this idea are fructifying now.

ASIAN COOPERATION DIALOGUE

In June 2002 Brajesh Mishra asked if I would be willing to go to Thailand to represent India at a meeting which the Thai prime minister was organizing to promote economic and financial cooperation among Asian countries. They had decided to call it the Asian Cooperation Dialogue (ACD) and had invited the foreign ministers of fifteen Asian countries, including those of India and Pakistan, to the meeting. Jaswant Singh, the foreign minister, was not free to attend. I agreed, as the discussions were going to be largely economic. After the formal opening by the Thai prime minister, the meeting became no-tie and informal, with the ministers sitting around in a lounge. The Thai foreign minister presided. As expected, the discussion centered on economic cooperation, and a finance minister attending the session was quite welcome. I could make a substantial contribution because it was a subject close to my heart. Unfortunately, the Chinese foreign minister read out a prepared statement, in which he talked about the India–Pakistan hostility. I protested, because the ACD was hardly the forum to raise such an issue; he also should not have read out a speech in an informal gathering.

THE INTER-GOVERNMENTAL COMMISSION WITH RUSSIA

India and Russia have a high-powered Inter-Governmental Commission (IGC) which covers all aspects of our bilateral relationship except defence. It is co-chaired by a deputy prime minister from the Russian side and the external affairs minister from the Indian side. When I.K. Gujral was prime minister, as he was foreign minister as well, he had appointed P. Chidambaram, the finance minister, as co-chair of the commission. Since Vajpayee held the external affairs portfolio himself initially, he followed the Gujral government precedent and appointed me as the Indian co-chair of the IGC.

I made my first trip to Moscow in November 1998. The weather was freezing, but the warm hospitality of the Russians was a good antidote to the cold. Deputy Prime Minister Maleokov, my counterpart, had served as an engineer in Bhilai. I had a sentimental attachment to Bhilai because my father-in-law, an ICS officer, had been general manager of the Bhilai Steel Plant in the early 1960s and I was married there in 1961. Maleokov was a very jolly person and I got along with him pretty well.

The Russian co-chairs changed from time to time. But I continued to head the commission, first as finance minister and, subsequently, as external affairs minister, for all the six years that the BJP was in government. In India, the IGC is serviced by the external affairs ministry and the foreign secretary is the vice-chairman of the commission.

During President Vladimir Putin's visit to India, I represented the government at his meetings with Indian businessmen and industrialists in both Delhi and Mumbai and finally saw him off at Mumbai on behalf of the government. The meetings were organized jointly by FICCI and CII. I remarked to President Putin that he had succeeded where we had failed, namely in bringing the two chambers together.

Mrs Putin is a very gracious lady. However, her remark when she reached the ceremonial lounge of the Mumbai airport left the Maharashtra ministers dumbfounded. She wanted to know why the buildings in Mumbai were so dirty and wondered why nobody bothered to paint them. An embarrassed silence followed her remark. The ministers tried to explain how the tenancy laws were responsible for it but the explanation did not convince Mrs Putin.

When I shifted to the external affairs ministry in July 2002, I sent a note to the prime minister suggesting that, since the IGC was concerned mainly with economic issues, it would be better if the finance minister continued to co-chair it from our side. My proposal was promptly rejected by the prime minister.

27

Facing Up to Controversy

A minister should be prepared to face his share of controversies. Looking back, I had, perhaps, more than my fair share. The first was the onion crisis.

In October 1998 onion prices shot up suddenly. It became a major issue, especially because the four states of Rajasthan, Madhya Pradesh, Delhi and Mizoram were going to the polls in November. Prices of other vegetables also went up, and we were short of pulses and edible oils. Malaysia and Indonesia had been affected by El Niño and their edible oil crop had been damaged. Imports of palmolein had become expensive. There was pressure on sugar prices as well. The Congress party took the fullest political advantage of the situation. People were baying for somebody's blood and I was the most obvious target. We put our act together quickly and started importing onions, edible oils and toor dal in order to get over the shortages. But we still had to pay a heavy political price for it; we lost in all four states. The general feeling was that we had lost because of the skyrocketing onion prices, though actually, there is never only a single reason for an electoral loss.

THE FIRST UTI CRISIS

I faced the first UTI crisis in October 1998. The Unit Trust of India (UTI), set up under an act of Parliament, is controlled by some important public financial institutions including the Industrial Development Bank of India, State Bank of India and Life Insurance Corporation of India. It has a vast number of subscribers and was one of the largest investors in the stock market. I was in Washington for the annual meetings of the IMF and the World Bank when the crisis hit. There was a great deal of speculation that UTI was about to collapse. On my return to India we were able to work out a formula and UTI was bailed out of the crisis. The problem had arisen because, in the past, UTI had been forced to buy shares of PSUs which were not doing well because of the market slowdown. The Net Asset Value of the US-64 portfolio—its main scheme—had gone down. We identified some of the weak PSU scrips in the US-64 portfolio, separated them from the other scrips and put them into a separate portfolio. The government decided to finance UTI to the extent of the losses on this portfolio in the hope that some day UTI would be able to recover the amount. A bail-out package of around Rs 3300 crore was prepared. It was budget neutral because we issued five-year bonds of the same amount.

But worse was to come later.

MOHAN GURUSWAMY:
A MISTAKE IN JUDGEMENT

I came to know Mohan Guruswamy in 1984 when the two of us started to work for Chandra Shekhar. He had been a Mason fellow at Harvard University. Chandra Shekhar was very impressed by him and was keen that we work together. We did so, until he drifted away from the Chandra Shekhar camp and went over to V.P. Singh. We met rarely, especially after I joined the BJP in 1993. Guruswamy had an overassertive style of functioning, contrary to my own low-key and quiet style.

In 1998, a few months after I became finance minister, Advani suggested that I appoint Guruswamy as my adviser. There was a group of people around Advani who were very keen that Guruswamy join the finance ministry. Vajpayee was not in favour of this idea. Ultimately, however, I succumbed to pressure. I must confess that here I showed weakness in handling the issue.

I was not happy with the way Guruswamy worked in the finance ministry. His style of functioning soon created many problems, and I decided to take up the matter with Advani, as I wanted Guruswamy to leave the ministry. Advani immediately rang up Dinanath Mishra, a journalist who was a Rajya Sabha BJP member, and asked him to tell Guruswamy to put in his papers. Later that evening, I got a call from Guruswamy informing me that he had got the message, and that he was willing to resign but asked if he could do so after his return from a trip abroad. I again made the mistake of agreeing to the request.

Before Guruswamy's return, someone informed me that the *Asian Age* was going to publish a story the next day about how Guruswamy was unhappy with the government in general and the prime minister in particular and had therefore decided to resign. He was also going to level serious allegations against the government. This was a clear breach of faith. I decided therefore not to wait for Guruswamy to put in his papers, but to dismiss him instead and inform the media. Both news items appeared in the media the next day—one saying that he had been dismissed, and the other that he had resigned.

The story did not end there. Before the budget session began in February 1999, Guruswamy wrote a series of articles in the *Asian Age* in which he levelled serious allegations against the prime minister, his foster son-in-law and me. These allegations provided readymade material for the opposition to use against us in Parliament. The opposition raised the issue in both Houses, first in the Rajya Sabha and then in the Lok Sabha, and forced a discussion. Manmohan Singh, as leader of the opposition in the Rajya Sabha, led the opposition charge and quoted extensively from Guruswamy's articles in order to put the government in the dock. Other opposition members also criticized us vehemently. I systematically demolished each and every charge. In fact, my reply was so effective that some Congress members expressed dissatisfaction with Manmohan Singh's performance. They felt that he had not been able to put forth the Congress party's point of view aggressively enough. In the Lok Sabha, the debate remained inconclusive, because, in the meanwhile, the government fell and the Lok Sabha was dissolved.

THE MAURITIUS TREATY ISSUE

In mid-April 2000, the Indian stock markets crashed. The BSE Sensex plummeted 365 points in one day. I was very surprised at this development because there was absolutely nothing in the fundamentals of the economy to justify the sharp fall. My inquiries revealed that the markets had crashed on account of FIIs selling. They were doing so because some income tax officials in Mumbai had passed orders that FIIs, covered by the double taxation avoidance treaty with Mauritius, were liable to pay taxes in India.

The tax treaty with Mauritius had been concluded way back in 1983, when Indira Gandhi was prime minister. The Mauritius route had been thrown open to FIIs in 1992, when Manmohan Singh was finance minister. So far, in all these years, no such order had been passed by the income tax officials anywhere in the country, even after the scrutiny of the tax returns of the FIIs. The SEBI chairman told me that, if the matter was not settled immediately, the FIIs, faced with the uncertainty on the tax front, would be compelled to start selling. This would completely destabilize the market in the coming days. My worst fears were aroused.

I used to worry about the Indian economy being destabilized by the FIIs selling heavily in the stock market and then converting the rupees into dollars, thereby creating pressure on the exchange rate. The FIIs had by then invested $9 to $10 billion in the Indian stock market and the repatriation of a few billion dollars out of India would have created chaos in the economy as a whole. We would have had a real crisis on our hands.

I asked the CBDT to examine the matter in depth. The CBDT suggested that we issue a circular clarifying the law once and for all. The CBDT had the power to issue such a circular. I was also told that the orders passed by the income tax officials were incorrect since they were based on a misunderstanding of the law. Once the circular was issued, and the worries of the FIIs taken care of, the markets stabilized.

The circular was issued on 13 April 2000 and everything was normal until the *Asian Age* carried a story wherein it accused me of issuing the circular to help my daughter-in-law Punita, an employee in an investment company. I was shocked. I was quite unaware that the company Punita worked for was registered in Mauritius. My sons and daughters-in-law lead independent lives; we never interfere in each other's work.

The circular had nothing to do with my daughter-in-law, as reported in the *Asian Age*. But the story was immediately picked up by other newspapers, and it was made to appear as if I was involved in a huge scandal. I called the media to inform them that my daughter-in-law was just an employee of the company and not its owner. Her remuneration was as per her terms of employment. The matter was blown all out of proportion and, soon enough, reached Parliament. I clearly put forward all the facts in Parliament.

I wanted to get to the bottom of the controversy and, when I started making inquiries, I discovered some startling facts. Three different income tax officers from three jurisdictions in Mumbai had passed those orders. I obtained a copy of one of the orders and went through it. It was a well-argued and well-written document. I then decided to look at the orders passed by the other two officers. To my surprise, I found that all three orders were absolutely identical to each other except for the names of the firms and the amount of tax assessed. Even the language used was the same. I wondered how three officers of three jurisdictions could pass orders that were absolutely identical. Officers of the CBDT explained to me that very often IT officers dealing with similar cases sat together to decide what they should write. One officer wrote the order, and the others just copied it. The explanation did not satisfy me. In fact, it was widely rumoured that some industrial houses were unhappy with me for not toeing their line. They constantly tried to malign me with the objective of getting me out of the finance ministry.

I personally felt greatly hurt by the Mauritius controversy. Not only were the allegations farthest from the truth, a section of the media went out of its way to malign me. *'Ek adesh se vitt mantri ne apni bahu ko crorepati bana diya'* (Through just one order the finance minister has made his daughter-in-law a millionaire) screamed a headline in a Hindi newspaper. I must mention that there were some journalists, however, who did their homework seriously, examined the deals Punita's firm had done in India and presented the correct picture. They also mentioned her qualifications as an IIT graduate with a doctorate in finance from the Wharton School of Business.

The matter was not allowed to rest. The Azadi Bachao Andolan decided to challenge the CBDT circular through a PIL in the Delhi High Court. The court declared the circular illegal in May 2002. Again, there was a hue and cry, especially in the media.

The government appealed against the decision in the Supreme Court in September 2002. By then I had shifted from the finance ministry. The Supreme Court passed an order in October 2003 setting aside the Delhi High Court judgement. In its judgement the Supreme Court said that Government of India had the power to enter into an agreement not only to give relief, where there is double taxation, but also to avoid potential double taxation by demarcating the respective areas of jurisdiction of taxation, even if no tax is levied presently in the other country. The issuance of the circular was declared legal and within the competence of the CBDT.

This was a great relief, a clear vindication of the step we had taken in 2000, in accordance with the law of the land and the exigencies of the situation.

MARKET SCAM OF 2001

Even though my 2001 budget was reform-oriented and was very well received, my luck ran out pretty quickly. In March 2001, the stock market was hit by a scam. I am still not sure if it can really be described as a scam. Fluctuations in stock markets is not a scam. Speculation is inherent in the nature of markets. Where exactly speculation stops and manipulation begins is a question which, perhaps, nobody has been able to answer so far. When the markets started to fall in March 2001, this was attributed to Ketan Parekh, a leading stockbroker, who was accused of borrowing huge sums of money from the Madhavpura Mercantile Cooperative Bank in Gujarat and the Bank of India to invest in the stock market.

Clearly, these borrowings were in violation of the rules. In the midst of all this confusion, on 13 March 2001, the Tehelka sting operation, which claimed to have caught on camera several defence ministry officials and also the president of the BJP, Bangaru Laxman, taking money, came like a bombshell, and the markets crashed. A discussion was already in progress in Parliament on the stock market scam. I was in the Rajya Sabha giving an account of the steps we had taken to streamline the functioning of the markets, including the corporatization of stock exchanges. When my speech concluded and we adjourned for lunch, I came back to my room in Parliament and switched on the TV. I was shocked to find that the markets had crashed. The Sensex had fallen by nearly 227 points. I did not know anything about the Tehelka disclosures then and wondered what had caused such a huge fall. The BSE index soon started improving and by the time I left for the afternoon session of Parliament the situation appeared to have improved.

At the end of my day's work in Parliament, I left to attend a cabinet meeting. It was there that I learnt about the Tehelka disclosures. Arun Jaitley had a transcript of the Tehelka tapes with him and the cabinet was apprised of its contents. At that point, none of us could figure out what its dimensions were.

I noticed that there was a reference to me too in the Tehelka tapes. R.K. Jain, the treasurer of the Samata Party, was caught boasting on the Tehelka camera that most politicians were corrupt and he was close to many ministers. He claimed that he knew me very well and could get anything done by me. He said that it was at his instance that I had sanctioned a loan of Rs 30 crore to his brother for a consideration. I decided to meet the issue head on and issued a legal notice, because I had never met this person in my life and knew that he was talking pure nonsense. Jain promptly apologized. In a letter to me he wrote, 'All statements against you made by me are false and incorrect and I had no intention to defame or hurt you or anybody's feelings. I would like to add that I have never met you, nor do I know you in person, nor do I have any access to you in any way, leave apart getting any work done from you. I now realise my folly and I was deeply shocked to see the casual conversation becoming public.'

An inquiry commission under Justice K. Venkataswami was set up to probe the Tehelka issue. In the meanwhile, George Fernandes, the defence minister, and Bangaru Laxman resigned. The Tehelka episode had a very adverse impact on the stock markets. The Sensex fell by more than 600 points within a month of the Tehelka disclosures.

I would like to make special mention of D.R. Mehta here, who was the chairperson of SEBI when I became the finance minister. I was in the thick of the budget exercise in February 2000 when the BSE Sensex crossed the 6000 mark. We were holding a budget meeting in the CBDT chairman's room. Incidentally, it was the room Lord Mountbatten had used during the Second World War as commander-in-chief of India and the Far East. The room has a plaque commemorating this. It was here that I received a call from Mehta informing me that the index had crossed the 6000 mark. I should have felt happy—the index had reached an unprecedented level, investor wealth had gone up and I could easily take the line that it reflected the strength of the economy. I knew, however, that it was not so. In fact, I felt worried at this unusual development, as the possibility of some people manipulating the market could not be ruled out. I asked Mehta to caution investors and take all steps to ensure that there was no manipulation of the market. Mehta was a solid civil servant and did his job honestly. After the market scam, when there was an attack on him in the Rajya Sabha, I vouched for his integrity. Many members did not like this, asking me why I had put my own reputation at stake for him. I felt it was my duty as minister to defend my officers; who else would defend them? The market scam did take place when Mehta was the chairman of SEBI, and he did come in for some criticism from the Joint Parliamentary Committee (JPC) for his acts of omission. Mehta is also a public-spirited person. He has played a leading role in setting up Jaipur Foot, an NGO which makes artificial limbs and helps physically challenged people. I saw for myself the excellent work being done by Jaipur Foot when I visited Jaipur after I had left the finance ministry.

THE SECOND UTI CRISIS

US-64, the flagship fund of UTI, is not an assured income scheme but a regular income scheme. In 1991–92 only 28 per cent of the total US-64 fund was invested in equity. The balance was invested in other instruments. It continued as a regular income scheme only on the strength of the bulk of its investments in non-equities. In subsequent years, the fund's exposure to equities increased gradually and by 1995–96, the last year of Narsimha Rao's rule, it had gone up to 66 per cent. Thus the fund did not remain a balanced fund. It became a largely equity-oriented fund with its income being entirely dependent on the fluctuations of the stock market.

The market crash in March, April and May 2001 created a crisis for UTI. As UTI's financial year is from 1 July to 30 June, it has to declare dividends and its balance sheet for the year immediately after 30 June. With the end of its financial year drawing close, the market crash became a nightmare for UTI. Had the crisis come at some other time of the year, UTI would not have been in the same kind of mess.

For three years, from 1994 to 1997, UTI had drawn heavily upon its reserves in order to declare high and unsustainable dividends for the US-64 scheme. In 1994–95 the dividend was 26 per cent. In 1995–96 it was 21 per cent, and in 1996–97 it was 20 per cent. As a result, the reserves turned negative. UTI had exhausted all other options such as borrowing from another fund. It had also made some bad investments over time which had turned into NPAs. Thus, by mid-2001, UTI found itself in a big financial mess. And it was not only the financial mess but the manner in which the situation was handled by UTI which further compounded the problem.

In June 2001 I had to go for medical treatment to the United States for about fifteen days. Before I left I came across newspaper reports, especially in the pink press, raising concerns about the financial health of UTI. I marked these reports to the finance secretary and inquired if everything was all right with UTI. I did not get any report about the poor financial health of UTI. In the meanwhile, P.S. Subramanyam, chairman of UTI, had sent a letter to the finance secretary, Ajit Kumar, and told the media that UTI was expected to do well despite the stock market crash.

On that fateful day of Monday 2 July, I had an important meeting with the prime minister at 11 a.m. I was preparing for it when my private secretary, Bharat Vyas, an extremely capable officer from the Jammu and Kashmir cadre, buzzed me on the intercom with a request that Subramanyam wanted to pay a brief courtesy call as he was in the building. I agreed but told Bharat that it would have to be really brief. When Subramanyam came in, he informed me he was in Delhi to attend the UTI board meeting. He also told me that he was planning to put a proposal before the board to freeze the sale and repurchase of US-64 units due to the financial problems facing the fund. I was shocked. I ended the meeting and called in the finance secretary, wanting to know if he was aware of this proposal. He told me that he had seen a letter that morning from the UTI chairman to this effect. I learnt later that the letter had actually been delivered at the finance secretary's residence on Friday evening.

The UTI chairman also claimed that he had mentioned it to Jaimini Bhagwati, joint secretary, capital markets, in the finance ministry on 29 June. The joint secretary claimed that Subramanyam had sought his personal opinion, and had not informed him of this matter in his official capacity. As Subramanyam had not sought any formal clearance or any formal reaction from the government, this development was not brought to my notice. I do not know if Bhagwati reported it to Ajit Kumar.

After a brief discussion with Ajit Kumar, I left for my meeting with the prime minister. We both felt that it would be best to wait for the UTI board to discuss the issue and find a solution. I was certain that the UTI board would not accept such an outrageous suggestion. In retrospect, it appears to me that I committed a mistake by not cancelling my meeting with the prime minister and calling an emergency meeting of my officials in order to act before the UTI board took its final decision. The UTI board met and approved the management's decision to freeze the sale and repurchase of US-64 units.

When Chidambaram was finance minister in 1997, the government's representative on the UTI board had been withdrawn. The argument was that, though the UTI was set up by an act of Parliament, it must be allowed to function completely independently of the government. Be that as it may, all hell broke loose as soon as the UTI board's decision became known. When I returned to North Block from my various meetings, mediapersons were waiting for me. I told them that the finance ministry had been kept in the dark about the financial problems of UTI and that I did not agree with the decision taken by the UTI board.

We acted without losing any time. I decided that Subramanyam must leave. I consulted Bimal Jalan about a replacement for Subramanyam and he suggested M. Damodaran, who had earlier worked with me as joint secretary in the banking division of the finance ministry. I thought well of him. In any case, there was no time to waste. I went to the prime minister with the suggestion. He approved my proposal at once. That was the first damage-control exercise that we undertook. Later, Subramanyam was arrested by the CBI for his alleged involvement in investing around Rs 30 crore in a private firm called Cyberspace Infosys. All this created further anxiety in the market. The UTI imbroglio had become a major story in the media day after day. On 9 July, a week after the UTI board's decision, I called a press conference to explain the ministry's position and my own. My explanation cut no ice. In fact, some very nasty pieces were written against me in a section of the media at the time.

Even before the UTI crisis hit us, it had been decided that we would set up a JPC to inquire into the market scam. Pramod Mahajan, who was the parliamentary affairs minister, had told the prime minister and me that if we did not agree to set up a JPC it would be difficult for us to face Parliament when it reassembled for the second part of the budget session. Jaipal Reddy, spokesperson of the Congress party, had already demanded that there should be a JPC on the lines of the earlier committee which had been set up to inquire into the 1992 scam. I told both the prime minister and Mahajan that the finance ministry had nothing to hide. I was ready for a JPC probe. So, when Parliament assembled, a resolution was moved by the government and a JPC was set up to inquire into the market scam. When the UTI development took place, there was a further resolution passed in Parliament and an inquiry into the affairs of the UTI was also added to the terms of reference of the JPC.

The debate on the market scam and the UTI crisis led to some very ugly scenes in Parliament. A question on UTI was raised in the Rajya Sabha on the first day Parliament reassembled for the monsoon session. I gave a detailed blow-by-blow account of what had happened on 2 July 2001 in response to a supplementary question asked by Pranab Mukherjee. I did not know then that there would be a JPC on UTI. I knew that in Parliament one must always speak the truth. I am glad that I made a very detailed statement in the Rajya Sabha that day because subsequently, when the issue came up before the JPC, I could tell the committee what I had told Parliament even before the matter was referred to the JPC.

There were inspired media reports, on the basis of which Kapil Sibal, who was then in the Rajya Sabha, filed more than one notice of breach of privilege against me. I replied to all the notices. Nothing ever came of the notices but, every time he filed a notice with the chairman of the Upper House, he was allowed to raise the issue and his statements were flashed in the media. The media reports gave the impression that I had already been held guilty of breach of privilege. There were also personal attacks on me alleging that I had influenced certain investment decisions of UTI and that there were taped conversations between Subramanyam and me, which he would be releasing to the media and the opposition.

In the Rajya Sabha, when the opposition finished with what it had to say, I rose to reply to the debate. I was repeatedly interrupted by the opposition members and not allowed to proceed with my reply. It took me three days to complete my reply, with repeated interruptions and adjournments. In the Lok Sabha, the opposition brought an adjournment motion and Priya Ranjan Dasmunshi, who was the chief whip of the Congress party, was supposed to lead the attack. Rumours were afloat in Parliament that he had the tapes and documentary evidence of my personal involvement in the UTI scandal. Dasmunshi's speech turned out to be a damp squib. He had nothing original to say. When I got up to reply I congratulated him on his speech on the motion and remarked that Rashtriya Janata Dal member Raghuvansh Prasad Singh's charges were so outrageous that I did not consider them worthy of a reply. This led to a huge uproar from the opposition. Raghuvansh Prasad Singh, Mani Shankar Aiyar and others came into the well of the House shouting slogans and shaking clenched fists at me. They created such an ugly scene that it became impossible for me to proceed with my reply. The Speaker was forced to put the adjournment motion to vote in the midst of the pandemonium itself. The motion was naturally defeated. In my entire parliamentary career in both the Rajya Sabha and the Lok Sabha, that was the worst day of my life. I have always spoken in Parliament with conviction and have generally been heard in silence by other members of the House. But on this occasion, it was complete chaos.

In the Rajya Sabha, for instance, I had referred to the large investment made by UTI in the shares of Reliance Industries earlier in an off-market transaction in one day. This was done when Manmohan Singh was finance minister. I asked if the then finance minister, who had had a representative of his ministry on the UTI board, was responsible for this deal. Naturally, there was no reply from Manmohan Singh. I then asked him how he could accuse me of being responsible for every deal, especially the bad ones, made by UTI. UTI made independent decisions and I did not interfere in its decision-making. But this was a charge which was continuously levelled against me. The whole UTI affair is a very sorry chapter of my tenure as finance minister.

I was determined to restructure UTI and set up an informal group consisting of experts from the financial sector to make suggestions. We spent long hours trying to work out a solution to the UTI mess. A financial restructuring package was prepared by the ministry and taken to the Cabinet Committee on Economic Affairs, which cleared the package in December 2001. Accordingly, US-64 became a net-asset-value-based scheme which was fully SEBI compliant from 1 January 2002. Though the cabinet committee approved the package, there were some who felt that it would lead to the government losing Rs 8000 to 10,000 crore. I explained that the UTI was running in loss largely on account of the depressed stock markets and only partly because of the bad investments it had made and the NPAs it had accumulated. I reassured the committee that once the stock markets went up UTI would be in a profitable position once again.

My assessment was not wrong. At the end of the day, UTI

did make substantial profits on the bail-out packages of both 1998 and 2002 when the stock market indices improved.

FLEX INDUSTRIES CASE

On my way back from China in 2002, I stopped for a day in Hong Kong on official business. The next day, as I was boarding the flight to Delhi via Bangkok, my son-in-law, who was consul general of India in Hong Kong and had come to see me off, casually started looking at the day's Indian newspapers on the internet in the VIP lounge. Suddenly, he came across a front-page report in the *Indian Express* accusing me of getting my election publicity material printed by Flex Industries, suggesting that I might have got it done for free. I had not yet become thick-skinned enough for such stories not to affect me. I boarded the flight in a very disturbed frame of mind. It appeared to be a part of the series of inspired personal attacks.

I arrived in Delhi around 10.30 p.m. When I reached my residence, I found that my staff had very thoughtfully kept a copy of the day's *Indian Express* on my table. I was able to study the report in greater detail.

Why was I being linked to Flex Industries? The reason was simple. The chairman of Flex Industries, Ashok Chaturvedi, was accused of bribing the chief commissioner of excise in Delhi. Both Chaturvedi and the chief commissioner had been arrested and put behind bars. The basic thrust of the allegation against me therefore was that I had a nexus with the notorious firm whose chairman had bribed an official of the finance ministry. How could I be expected to do justice in the case? I should therefore quit as finance minister.

Before I come to the merit of the case, I must mention how the *Indian Express* got the story. I had in my personal staff a man from Bihar who had worked with me for many years. He continued working for me when I became finance minister. He was the custodian of all my personal papers. I generally trusted him, though there had been occasions when I had found that he had not behaved honestly. In 2001 when I returned from my medical trip to the United States, I learnt that he had approached an official of Gujarat Bhavan to get 'my nephew' admitted in Sardar Patel Vidyalaya in Delhi. I was told that he had exerted enormous pressure on the official, and finally succeeded in getting the child admitted in the school. Actually it was his own nephew, not mine, for whom he had pulled strings and misused my name. I was extremely disappointed when I learnt of this from a Gujarat Bhavan official, since I expect my personal staff to be absolutely honest and truthful. In fact, I told this particular staffer that, if he had made the request to me, I would have tried to get his nephew admitted in the school. He should not have given a false statement, and I could no longer keep him on my staff. Surprisingly, this time he did not plead with me to forgive him as he had on earlier occasions.

Obviously the man had better ideas. He rushed to meet Congress party leaders and fed them with tales he made up about me. Obviously delighted to hear the stories, they persuaded him, as I learnt later, to put it all in a sworn affidavit. I soon learnt that what had appeared in the *Indian Express* was only a part of the affidavit, in fact only the tip of the iceberg. More juicy material was to follow. I tried to get a copy of the affidavit, but failed to find one.

Returning to the original accusation of taking free election material from Flex Industries, someone (who is today an important person in politics and a Congress party MP) had brought the chairman of Flex Industries to meet me a few weeks before the general election of 1999. He had initially asked for an appointment with me at my house. When he came, he was accompanied by the chairman of Flex Industries, whom I met for the first time that day. The MP told me that Flex Industries made plastic-coated pouches for paan masala, and they could print attractive election publicity material for me. He suggested I should get all my election publicity material supplied by them. He also told me that Flex had supplied election material to top leaders of the Congress party and the

BJP. I told him that I might be interested in getting some material for the campaign made by him, but only on condition that I would pay for it. The whole matter was thus absolutely open and above board. I had, in fact, bought some publicity material from a few printers in Delhi for my Lok Sabha campaign in 1999 and Flex Industries happened to be one of them.

The material from Flex was prepared and sent to my house in Delhi. My staff was responsible for dispatching the material to Hazaribagh by rail. For the supplies received from Flex Industries, as indeed from other printers, regular bills were raised by these firms and full payment made to them. Flex Industries had submitted five bills amounting to Rs 45,583. The amount was paid by me and incorporated in my statutory return on election expenses filed with the district election officer of Hazaribagh Lok Sabha constituency and was available with the Election Commission. This was the first and last meeting I had with the chairman of Flex Industries. But in the media it was projected as if a great scandal had been uncovered.

Parliament was in session and members of the Congress party raised the matter in both Houses. In the Rajya Sabha Arjun Singh raised the issue and demanded my dismissal from the government. Pramod Mahajan must have been very upset that I was under attack in Parliament. The next day, I was called by the prime minister to his Parliament House office. Pramod Mahajan was also present. They wanted to know the facts of the case. I told them there was no reason to worry and placed all the facts before them. Mahajan then suggested that I make a statement in Parliament. I readily agreed. I collected a copy of my election accounts which I had submitted to the district election officer three years ago in 1999 and made my statement in the Lok Sabha. Everyone was satisfied. Those who thought I was in deep trouble were disappointed.

In the afternoon, I went to the Rajya Sabha to make my statement. We have a tradition in the Rajya Sabha that a statement made by a minister remains open for discussion and members can seek clarifications. The statement I made in the

Rajya Sabha was, however, a personal explanation and seeking clarifications was not permitted under the rules. After I made my statement, many Congress members, including Arjun Singh, demanded that they be allowed to seek clarifications. It was a Congress member, Suresh Pachauri, who was in the chair then and he ruled that clarifications could not be permitted under the rules. As I came out of the House I met Arjun Singh in the lobby. He told me that all he had wanted to say was that after my statement he had no further questions and everything was clear. Mulayam Singh Yadav, a member of the Lok Sabha, and Amar Singh, general secretary of the Samajwadi Party and member of the Rajya Sabha, supported me by issuing statements in my favour. Mulayam Singh also told me that he admired the meticulousness with which I had recorded the expenditure details of my election campaign, particularly since during an election campaign one is so busy running from one place to another that it is difficult to keep track of every rupee spent. Clearly, I was an exception.

The *Indian Express*, however, was not done with me yet. A few days later, I got a telephone call from their correspondent, who said that she was going to do a story about my house in Noida which was on rent to an executive of Flex Industries. This was further proof of my nexus with the company. I agreed to explain it all in writing. When my house in Noida fell vacant we took out an advertisement for putting it out on rent again. An estate agent called us to inquire about the house. He did so on behalf of an executive working for the company. The whole process of giving the house on rent was done in the usual, normal way. The additional point I made was that whereas my earlier tenant paid a rent of Rs 50,000 a month, not including the basement, which had remained under my possession, in the present case I had also rented out the basement at the same rent. So there was nothing wrong with this transaction. My statement was published in the newspaper, although they still carried their story on the front page, repeating their assertion that I had rented my premises to a Flex Industries executive, which further proved my nexus with them. The paper did not stop there. A year later, it celebrated the anniversary of the disclosure by declaring how it had exposed me by publishing the stories. Such is life.

My suspicion was once again confirmed that there were at least some people who wanted to destroy me since I did not suit them as finance minister. If one looks at all the allegations, starting with the Mohan Guruswamy episode, the personal attacks which were levelled against me in the Mauritius treaty case, the UTI imbroglio and the market scam and subsequently in the Flex Industries case, it will clearly show that, while there was no substance in the charges, some people did try their best to malign me and damage my reputation by making baseless allegations against me repeatedly the entire time I was finance minister. I also learnt later that these elements did their best to defeat me in the 1999 elections. They sent money to my opponents in Hazaribagh to ensure my defeat. They may have finally succeeded in 2004, when I lost the election in Hazaribagh.

RELATIONS WITH THE
BJP PARLIAMENTARY PARTY

Perhaps what was most distressing during my tenure in the finance ministry was the opposition I sometimes faced from my own colleagues within the party. This opposition was most pronounced in the BJP parliamentary party. The worst part was that these discussions did not remain confidential; they became public and were highlighted in the media; and the impression gained ground that I did not enjoy the confidence of the entire party.

The parliamentary party of the BJP consists of all its Lok Sabha and Rajya Sabha MPs. When Parliament is in session, the parliamentary party meets every Tuesday at 9.30 a.m. When we were in government, it was presided over by the prime minister and in his absence by Advani. The parliamentary affairs minister briefs the MPs about business in both Houses for the coming week and the strategy for meeting the challenges posed by the opposition parties. Other ministers are also called upon to brief the party MPs about important business relating to their ministries. Members are also free to raise issues of public importance at these meetings.

As finance minister, whenever I took a step which was not popular, there was invariably a demand from the party MPs to roll it back. Most of our MPs naturally had concerns regarding agriculture and rural development schemes and the budgetary allocations for them. A sizeable number, representing the industrially advanced states, was also concerned with the impact of the budget on industry, especially on the small-scale and cottage industries. Since most MPs were concerned with sectional interests, they rarely saw the larger picture. My compulsions on the fiscal front were of little importance to them. The maximum criticism was reserved for increases in subsidized prices.

After the presentation of each budget, a separate and special meeting of the parliamentary party was held in which I used to explain the philosophy of the budget and its various provisions. Members were free to express their views and, on many occasions, they were quite critical; my clarifications to their questions would not satisfy them. Sushma Swaraj, one of our more vocal and eloquent leaders, was a great critic of the economic policies of the government, in both the parliamentary and party forums, during the period when she was out of the cabinet.

Some members did understand the economic situation, appreciated the steps taken in the budget and lent me their support in the parliamentary party meetings as well as in Parliament. But for them, I would have felt lonelier in the two Houses. And I often found that our allies in the NDA were at times more critical of my budget than even the opposition.

I recall a meeting of the national executive of the party scheduled to be held in Nagpur in 2000. I was not planning to attend the meeting as I was not well. A day before the meeting, however, I got a call from the prime minister suggesting that I accompany him the next day. I accepted the prime minister's invitation and we travelled together to Nagpur.

Upon reaching there, we went straight for the meeting. Murli Manohar Joshi, who was seated on the dais, came down and told me that Sushma Swaraj had been extremely critical of the economic policies of the government and the prime minister wanted to know whether I would like to respond to her now or later. I told Dr Joshi that I would prefer to respond later because I would like to first find out what she had said. I answered her criticism the next day. Looking back, I realize that the prime minister must have got wind of the fact that the economic policies of his government would be under attack from members of the executive and had therefore persuaded me to accompany him to Nagpur.

28

Farewell to North Block

After the success of my 2001 budget and before the stock market scam surfaced, I personally felt that I had had enough of the finance ministry and perhaps a change would be welcome. I wanted to move to the external affairs ministry. Before taking it up with Vajpayee, I decided to sound out two friends in the PMO, Brajesh Mishra and N.K. Singh. Brajesh Mishra offered to meet me personally to discuss the matter further. I did not mention the idea to anyone else.

Brajesh was to meet me at my residence on a Sunday. A little before his arrival, I received a telephone call from Vajpayee. He told me that I was doing a good job as finance minister and therefore there was no question of my shifting to any other ministry. If I had any such thoughts, I should give them up. There now seemed no point in my discussing this idea with anyone else. I do not know how the prime minister got to know that Brajesh Mishra and I were meeting to discuss this matter. I thought Brajesh Mishra might have informed him of my plan, but when Brajesh arrived he said that he had not talked to the prime minister at all on this matter. We both agreed that there was no point in pursuing the matter further. It dawned on me once again how extremely well informed the prime minister generally was.

The first time I had a taste of this was after a meeting with Jayalalitha some time towards the end of 1998. I had not had an occasion to meet her after I took over as finance minister. Janardanan, an MP from her party who worked with me as minister of state, informed me one day that 'Madam' was very keen to meet me. Could I make a trip to Chennai to see her? I agreed to meet her when I went to Chennai next. I knew that my meeting with Jayalalitha, against whom there were so many revenue cases, would be publicized out of proportion. I was not at all keen on that kind of publicity.

In the normal course, after a couple of months when a visit to Chennai came up, I decided to consult the prime minister on the matter. I told him of the invitation from her and inquired whether I should meet her during my trip. The prime minister was of the view that I should meet her. I informed Janardanan that since I would be visiting Chennai he could fix a meeting with Jayalalitha, if it was convenient to her. He got back to me soon enough—Jayalalitha had invited me for lunch. I fixed my programme in Chennai accordingly. Dilip Ray, minister of state for coal, told me that he had also been invited for the lunch. He was close to Jayalalitha.

In Chennai, after completing my programme in the forenoon, I quietly left for Jayalalitha's residence. Fortunately, there were no photographers waiting there. I was ushered into the living room, where she waited for me. We chatted for a while, and then went for lunch. There were only the three of us for lunch—Jayalalitha, Ray and myself. The lunch was delicious, served by liveried bearers wearing white gloves; everything was done in great style. As I was about to leave, Jayalalitha handed me an envelope. Later, when I opened it, I found it was a note about her income tax cases. I did not act on the note because as a policy I did not interfere in such cases.

I met the prime minister a few days later and reported the details of my meeting with Jayalalitha in Chennai, but forgot to mention the envelope. After I had finished my narration, Vajpayee innocently asked me about the envelope she had given me and its contents. I was taken aback. Obviously, the Prime Minister of India gets to know everything, if he so wishes. Is it a matter of surprise, then, that Vajpayee came to know about my meeting with Brajesh Mishra and the subject we were going to discuss?

One reason for my unhappiness in the finance ministry was that I had lost the confidence of the Swadeshi Jagran Manch and the RSS, with whom I had worked so closely earlier in the swadeshi movement. I was always of the view that we should take them into confidence, have discussions with them and explain why we had done what we had. I had no doubt in my mind that our explanations would have removed their doubts and satisfied them, but the meetings could not take place regularly due to lack of time. Thus there was a widening communication gap between them and us. In fact, the misunderstanding became so serious that Dattopant Thengdi, one of the seniormost leaders of the RSS, known as the patron saint of swadeshi, went to the extent of calling me an *apraadhi* (culprit) in a public meeting in Delhi in April 2001. He described how I had deviated from the path of swadeshi after I had become finance minister. I sought a meeting with him to explain my position, but there was no response from his side. He passed away some time later and it will forever remain my regret that I could not meet him to explain my point of view.

Dattopant Thengdi's statement affected me greatly. I drafted a brief letter of resignation and was planning to go to the prime minister to hand it over when perchance I got a telephone call from Advani. Towards the end of the call, I asked him if he had seen what Thengdi had said about me. He had. I told him that I was very hurt and was planning to hand over my resignation to the prime minister. I could not continue in the government any more. Advani was equally upset, but said that I should not take such a drastic step. He suggested he would discuss the matter with the prime minister, and also talk to the Sangh, and that I should not take any precipitate action. Advani's pep talk made me give up the idea of resigning. Instead, I went to the parliamentary party meeting which was scheduled for that day. In that meeting Vajpayee, in his intervention, talked briefly about the economic policies of the government and asserted that we were on the right track. This statement helped restore my morale.

The 2002 budget did not turn out to be a popular budget. My own party members were unhappy and complained loudly that I was alienating the middle class by lowering interest rates, taxing perquisites and dividend income, and not extending more income tax concessions. The Delhi municipal elections were held in March 2002, immediately after the budget, and we lost the election badly. Many Delhi state BJP leaders blamed me for the loss, claiming that it was the budget and the falling interest rates which had alienated the government employees and the middle class from us. In April 2002 the national executive of the party met in Goa. Parliament was in recess then. It was very clear that I would come under attack for my economic policies at this meeting. There was also strong speculation in the media that I was not only going to be shifted from the finance ministry, but also dropped from the cabinet.

For the meeting, I prepared a PowerPoint presentation on the state of the economy and also collected some very relevant facts about the Delhi municipal elections. When the issue regarding the economy was raised, I used my presentation to inform the executive members about the state of the economy and why we had to do what we were doing, how falling interest rates had to be looked at in the context of falling inflation, what the real interest rates were and how it was beneficial for the economy. Since nobody had blamed me directly for our loss in the Delhi municipal elections, I did not touch upon that issue. The presentation did make an impact; a number of my party colleagues told me later they were not aware of many facts I had presented and asked if I could make available copies of my presentation to them. K. Jana Krishnamurthy, the party president, remarked at the end of my presentation that we had to remain in power in order to implement the policies that I advocated. If, as a result of these policies, we were voted out, then all these policies would remain on paper. He was absolutely right. This was a dilemma the political system faced. Elections were important and winning them was also important. But we had to remember our responsibility not only to the present but also to the future. Good economic policies could not, and should not, be sacrificed at the altar of political gain for the present.

I always talked of inter-generational equity in various other interventions in Parliament and elsewhere. We have no right to leave an unbearable burden on future generations because we are helpless before the populism of the present. I am still convinced that no person or party has the right to think only of the present, and let the future be damned. Governments cannot function on the basis of the theory 'after me the deluge'. But irrespective of what happened in Goa, the media continued to speculate about my being shifted from the finance ministry and being dropped from the government.

After the meeting in Goa and while Parliament was still in recess, I sought a meeting with the prime minister. I told him that he should indeed shift me from the finance ministry, explaining that since the budget was only midway in Parliament, and was yet to be passed, my successor could make the changes he wanted, especially in the finance bill. He would, at least, have the satisfaction of part ownership of the budget. Otherwise, he would have to implement a budget that was wholly mine. I pleaded therefore that he should make the change during the parliamentary recess itself. For the first time I noticed that Vajpayee did not reject the idea outright. Instead, he asked where I would like to go. I replied I preferred to remain an ordinary MP, defending the government in Parliament whenever needed. I had performed this role very ably after I had refused to join the V.P. Singh government, and he should not be unduly concerned about my being accommodated elsewhere. But when he insisted that I should remain in government, I expressed my wish to be shifted to the Ministry of External Affairs. Since Jaswant Singh was doing a fine job and had built up personal rapport with leaders the world over, Vajpayee was not in favour of shifting him from external affairs. We left the matter at that.

After my conversation with Vajpayee, I knew that my

leaving the finance ministry was only a question of time. So I sought a meeting with Advani and conveyed the same message to him, that if I had to be shifted and still be retained as a minister the only portfolio I would like to handle was external affairs. Advani was sympathetic and assured me that he would try his best for me.

Towards the end of June 2002, I got a telephone call from Vajpayee in my office in North Block, asking me to meet him. I knew what the call meant; either there would be a change of portfolio or I would be asked to leave the government. I went to see him straightaway at 7 Race Course Road. Vajpayee started the conversation by saying that I was doing a good job in the finance ministry, but the public perception was unfortunately different. As public perception had to be taken note of, he had decided to shift me from the Ministry of Finance. I thanked him for his decision, expressed my gratitude for all the support he had extended to me in the finance ministry and left. It almost sounded like a farewell speech.

A few days later, the changes in portfolios were formally announced. I was shifted to external affairs and Jaswant Singh to finance. I was happy because I had got what I wanted. My only regret was that I was shifted because the 'perception' about my tenure in the finance ministry was not favourable about me.

Perhaps a lot of people were glad that I had finally left charge as finance minister. I do not know if I could have played the game differently, could have propitiated the powers that be in a different way. I am not merely referring to the powers that be in the party and in the government but to those out there in Mumbai and other places. I could have curried favour with them; I could have obliged them when they came to me for favours. Perhaps, if I had wanted to survive in the finance ministry, I should have persuaded myself to do things differently. In retrospect, I know I worked hard and did my best, for the people and for the future of this country—and that is the greatest satisfaction of all. It was only when I shifted to the Ministry of External Affairs that I realized just how hard I had worked in the finance ministry.

29

The Life of a Finance Minister

The finance ministry is perhaps the largest ministry in the Government of India. It has a large number of departments, attached and subordinate offices and big cadres of officers and staff. It generates a huge quantity of work on a daily basis. The finance minister has to attend the largest number of meetings. He is also very busy in Parliament. The preparation of the annual budget is an onerous task.

I soon realized that I had more work to do in Parliament than any other colleague. It was not merely parliamentary work relating to the budget; I also had the largest number of legislations to steer through Parliament. I answered the largest number of questions in every session, and had to reply to discussions on issues raised under the various rules. The four years I spent in the finance ministry gave me a thorough understanding of the functioning of Parliament, one I would not have acquired had I been serving in any other ministry.

There is no doubt that irrespective of his political standing the finance minister is the most important minister in the government. No other minister deals with the affairs of the entire government and all the ministries. The finance minister also has to maintain a close link with the state governments and with people at the grass-roots level, just as he has an international profile through the various multilateral organizations in which he represents the country. Nobody was more acutely aware of this than I, which is why I went to Vajpayee on the very first day of my appointment in 1998 and told him that I needed all his support and confidence as finance minister. While Vajpayee might have promised me that support, and even extended it to me unflinchingly, the fact remains that there were people within the party who were unhappy with me as finance minister. They probably felt that since I was a comparative newcomer to the party, having joined it only in 1993, I should not have been made one of the more senior ministers of the government.

I have no hesitation in accepting that my political profile within the party did not justify the allocation of the finance portfolio to me. In the Chandra Shekhar government I had no such problem, because I was a close confidant of Chandra Shekhar. I was also politically important within my own party. I was the leader of my party in the Rajya Sabha and by virtue of that, the Leader of the House. As such, I did not suffer from the sense of political inadequacy that I felt when I was made finance minister in 1998.

During this period, there were several occasions when a Group of Ministers (GoM) was formed. The first name which appears in the list of a GoM is the chairperson of the group. Since I held the finance portfolio, more often than not this responsibility was cast on me. I perhaps chaired more than 90 per cent of the GoMs which were constituted to deal with various issues. Since many of my colleagues felt that they were politically senior to me, they insisted in the beginning that the meetings of the group be held in their ministries rather than in the finance ministry, though I headed the group. I never cared much for such niceties, never made them matters of prestige, and without any hesitation went to the offices of other ministers to attend the meetings. But gradually, all this changed automatically. I found that senior colleagues no longer had any difficulty in coming to my office in the finance ministry to discuss any issue or to attend a GoM or other meetings. The only two ministers on whom I invariably offered to call whenever something had to be discussed were Advani and

Dr Murli Manohar Joshi, both former presidents of the party. I extended the same courtesy to George Fernandes, though George was too decent a person to care about such formalities. But everyone was not like him.

In one cabinet meeting the issue of the corporatization of the Department of Telecommunications came up. After some discussion, it was decided that a GoM be formed to examine the matter further. When the prime minister announced the group, my name was listed at the beginning, which meant that I was to chair the group. In the next day's newspapers, however, it was reported that Ram Vilas Paswan, who was the Minister for Telecommunications, would head the group. I was naturally surprised and curious. It appears that after the cabinet meeting, Paswan had gone to Vajpayee and pleaded with him that he be made the chairman of the group as it was a question of his *izzat* (prestige). The prime minister agreed and Paswan became chairman of the group.

It did not really matter who headed the group or where the meetings were held because no decision could be taken without my approval. I was aware of Paswan's tendencies. I had been told how, as member of a GoM in the I.K. Gujral government, he had been instrumental in giving a bonanza to government employees when the Fifth Pay Commission report was under consideration. I was very cautious of him and always tried to keep him in check. But he had a certain style and used to give the impression to the trade unions that he was their only messiah. In the interest of revenue, it was left to me to argue with the trade unions as well as with him. He served sumptuous meals when the meetings continued late into the evening. My style was more parsimonious—whenever I headed a GoM I only served tea and biscuits!

An important job of a finance minister is to scrutinize the proposals that emanate from other ministries. While sending proposals to the finance ministry, each minister expects his proposal to go through without a hitch. The finance ministry, however, may disagree. This often led to arguments in cabinet meetings or in front of the prime minister. Sometimes my colleagues took it personally. I remember one such occasion, in the very first year, when a proposal came to me from the Ministry of Power. My very dear friend, Rangarajan Kumaramangalam, was the minister. I did not support the ministry's proposal, and when the matter came up before cabinet I naturally opposed it. Perhaps Ranga had got out of the wrong side of the bed that morning, because he suddenly flared up and started shouting at me. He felt it was impossible for him to work as power minister with me as finance minister, and even went to the extent of saying that he would not like to remain in the power ministry; the finance ministry could run the power ministry as well. I was completely taken aback by his outburst. Surprisingly, the person who spoke up for me equally vehemently was Sikander Bakht, the industry minister. He was categorical that no minister could behave in such a manner with his cabinet colleague. This helped cool tempers.

On many such occasions, including this one, I had to remind the prime minister that, as long as I was in charge of the finance ministry, I must be allowed to have my say; otherwise I would not be true to my responsibility. After shifting to external affairs, I was amused when Jaswant Singh had to carry the can on such occasions. Situations such as these were always tricky, and the decision depended on the prime minister.

There is such an enormous amount of work to be done in the finance ministry that I had no time for family, friends, social events or anything else during those years. In fact, I did not look forward to being invited to dinner by anyone, because that meant I either had to work until the early hours of the morning or else leave the work pending. I knew of many ministers who followed what is generally known as the 'peshi' system, under which the private secretary puts up the file to the minister, explains what the file contains and also suggests what order should be passed by the minister. If a mere signature by the minister is needed, he/she would put his/her signature, but if something had to be noted on the file, the private secretary would be asked to prepare a draft of the minister's minutes which would then be signed by the minister. During my days as a civil servant, I worked as principal secretary to two chief ministers of Bihar, where this system was in vogue. I studied the files, presented them to the chief minister and suggested what the order should be. If it was to be a written order, I prepared the draft and put it up for the chief minister's approval. I never followed this system myself when I became a minister.

On a typical day, I would wake up at around 7 a.m. and spend about an hour having tea and reading as many newspapers as I could. Though it was important for me to read all the newspapers, it was not possible to do so. My wife supported me by reading all the remaining papers, telling me if there was anything I needed to know or act upon.

I had earmarked two days in the week for a janata darbar at my residence, to meet people from 9 a.m. to 10 a.m. The time limit was hardly ever honoured, and the meeting usually stretched well beyond the appointed time. Also, since my doors were kept open for people from my constituency on all days of the week, others walked in too. Once they were in I had to meet them.

After meeting visitors at home, I used to go to my office. The entire day would be consumed in meetings, or in discussions with ministry officials. It was late in the evening, at around 8.30, that I would be done with the busy schedule, only to realize that the day was already over. I would then inquire from my staff the number of files which had accumulated during the day, the people who had phoned, the requests received for meetings and the schedule for next day's meetings and appointments. After getting this information, I would give instructions about the people I wanted to meet with, meetings I wanted arranged or wished to attend the next day and any other matter. Only then would I leave office, along with all the papers and files which constituted my home work.

Reaching home at around 9 p.m., after a quick dinner, I would work in my office at home. The work I took home would generally consist of a large number of acknowledgements and replies to letters from MPs and other VIPs which I had to sign, files, letters and correspondence, and briefs for the next day's meetings. The briefs had to be studied carefully, because I like to go to meetings fully prepared on the subject. In addition, I often took additional, oral briefing from my officers before a meeting. After this, there were telephone calls which had to be returned, for there was always a backlog. Along with attending to papers and files, I would begin returning the calls. This would go on till 11 p.m. or so. After that it was too late to call. But I would continue looking at the files and went to bed only after I had disposed of the last piece of paper. Often it went on until well past midnight.

When I shifted to the Ministry of External Affairs, it dawned on me how my other colleagues had so much time for politics while I had had none at all as finance minister. Being one of the largest ministries, the finance minister has to look at the largest number of files. Hundreds of files used to await me when I returned to the capital after a trip. When Parliament was in session the burden used to multiply manifold.

I am not an early riser, which is why I could not afford to leave anything for the next day. I believed in disposing of all my work the same day. This was the practice I had followed even when I was in the bureaucracy. I never left anything pending. The only person who assisted me was a peon. He opened the boxes, put the papers on the table and removed the boxes when they got filled with the files that had been dealt with. Sometimes I tried to make light of the work by picking up the fat files first, because that helped reduce the physical bulk of the pending work. If I came across a complex file I would deal with it towards the end. My personal staff was under instructions not to keep any file pending with them, either on its way to me or on the way back. And it was the responsibility of my private secretary to ensure that everything, including the last bit of paper, was put up to me the same day it was received.

It was my training as a civil servant that held me in good stead to deal with all these files. I had developed the knack of separating the grain from the chaff, the important from the trivial. It was not possible for anyone to take me for a ride. I could take a decision and dispose of files the same day, although my officers would have spent considerably more time on the decision, often inordinately delaying a file. There were occasions when I differed with the recommendations made by my officers and recorded my own arguments in response.

IN CONCLUSION

Just as I had more than my fair share of controversies during my tenure as finance minister, I also had more than my fair share of man-made and natural disasters and misfortunes during this period. When we came to power in March 1998, the East Asian crisis was raging, our foreign exchange reserves were depleting, interest rates had been hiked and the economy was on a downward swing. To this was added the burden of the Fifth Pay Commission on the expenditure side. Then came the nuclear tests of May 1998 followed by economic sanctions. In 1999 the country was plunged into the throes of political instability. The government lost the vote of confidence by one vote and we had to go in for general elections. The conflict in Kargil soon followed, creating its own pressure on the expenditure front. Nature showed its fury when the super-cyclone hit Orissa in 1999, followed by the Gujarat earthquake of January 2001. These two massive natural disasters had to be provided for adequately in the budgets.

The year 1998 was a normal one, even a good one from the point of view of the performance of the monsoon. Twenty meteorological sub-divisions had normal rainfall, thirteen had excess rainfall and only two sub-divisions had deficient/scanty rainfall. The long period average rainfall for the country as a whole was 105 per cent. But that is about as long as my luck lasted. The next four years were bad. The percentage of districts with normal/excess rainfall declined from 83 per cent in 1998 to 67 per cent in 1999, 66 per cent in 2000, 68 per cent in 2001 and 39 per cent in 2002. The long period average rainfall for the country as a whole declined from 96 per cent in 1999 to 92 per cent in 2000, 91 per cent in 2001 and 81 per cent in 2002. It had its impact on agricultural production and the growth rate in agriculture. We often forget the role of natural disasters and their impact on the economy when we talk of growth rates, and tend to compare oranges with apples when we compare a normal year with a bad year. The year 2002 was the worst. It witnessed the worst drought ever, since we started recording monsoon rain figures.

The market scam of 2001 played havoc with investor sentiment, which had been preceded by the global collapse of technology stocks in 2000. International petroleum prices went through the roof in 2000 and 2001, creating pressure on our foreign exchange reserves. The terrorist attack on the twin towers in New York on 11 September 2001 unleashed its own cascading effect on a large number of economic activities even in India. The mobilization of Indian troops along the entire border with Pakistan after the terrorist attack on our Parliament on 13 December 2001 was an expensive exercise.

World trade and world growth rates were also sluggish during this entire period on account of various crises. There was hardly a year during my four years as finance minister that could be called normal. It was a period of struggle, often reminiscent of the fire-fighting I had had to do in 1990–91.

The Congress party moved a motion of no confidence against the government in the Lok Sabha on 18 August 2003. Sonia Gandhi led the charge. Speaking on the economy she said, 'During the previous Congress government's rule, I am talking now of our economy, the economic growth averaged 6.7 per cent per year. Is it not true?' she asked, and added, 'Last year it came crashing down to just 4.3 per cent or thereabouts.' She obviously spoke as briefed. But the picture of lower growth rates during the NDA regime has been sought to be perpetuated by resorting to a simple untruth. Take the best years of the earlier Congress rule, namely that of Narasimha Rao, and compare it with the worst year of Vajpayee's rule. The facts speak otherwise.

During the five years of Narasimha Rao rule, the annual growth rate of the economy was 1.3 per cent in 1991–92, 5.1 per cent in 1992–93, 5.9 per cent in 1993–94, 7.3 per cent in 1994–95, and 7.3 per cent in 1995–96. The annual growth rate during the six years of the Vajpayee government was 6.5 per cent in 1998–99, 6.1 per cent in 1999–2000, 4.4 per cent in 2000–01, 5.6 per cent in 2001–02, 4.3 per cent in 2002–03, and 8.5 per cent in 2003–04. But without wasting time on a meaningless controversy of this nature, I shall return to my basic theme of India's economic security. Four chronic problems have bedeviled the Indian economy since independence. It was the persistence of these four problems which made the Indian economy insecure, unstable, vulnerable to crises and dependent on foreign help. I can say with a reasonable degree of confidence that, at the end of the four years during which I was finance minister, these four chronic problems were effectively tackled and resolved for good.

The first of these was the problem of a precarious balance of payments. When we came into office, foreign exchange reserves stood at a little over $29 billion. On 31 May 2002 the reserves were almost $50 billion and growing. What is even more remarkable is that for the first time after twenty-three years India recorded a current account surplus of 0.3 per cent of the GDP in 2001–02. The external-debt-to-GDP ratio, signifying the extent of external debt vis-à-vis domestic output, declined from 24.3 per cent at end-March 1998 to 20.1 per cent at the end of September 2002. The debt-service-to-current-receipts ratio, which signifies the capacity of the country to meet its debt service obligation, improved from 19.5 per cent in 1997–98 to 13.8 per cent in 2001–02. Short-term debt also declined from $5.05 billion at end-March 1998 to $2.75 billion at end-March 2002.

In fact, our management of the external sector of the economy earned praise even from our erstwhile critics abroad and became a model for other developing countries.

The second chronic problem was perpetual food shortages and import of food grains. Through deft management of the food economy and procurement prices, it became possible for us to procure larger quantities of food grains from farmers, extend the area of procurement to other states, build large stocks of food grains in government godowns, launch food security schemes such as Annapoorna and Antyodaya and even emerge as one of the leading exporters of food grains globally. We never even considered importing food grains to shore up our stocks as governments immediately before and after us have done.

The third chronic problem that we overcame was inflation. After the bitter onion and potato debate in Parliament in 1998, I cannot recall a single occasion when rising prices agitated MPs. Government figures show that the annual average WPI-based inflation, which was 10.6 per cent between 1991–92 and 1995–96, came down to 5.1 per cent between 1996–97 and 2000–01 and further to 4.1 per cent between 2001–02 and 2003–04.

The fourth chronic problem of the Indian economy is infrastructure. Vigorous measures were taken in all areas of infrastructure to develop world-class facilities. Telecom and highways are the more publicized success stories. But the achievements in the port sector where the average turnaround time dropped from 7.5 days in 1996–97 to 3.5 days in 2001–02, in housing where the target of twenty lakh houses a year was significantly exceeded, the financial sector reforms and reforms in the area of human resource development are no less impressive.

Most importantly, the Indian economy, which in the past had been so prone to crisis, became safe and secure, not only for the present, not only temporarily, but for decades to come. The resolve which I had made on that hot and sultry day in Patna in 1991, to make the country economically secure and self-reliant, stood largely fulfilled when I left the Ministry of Finance.

Epilogue:
A Vision for the Future

India lives in every century of time. One does not have to travel too far from a city to discover this. Some tribal communities in my own district live in a way which can only be described as prehistoric. We have to remember this while making policies for our people hoping to give them a better quality of life. One cap cannot fit all even in one district of India, leave aside the whole country. A better quality of life for the common man is the demand of our times, which can neither be avoided nor postponed any longer. In effect it means removal of poverty and provision of basic amenities. To achieve these twin objectives we need economic growth on the one hand and targeted policies for the poor and the deprived on the other.

Growth means creation of additional wealth, which, when properly distributed, gets reflected in higher per capita income for the poor. Much of the poverty in India can be ascribed to low growth and low per capita income in the past. Higher growth will enable us to eradicate poverty faster. Double-digit growth, which can dramatically change the face of the country in a decade or two, is not merely an academic exercise but a crying need. While all sectors of the economy must grow, it is the agricultural sector, supporting over 60 per cent of our people, which needs the most attention. Unfortunately, the contribution of agriculture to our GDP has declined to reach the alarming figure of 18.5 per cent.

India has set itself the target of becoming a developed country by 2020. When the NDA demitted office in May 2004, the annual growth rate of the economy for 2003–04 had already leaped over 8 per cent, in fact, registering a growth of 8.5 per cent in that year. In 2003–04 all sectors of the economy—manufacturing, services and agriculture—registered an impressive performance. Though the slogan 'India Shining' was ridiculed, there is no doubt that the NDA left behind an India which was shining as never before. The Tenth Five Year Plan target of 8 per cent growth, once described as '*Mungeri Lal ke sunehary sapne*' (The sweet dreams of Mungeri Lal) by Sonia Gandhi, has actually been achieved. Double-digit growth rate now certainly appears to be within our grasp.

But before we present the policy framework needed to achieve double-digit growth, it is important to look at the policies India followed in the past, learn from any mistakes and then move forward.

It is one of the ironies of history that, while we embraced competition in almost all walks of life after we gained independence, in the economic field we followed policies which discouraged, nay, actually killed, competition. In the political field we adopted democracy and rightly so. Political parties were required to compete with each other for peoples' mandate in order to secure the right to govern. Recruitment to the various civil services and the armed forces was through competitive examinations. Professionals qualified and could progress in their profession only through competition. In fact, competition became the way of life in all areas of activity except the economy. Our economic policies favoured a mixed economy with a strong socialist bias. The Congress party, which ruled at the centre uninterruptedly for three decades, had adopted the socialistic pattern as its creed. In theory, it meant that the commanding heights of the economy would be controlled by the government through the public sector. In fact, it meant control of all sectors of the economy by the government. Even in sectors like homoeopathic and Ayurvedic medicines, if the private sector was not forthcoming, the government set up its own company. A shortage of bread led to the setting up of a company to manufacture bread. Government in business became all-pervasive. Wherever the private sector was allowed to exist, it could do so only under a strict licence. Allocation of financial and physical resources was strictly controlled by the government. Every economic activity had to secure the permission of some authority or the other. Thus, the regime of rationing and controls erected during the Second World War, instead of being dismantled after independence was further strengthened and an elaborate licence-quota-permit raj came into existence. Everyone flourished under this system. Officials and ministers of the government wielded enormous powers. The public sector was their happy hunting ground. Nepotism soon led to overstaffing in the public sector, while productivity and profitability became dirty words. Losses were worn as a badge of honour. PSUs became extensions of the ministries they were attached to, to be preyed upon by unscrupulous elements in government. There was a scramble among private entrepreneurs for licences, permits and quotas. Those who secured them made huge profits. Vested interests developed everywhere. Competition became anathema. Naturally, both production and productivity suffered, scarce capital was inefficiently utilized, growth became a casualty and the common man suffered the most because for him everything was scarce, expensive and of poor quality. The economy became prone to crises. As a nation we were barely able to make both ends meet. India became a byword for poverty, corruption and inefficiency. We went round the world with a begging bowl and led, as Deen Dayal Upadhayay said, a ship-to-mouth existence. In those years, because there was hardly any wealth creation, we distributed poverty in the name of equity and social justice.

The continued mismanagement of the Indian economy ultimately led to the worst crisis in independent India's history when we were left with only $1 billion in foreign exchange reserves in January 1991. Reforms were initiated under compulsion in 1991 and abandoned as soon as the compulsion was over. Economic reforms were resumed systematically, strongly and on our own volition only when Vajpayee became the Prime Minister of India in March 1998.

The Congress government under P.V. Narasimha Rao followed the reform path for only about three years. Losses in state assembly elections and mounting opposition within the Congress party forced the government to more or less abandon reforms after 1994. In fact, in some areas reforms were reversed. Rising inflation forced the government to adopt a tight money policy, raise interest rates and curb consumption. Combined with political instability in India and the East Asian crisis of 1997, this had an adverse impact on the Indian economy with the result that the growth rate of the economy dived to 4.8 per cent in 1997–98 compared to 7.8 per cent in 1996–97. The major and chronic problems of the Indian economy remained unresolved.

A sustained and sustainable double-digit growth for the next ten to fifteen years can be achieved only through continued economic reforms. We cannot afford to rest. New situations will demand a new set of policies, new reforms. Getting rid of our chronic problems is a major achievement of the Vajpayee government. We must ensure that they do not return. We must also ensure distributive justice. The poor must not be excluded from the benefits of reform or the fruits of growth. But an intellectual shift is necessary here. Instead of distributing poverty as we have done in the past, we must distribute wealth in the future. This is not an easy shift. There are many who believe that equity lies in the country remaining poor. We shall have to get rid of the mindset that creating wealth is sinful.

Secondly, double-digit growth will require matching investment. There cannot be growth without investment. Investment will come mainly out of domestic savings. Fortunately, domestic savings showed a very healthy growth during the NDA regime, rising from 21.5 per cent in 1998–99 to 29.7 per cent in 2003–04. But what is worrisome is the low rate of public savings. Our policy therefore should be to continue to encourage household savings and private sector savings and ensure that public savings, for which the government is responsible, also remains healthy. This can be done by keeping fiscal deficit under control and making the public sector profitable.

We will also need foreign investment to meet the balance of our requirements. It must be noted here that India has received, over the years, only a fraction of the foreign investment that other major developing countries have received. There is much needless and uninformed opposition to foreign investment in India. Foreign investment has generally contributed the equivalent of only about 1 per cent of our GDP annually to the gross investment in our economy. So, certainly there is scope for more. FDI must remain the preferred form of foreign investment. But, we should not turn away other forms of foreign investment. We should also encourage Indian companies to raise both equity and loans abroad, especially if they are cheaper.

Efficient utilization of capital is a given for building an efficient economy. We must ensure a good capital output ratio. History has proved that the state is a poor and inefficient allocator of resources and an inept owner of the means of production. The role of the state therefore should be limited to ensuring fair play amongst private and public players in the market. While socialism clearly stands discredited as a system for the management of economy, capitalism also has not covered itself with glory. Thus, while the capitalist theory of free play of market forces is a better system for more production and higher growth, that by itself is incapable of ensuring distributive justice and meeting the rising aspirations of people, especially in a democratic society. The state must play its role and provide basic amenities like roads, electricity, water, education and health to the people. It must also ensure, by setting up regulatory mechanisms, that the market functions fairly for everyone, monopolies are not able to establish themselves, prices, quality and availability of products are to the satisfaction of the people, and market manipulation and aberrations are dealt with firmly and swiftly.

The state must be at the forefront of the fight against poverty; by 2020, India must get rid of the scourge of all kinds of poverty. Poverty can be of various types. The first is the poverty of the individual. If a person is unemployed and unable to earn his livelihood, he will remain poor unless he was born rich. Then, a family can be poor if only one member of the family is earning and other adult members who are capable of earning do not. The third type of poverty is poverty of the community. An individual or a family may have adequate income and a reasonable standard of living but, if there is no electricity, water, road, educational and health facilities available in the community and the people in general are poor, then the individual or the family and naturally the whole community will still experience a sense of poverty. And finally, there is poverty at the national level. As long as a sizeable section of this country is compelled to live below the poverty line, India will continue to be a poor country, irrespective of the prosperity of an individual, a family, a community, or even a region. All these forms of poverty have to be tackled and eliminated.

The best and long-term solution to eliminating poverty is remunerative employment. The state's economic policies must therefore facilitate productive employment generation. There is need for the greatest caution here since the dividing line between productive employment and wasteful expenditure is very thin. There is also the added danger of mismanagement and corruption in government-run schemes. In my view, maximum employment can be generated through the creation of physical and human infrastructure. The road building programme of the NDA government is an example. In rural areas, we need roads, irrigation, housing, electricity, drinking water, education, health and other kinds of services. All these have the potential to generate large-scale employment. Similarly, in urban areas, all these schemes and many more can generate enough employment. In the economy as a whole, the manufacturing sector and some of the service sectors have great employment potential. Their growth must be encouraged. In other words, through well-conceived policies, we must be able to eliminate unemployment by 2020, and by providing infrastructure and services, poverty in all its forms. There is an umbilical link between employment generation and poverty eradication on the one hand and infrastructure creation, economic growth and a better quality of life for the people on the other. Once we establish this virtuous cycle, we shall win the war against poverty.

Inflation—rising prices for the common man—must be tackled with all the instruments at a government's command. Inflation, as all economists agree, is the worst kind of tax on the poor, since it does not discriminate between them and the rich. Inflation also induces higher interest rates, which makes the economy uncompetitive globally. In fact, the biggest drawback of the Indian economy since independence has been a vicious cycle of high inflation and high interest rates. The high cost of money was one of the main reasons for the uncompetitiveness of the Indian economy. This vicious cycle was successfully broken and replaced by the virtuous cycle of low inflation and moderate interest rates by the NDA government. The increase in essential consumption by the common man and the housing revolution which was unleashed during that period can be directly ascribed to low interest rates and the easier availability of finance by banks and other lending institutions. In 2007 higher inflation is already creating pressure on interest rates. If this is allowed to go on, it is bound to cause great harm to the economy.

Progress is not possible in any sector unless we have power. Responsibility for this sector rests with the state governments. They must move more purposefully to clean up this sector, make it more efficient, cut losses and generate resources for further investment. All sources of energy must be simultaneously developed.

The other area to which the greatest attention must be paid is water resources. Not only must we ensure every parched throat and every dry field has access to water, efforts must be made to save every drop of water in every possible way. No amount of money is too much to spend on this sector.

Governments must be lean and efficient. Many of the activities of the government have already become redundant as a result of liberalization and shrinking of government's functions. Government needs to shed more flab. They must also set examples in austerity. All this can be achieved through focused administrative reforms. Governments will always need to collect taxes. A lot of tax reform has already taken place. This must be carried forward. Our customs tariffs especially need to be aligned to world levels. Tax administration must also be made as people-friendly as possible.

Only through a lean and efficient government, higher growth, soft interest rates, proper user charges, moderate taxation, properly targeted subsidies and higher return on government investments can India achieve a better and sustainable fiscal balance. In this connection, the Fiscal Responsibility and Budget Management Act passed by Parliament during the NDA regime is of great significance.

The external sector of the Indian economy was well managed during NDA rule. In fact, it became a model for others. The process must continue. The re-emergence of large current account deficits is not yet a matter of concern, but it is no cause for celebration either. Comfortable foreign exchange reserves have given India a lot of elbow room globally, including in foreign policy. We have become a net lender to the IMF instead of being a borrower. India has also emerged as a large giver of aid to other developing countries while signing off on aid with many developed countries. For all practical purposes, India is already a member of the G7. The rupee is largely convertible even on the capital account. The time has come for India to take the plunge and make the rupee fully convertible.

Globalization is a fact of modern life. The question whether India should globalize or not is moot. The more relevant question is how we should manage its impact. Globalization can be both good and bad. It should be our effort to filter the bad and embrace the good. India has managed the impact of globalization better than most developing countries. In the last decade itself, the benefits of globalization have become evident in the information technology, manufacturing and services sectors. Cities like Bangalore and Hyderabad have become global, even though outsourcing is creating an outcry in many Western countries, especially in the United States. Indian professionals are all over the world, managing multinational companies. Indian companies are becoming multinationals themselves. More and more Indians are travelling abroad, investing abroad. Bollywood and chicken tikka are conquering the world.

We must be careful to ensure globalization is not exploitative—for us and for others. No country is better suited to carry this message of benign and fruitful global cooperation than India. Our interaction with the rest of the world throughout history has been non-violent and non-exploitative. It has been based more on soft power than on military might. The world should be persuaded to believe in Vasudhaiva Kutumbkum (Universal Brotherhood) just as we believe in it.

Much of our recent success, both at home and abroad, can be directly ascribed to India's human resource. We are a young nation today. This is going to be the biggest advantage for the next four decades or so. Even though only a small fraction of our people have access to institutions of excellence, it has brought more credit to India than all the governments put together since independence. India is well-known today not merely as a supplier of cheap and skilled manpower, but more famously for its prowess in science and technology including cutting-edge technologies. In the knowledge-based economy of the future, India must emerge a major player. This is achievable by creating access to more institutes of excellence for larger numbers. While the Sarva Shiksha Abhiyan, started by the NDA government, will no doubt lay a stronger foundation for it, we must also set up more technical and professional institutes like the IITs and IIMs.

At the same time we must also look after the health of our human resource. Quality medical facilities must be made available in the remotest areas. While the private sector will no doubt play an important role in both education and health, the primary responsibility must continue to lie with the state.

Double-digit growth will be difficult to achieve if there is no peace within the country. Threats to peace and law and order will therefore have to be tackled by the government with strength and determination. Cross-border terrorism, insurgency, organized crime, economic offences and social unrest must be effectively tackled so that development takes place without let or hindrance. We must work with our neighbours to ensure peace and stability in the region.

People generally, and investors in particular, must have the assurance of the durability of our policies. Surprises, especially unpleasant surprises, must be avoided. The direction of economic policy must be clearly laid out. The unfinished agenda of reforms must be carried forward on the basis of consensus. Privatization of PSUs, labour market reform, pension reforms, financial sector reforms, role of foreign investment, globalization, role of governments, quality of expenditure, subsidies and user charges, etc. are issues on which there is no national consensus today. In fact, the fragile consensus that seems to have existed so far is also fast disappearing. The constituency for economic reforms is shrinking.

Economic reforms do not merely relate to the stock markets or to privatization of PSUs. Economic reforms, as understood by us during the Vajpayee era, have to be comprehensive and people-friendly. No economic reform in India can be worthwhile unless it includes the reform of agriculture and the rural economy. Unfortunately, in our country the debate on economic reforms has been confined to a few issues only. This has created enormous misunderstanding about the concept, nature and impact of economic reforms. We need to debate afresh to rebuild consensus. I had recently asked the Minister of Labour and Employment about the total number of people who had become unemployed as a result of closure of factories in the last five years. The minister's reply is revealing—11,904 in 2000; 11,599 in 2001; 10,025 in 2002; 8673 in 2003; and 9759 in 2004. It is not in millions as claimed by some people. The Economic Survey 2006–07 has brought out some of the benefits of economic reforms carried out during the NDA regime. It takes note of the efficiency improvements in the economy since 1999–2000. The ratio of net capital stock to gross value added in the economy went down from 2.78 to 2.6 between 1999–2000 and 2004–05. The improvement covers both agriculture and industry.

While in government, we faced a lot criticism for the declining rate of employment generation. To quote the Economic Survey:

> The results of the NSSO's 61st Round large–scale quinquennial survey on employment and unemployment conducted during 2004–05 throws a lot of light on the heated debate on jobless growth under reforms. The survey results show how the annual growth rate of employment, which had declined from 2.1% during 1983–94 to 1.6% during 1993–2000, went up to 2.5% during 1999–2005.

The Survey also notes that the incidence of poverty came down to about 22 per cent in 2004–05 from a level of 26.1 per cent in 1999–2000.

Some pain in any adjustment is inevitable. This pain is directly felt by the people when it relates to any increase in user charges or any reduction in subsidies. Over a period of time, our people had got used to some of these free lunches, without thinking about where the money comes from. Obviously, the state is bearing the burden. The capacity of the state to bear this burden has long vanished. Governments have borrowed more and more to keep the old system going. In the process, they have done great damage to the economy. Electricity is a case in point. Free electricity to farmers has often meant no electricity at all. The same is true of other services as well.

The gain to the people through many of these populist schemes is ephemeral. Large borrowings by the government mean higher prices, among other things. The laws of economics are as ruthless as the laws of nature. The consequences are unavoidable. The choice is clear—we can produce wealth and distribute it among the people by using our resources wisely or we can waste them on doles and perpetuate poverty. Winning elections is important, but not more important than the future of our country and the well-being of generations still unborn.

It is now increasingly being realized that democracy, far from being a drag, has actually been our strength. Our democracy must therefore be fully protected and preserved. The cancer of the four Cs, namely, criminalization, corruption, casteism and communalism, must be tackled resolutely and effectively by the political class in order to ensure that the state facilitates and does not obstruct the realization of the legitimate aspirations of the common man to improve his quality of life.

This is the only way to see an economically strong, secure, self-reliant India—a true testimony to 'swadeshi'.

Index